Essential
Neurology

Dedication

To both Biddies with love

FOURTH EDITION

Essential Neurology

Iain Wilkinson

BSc, MD, MA, FRCP
Formerly Consultant Neurologist
Addenbrooke's Hospital
Cambridge
and
Fellow of Wolfson College
and Associate Lecturer
University of Cambridge Medical School

Graham Lennox

BA FRCP
Consultant Neurologist
Addenbrooke's Hospital
Cambridge
and
West Suffolk Hospital
Bury St Edmunds

Blackwell
Publishing

© 2005 by Blackwell Publishing Ltd

Blackwell Publishing, Inc., 350 Main Street, Malden, Massachusetts
  02148-5020, USA
Blackwell Publishing Ltd, 9600 Garsington Road, Oxford OX4 2DQ, UK
Blackwell Publishing Asia Pty Ltd, 550 Swanston Street, Carlton,
  Victoria 3053, Australia

The right of the Author to be identified as the Author of this Work has been
asserted in accordance with the Copyright, Designs and Patents Act 1988.

First published 1988
Reprinted 1989, 1992
Four Dragons edition 1989
Reprinted 1992
Second edition 1993
Reprinted 1994, 1995, 1996

Four Dragons edition 1993
Reprinted 1994, 1997, 1998
Third edition 1999
Reprinted 2000, 2001, 2002, 2004
Fourth edition 2005

Library of Congress Cataloging-in-Publication Data

Wilkinson, I.M.S.
  Essential neurology / Iain Wilkinson, Graham Lennox.—4th ed.
      p. ; cm.
  Includes bibliographical references and index.
  ISBN-13: 978-1-4051-1867-5
  ISBN-10: 1-4051-1867-9
  1. Neurology.   2. Nervous system—Diseases.
  [DNLM: 1. Nervous System Diseases.   WL 140 W686e 2005]
I. Lennox, Graham.   II. Title.

RC346.W55   2005
616.8—dc22   2004019636

ISBN-13: 978-1-4051-1867-5
ISBN-10: 1-4051-1867-9

A catalogue record for this title is available from the British Library

Set in 9.25 on 12 pt Palatino
by SNP Best-set Typesetter Ltd., Hong Kong
Printed and bound in India by Replika Press Pvt, Ltd, Kundli

Commissioning Editor: Vicki Noyes
Editorial Assistant: Nicola Ulyatt
Development Editor: Lorna Hind
Production Controller: Kate Charman

For further information on Blackwell Publishing, visit our website:
http://www.blackwellpublishing.com

The publisher's policy is to use permanent paper from mills that operate a
sustainable forestry policy, and which has been manufactured from pulp
processed using acid-free and elementary chlorine-free practices.
Furthermore, the publisher ensures that the text paper and cover board used
have met acceptable environmental accreditation standards.

Contents

Preface to
the fourth edition

The three previous editions of this book were written by only one of us. The addition of a younger and enthusiastic second author has undoubtedly improved the book. It is more accurate and thoroughly modern. Both authors have been single-minded in their intention to present, clearly and concisely, that neurology and neurosurgery which is required by medical students at the time of graduation.

The revision of diagrams, use of colour, clarification of text, and inclusion of illustrative case histories have all helped, but it is the authors' discipline to adhere closely to the title of the book, *Essential Neurology*, which makes them hope that the textbook remains helpful to its readers.

I.W. and G.L.

Preface to the first edition

Excellent textbooks of neurology already exist, which deal with the subject in a detailed and comprehensive manner. This is not what the majority of clinical medical students require.

In writing this textbook, I have been preoccupied with the following questions:

- Have I kept to basic principles?
- Have I made each topic as easy as possible to understand, both in the text and in the diagrams?
- Have I omitted all unnecessary detail?

There is no section in the book specifically dedicated to 'How to examine the nervous system'. I believe each student has to learn this by apprenticeship to clinical neurologists in the ward and in the clinic.

Every effort has been made to ensure that this book lives up to its name, in setting out clearly all that the student needs to know about the common neurological and neurosurgical conditions.

I.W.

Acknowledgements

We both want to acknowledge the very great help of Drs N. Antoun and J. Gillard in preparation of the neuroradiological images.

Abbreviations

BG	basal ganglia
C	cerebellum
CNS	central nervous system
CSF	cerebrospinal fluid
CT	computerized tomography
ECG	electocardiogram
EEG	electroencephalogram
EMG	electromyogram
LMN	lower motor neurone
MR	magnetic resonance
NMJ	neuromuscular junction
S	sensation
UMN	upper motor neurone

CHAPTER 1

Clinical skills, physical signs and anatomy

'There's something wrong with my left leg, and I'm not walking properly.' In this chapter we are going to use this clinical problem to remind us:

- how important the details of the history are in making a neurological diagnosis, especially the clear definition of how the problem has evolved with respect to time;
- of the components of the nervous system involved in normal movement, their anatomy (which isn't complicated), and the physical signs produced by lesions in the various components;
- of the common patterns of neurological malfunction, affecting any part of the body, such as a leg;
- of the importance of the patient's response to his malfunctioning limb, in defining the size and nature of the whole illness;
- of the reliability of the clinical method in leading us to a diagnosis or differential diagnosis and management plan;
- how important it is to explain things clearly, in language the patient and relatives can understand.

At the end of the chapter are a few brief case histories, given to illustrate the principles which are outlined above and itemized in detail throughout the chapter.

Our response to a patient telling us that his left leg isn't working properly must not just consist of the methodical asking of many questions, and the ritualistic performance of a complex, totally inclusive, neurological examination, hoping that the diagnosis will automatically fall out at the end. Nor must our response be a cursory questioning and non-focused examination, followed by the performance of a large battery of highly sophisticated imaging and neurophysiological tests, hoping that they will pinpoint the problem and trigger a management plan.

No, our response should be to listen and think, question and think, examine and think, all the time trying to match what the patient is telling us, and the physical signs that we are eliciting, with the common patterns of neurological malfunction described in this chapter.

History

We need all the details about the left leg, all the ways it is different from normal. If the patient mentions wasting, our ideas will possibly start to concentrate on lower motor neurone trouble. We will learn that if he says it's stiff, our thoughts will move to the possibility of an upper motor neurone or extrapyramidal lesion. If he can't feel the temperature of the bath water properly with the other (right) leg, it is clear that we should start to think of spinal cord disease. If it makes his walking unsteady; we may consider a cerebellar problem. Different adjectives about the leg have definite diagnostic significance. We will ask the patient to use as many adjectives as he can to describe the problem.

Details of associated symptoms or illnesses need clarification. 'There's nothing wrong with the other leg, but my left hand isn't quite normal'—one starts to wonder about a hemiparesis. 'My left hand's OK, but there's a bit of similar trouble in the right leg'—we might consider a lesion in the spinal cord. 'I had a four-week episode of loss of vision in my right eye, a couple of years ago'—we might wonder about multiple sclerosis. 'Mind you, I've had pills for blood pressure for many years'— we might entertain the possibility of cerebrovascular disease. These and other associated features are important in generating diagnostic ideas.

Very important indeed in neurological diagnosis is detail of the mode of onset of the patient's symptoms. How has the left leg problem evolved in terms of time? Let's say the left leg is not working properly because of a lesion in the right cerebral hemisphere. There is significant weakness in the left

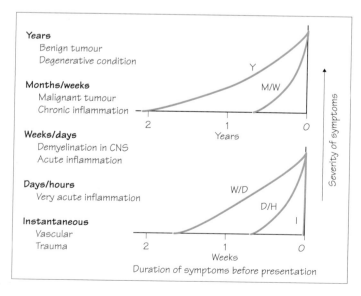

Fig. 1.1 The patient's history indicates the probable pathology.

leg, slight weakness in the left hand and arm, some loss of sensation in the left leg and no problem with the visual fields. This same neurological deficit will be present whatever the nature of the pathology at this site. If this part of the brain isn't working there is an inevitability about the nature of the neurological deficit.

It is the history of the mode of evolution of the neurological deficit which indicates the nature of the pathology (Fig. 1.1).

Components of the nervous system required for normal function; their anatomy; physical signs indicating the presence of a lesion in each component; and the common patterns in which things go wrong

The basic components of the nervous system required for normal movement are shown on the simple diagram below.

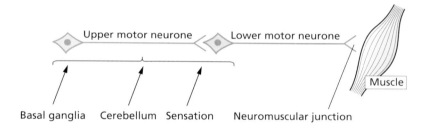

Lesions along the primary motor pathway, UMN–LMN–NMJ–M, are characterized by weakness or paralysis. We will see that the characteristics of the weakness are different in each instance; for example, UMN weakness has different characteristics from LMN weakness. Knowledge of these characteristics is fundamental to clinical neurology.

Normal basal ganglia, cerebellar and sensory function is essential background activity of the nervous system for normal movement. Lesions in these parts of the nervous system do not produce weakness or paralysis, but make movement imperfect because of stiffness, slowness, involuntary movement, clumsiness or lack of adequate feeling.

So we will be questioning and examining for weakness, wasting, stiffness, flaccidity, slowness, clumsiness and loss of feeling in our patient's left leg. This will help to identify in which component of the nervous system the fault lies.

To make more sense of the patient's clinical problem, we have to know the basic anatomy of the neurological components, identified above, in general terms but not in every minute detail. This is shown on the next three pages.

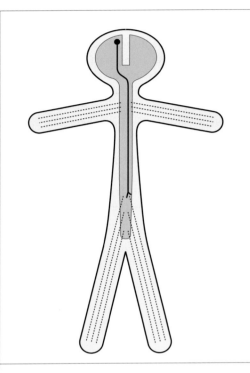

An upper motor neurone involved in left leg movement

Cell body in motor cortex of right cerebral hemisphere

Axon:
- descends through right internal capsule
- crosses from right to left in the medulla
- travels down the spinal cord on the left side in lateral column
- synapses with a lower motor neurone innervating left leg musculature

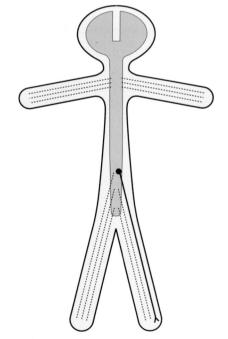

A lower motor neurone involved in left leg movement

Cell body at the lower end of the spinal cord on the left side

Axon:
- leaves the spine within a numbered spinal nerve
- travels through the lumbosacral plexus
- descends within a named peripheral nerve
- synapses with muscle at neuromuscular junction

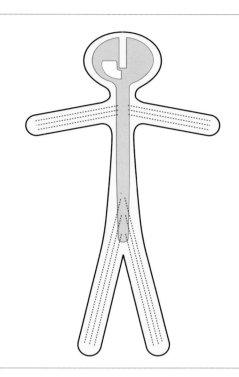

Basal ganglion control of the left leg

The structures involved in extrapyramidal control of the left side of the body reside in the basal ganglia and cerebral peduncle on the right

Basal ganglion function is contralateral

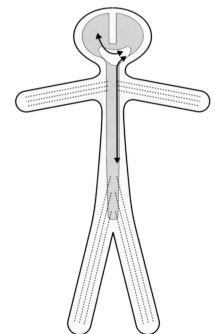

Cerebellar control of the left leg

The left cerebellar hemisphere has two-way connection with the right cerebral hemisphere and the left side of the body, via the cerebellar peduncles, brainstem and spinal cord

Cerebellar function is ipsilateral

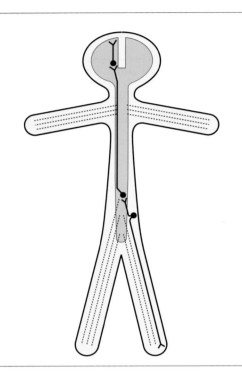

Pain and temperature sensation in the left leg

Third sensory neurone:
- cell body in thalamus
- axon travels to sensory cortex

Second sensory neurone:
- cell body in lumbar spinal cord on the left
- axon crosses to the right and ascends to thalamus in lateral column of spinal cord

Dorsal root ganglion cell:
- distal axon from the left leg, via peripheral nerve, lumbosacral plexus and spinal nerve
- proximal axon enters cord via dorsal root of spinal nerve, and relays with second sensory neurone

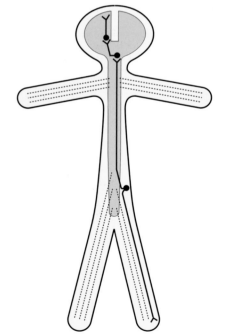

Position sense in the left leg

Third sensory neurone:
- cell body in thalamus
- axon travels to sensory cortex

Second sensory neurone:
- cell body in gracile or cuneate nucleus on left side of medulla, axon crosses to the right side of medulla and ascends to thalamus on the right

Dorsal root ganglion cell:
- distal axon from left leg, via peripheral nerve, lumbosacral plexus and spinal nerve
- proximal axon enters cord, ascends in posterior column on the left to reach the second sensory neurone in left lower medulla

The final piece of anatomical knowledge which is helpful for understanding the neurological control of the left leg, is a little more detail about motor and sensory representation in the brain. The important features to remember here are:

- the motor cortex is in front of the central sulcus, and the sensory cortex is behind it;
- the body is represented upside-down in both the motor and sensory cortex;
- the axons of the upper motor neurones in the precentral motor cortex funnel down to descend in the anterior part of the internal capsule;
- the axons of the 3rd sensory neurone in the thalamus radiate out through the posterior part of the internal capsule to reach the postcentral sensory cortex.

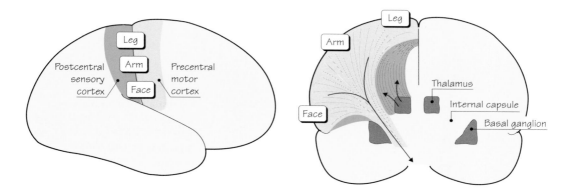

Having reviewed the components of the nervous system involved in normal function of the left leg, and their basic anatomy, we now need more detail of:

- the clinical features of failure in each component;
- the common patterns of failure which are met in clinical practice.

The next section of this chapter reviews these features and patterns.

Upper motor neurone

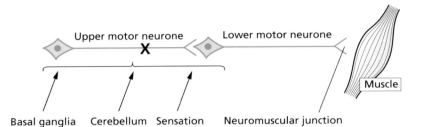

Characteristic of upper motor neurone lesions:
- no wasting;
- increased tone of clasp-knife type;
- weakness most evident in anti-gravity muscles;
- increased reflexes and clonus;
- extensor plantar responses.

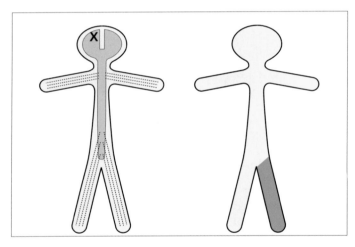

Contralateral monoparesis
A lesion situated peripherally in the cerebral hemisphere, i.e. involving part of the motor homunculus only, produces weakness of part of the contralateral side of the body, e.g. the contralateral leg. If the lesion also involves the adjacent sensory homunculus in the postcentral gyrus, there may be some sensory loss in the same part of the body.

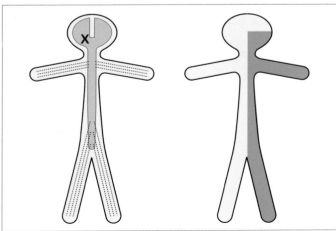

Contralateral hemiparesis
Lesions situated deep in the cerebral hemisphere, in the region of the internal capsule, are much more likely to produce weakness of the whole of the contralateral side of the body, face, arm and leg. Because of the funnelling of fibre pathways in the region of the internal capsule, such lesions commonly produce significant contralateral sensory loss (hemianaesthesia) and visual loss (homonymous hemianopia), in addition to the hemiparesis.

Ipsilateral monoparesis

A unilateral lesion in the spinal cord below the level of the neck produces upper motor neurone weakness in one leg. There may be posterior column (position sense) sensory loss in the same leg, and spinothalamic (pain and temperature) sensory loss in the contralateral leg. This is known as dissociated sensory loss, and the whole picture is sometimes referred to as the Brown-Séquard syndrome.

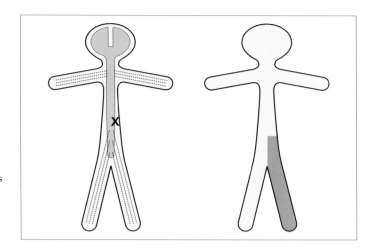

Ipsilateral hemiparesis

A unilateral high cervical cord lesion will produce a hemiparesis similar to that which is caused by a contralateral cerebral hemisphere lesion, except that the face cannot be involved in the hemiparesis, vision will be normal, and the same dissociation of sensory loss (referred to above) may be found below the level of the lesion.

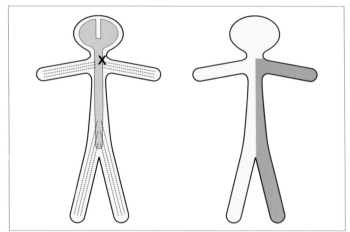

10   CHAPTER 1

A spinal cord lesion more usually causes upper motor neurone signs in both legs, often asymmetrically since the pathology rarely affects both sides of the spinal cord equally.

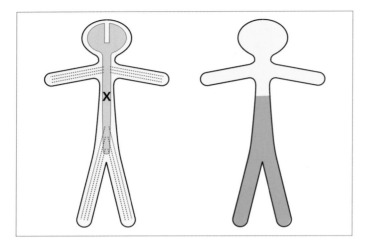

Paraparesis, if the lesion is at or below the cervical portion of the spinal cord.

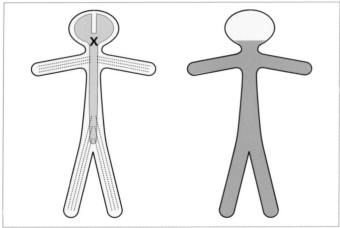

Tetraparesis or quadriparesis, if the lesion is in the upper cervical cord or brainstem.

Lesions anywhere between the midbrain and lower spinal cord may, in addition, involve ascending sensory pathways and fibre tracts involving sphincter function. There may therefore be sensory loss below the level of the lesion, and the possibility of bladder, bowel and sexual symptoms.

There may be physical signs which indicate the level of the lesion very accurately:

- LMN signs, loss of reflexes, dermatome pain or sensory loss, at the level of the lesion in the spinal cord;
- cerebellar signs or cranial nerve palsies when the lesion is in the midbrain, pons or medulla.

Lower motor neurone

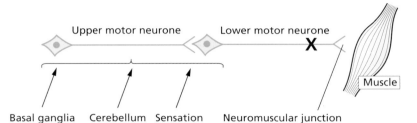

Characteristics of lower motor neurone lesions:

- wasting;
- fasciculation;
- decreased tone (i.e. flaccidity);
- weakness;
- decreased or absent reflexes;
- flexor or absent plantar responses.

Generalized LMN weakness may result from pathology affecting the LMNs throughout the spinal cord and brainstem, as in motor neurone disease or poliomyelitis. Generalized limb weakness (proximal and distal), trunk and bulbar weakness characterize this sort of LMN disorder.

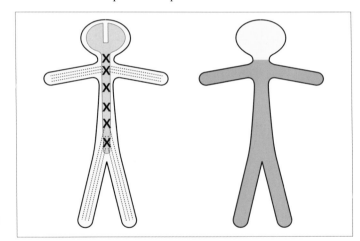

Generalized LMN weakness may also result from widespread damage to the axons of the LMNs. This is the nature of peripheral neuropathy (also called polyneuropathy). The axons of the dorsal root sensory neurones are usually simultaneously involved. The LMN weakness and sensory loss tend to be most marked distally in the limbs.

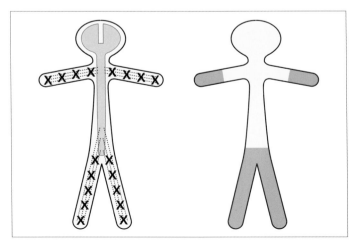

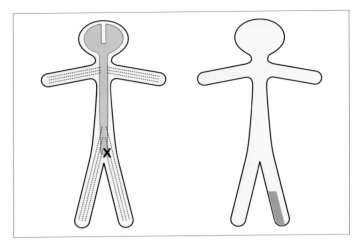

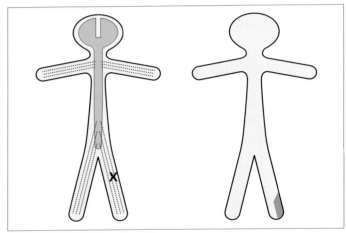

LMN weakness may be confined to the distribution of one spinal root (above) or one individual peripheral nerve (below). In such circumstances, the LMN signs are found only in the muscles supplied by the particular nerve root or peripheral nerve in question. Almost always there is sensory impairment in the area supplied by the nerve or nerve root. Examples of such lesions are an S1 nerve root syndrome caused by a prolapsed intervertebral disc, or a common peroneal nerve palsy caused by pressure in the region of the neck of the fibula.

Neuromuscular junction

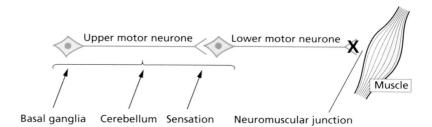

The classic disease of the neuromuscular junction is myasthenia gravis. Characteristics of myasthenia gravis:

- uncommon;
- no wasting;
- tone normal;
- weakness;
- fatiguability;
- reflexes normal;
- positive response to anticholinesterase.

The pattern of muscle involvement in this rare disease:

- ocular muscles common:
  ptosis;
  diplopia;
- bulbar muscles fairly common:
  dysarthria;
  dysphagia;
- trunk and limb muscles less common:
  limb weakness;
  trunk weakness;
  breathing problems.

More common paralysis due to neuromuscular blockade is that which is produced by anaesthetists during operative surgery.

Myasthenia gravis would not be a likely diagnosis in a patient presenting with left leg malfunction.

Muscle

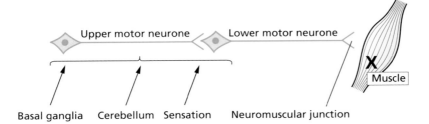

Characteristics of primary muscle disease:
- uncommon;
- wasting;
- no fasciculation;
- weakness;
- tone normal or reduced;
- reflexes normal or reduced.

Proximal muscle weakness typifies most primary muscle disease. The patient has difficulty in lifting his arms above shoulder level, and in rising from a chair into the standing position. He needs to use his arms to help him do this. In the standing position, the trunk muscle weakness often allows an abnormal amount of extension of the lumbar spine, so that the abdomen protrudes forwards. When walking, the abdominal and pelvic muscle weakness allow downward tilting of the pelvis when the leg is off the ground. This is known as Trendelenburg weakness.

A diagnosis of muscle disease would be unlikely in a patient presenting with unilateral leg malfunction. This is partly because muscle disease is rare, and partly because it usually produces bilateral symmetrical weakness.

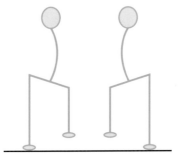

Basal ganglia

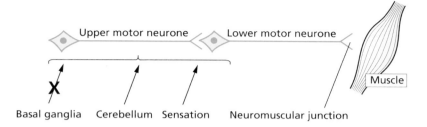

Two main syndromes, each with different characteristics:
1. Parkinson's disease:
   - common;
   - tremor at rest;
   - increased tone;
   - bradykinesia;
   - flexed posture.
2. Involuntary movements:
   - uncommon;
   - involuntary movements at rest and during action;
   - tone increased, normal or reduced;
   - normal speed of movement;
   - all sorts of postural abnormalities.

No weakness in either.

These syndromes may be unilateral and are commonly asymmetrical, the pathology being in the basal ganglia of the contralateral cerebral hemisphere.

It is not at all improbable that a patient complaining of left leg malfunction, and difficulty in walking, might be presenting with Parkinson's disease.

Cerebellum

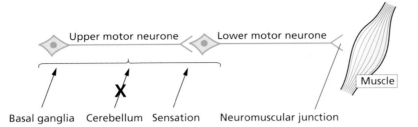

Characteristics of cerebellar lesions are:

1. Incoordination of muscle activity:
   - in the head: nystagmus, dysarthria;
   - in the arms: finger–nose ataxia, kinetic tremor, difficulty with rapid alternating movements (dysdiadochokinesia);
   - in the legs: heel–knee–shin ataxia, gait ataxia, falls.

2. There is no weakness. (Alcohol in large doses impairs cerebellar function. Intoxicated people show all the features of muscular incoordination mentioned above, but may be very strong.)

3. In a unilateral cerebellar lesion, the neurological deficit is ipsilateral to the side of the lesion. A patient complaining of malfunction of the left leg due to a left cerebellar lesion would have heel–knee–shin ataxia most marked in the left leg, and gait ataxia with deviation to the left. There might also be left arm cerebellar signs, and nystagmus most marked looking to the left.

Sensation

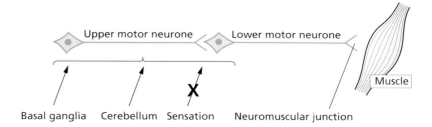

Characteristics of movement in the presence of sensory loss:
- ataxia or clumsiness of movement due to loss of sense of position mainly, but also due to loss of touch sensation;
- partial compensation by active monitoring of movement by the eyes;
- no weakness.

There are three main clinical syndromes where sensory loss may play an important role in impairing movement and function.

Cerebral hemisphere lesions: impaired accurate movements of the contralateral limbs because central registration of limb position is lost.

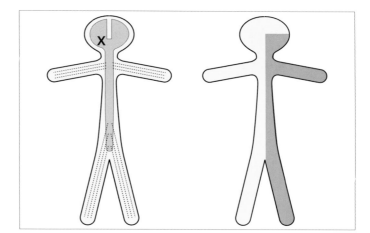

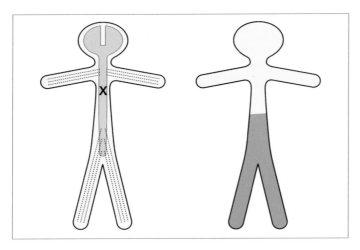

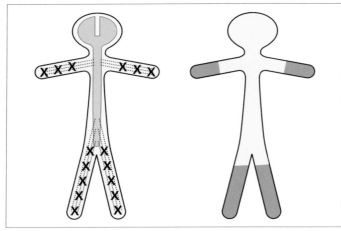

Loss of proprioceptive sense in the legs and feet may occur as a result of either spinal cord disease (above) or peripheral neuropathy (below). The loss of sense of position gives rise to clumsiness of leg movement when walking, unsteadiness, and the need to watch the feet and floor carefully. There is marked unsteadiness and falling when vision cannot compensate, e.g. in the dark, in the shower, when washing the face, when putting clothes over the head. Romberg's sign (stance steady with eyes open, but unsteady with eyes closed) is positive in such patients.

The patient's response to his symptoms

Hopefully the nature of the patient's physical illness causing the left leg malfunction will emerge from the history and examination, carried out against this background knowledge of common patterns of neurological failure. Just as important, and to be conducted during the same history and examination, is an evaluation of the patient's response to the illness. How much is the imperfect function in the left leg bothering him? What are the practical consequences of having the problem in his everyday life? What does he think is the matter? Has he worried about a really serious cause? Is he anticipating recovery or further disability?

In this section we recognize that the total illness in any patient is the sum of the physical illness plus the patient's psychological reaction to the physical illness. The latter may be appropriate and entirely understandable. Sometimes, however, the reaction is exaggerated for some reason, making the whole illness a bigger one for the patient, his family and the medical staff looking after him. Recognition of the two elements of illness, and the management of both, are particularly appropriate in patients with neurological disorders.

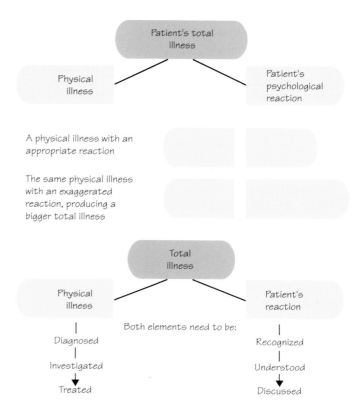

Diagnosis, explanation and planning

A diagnosis, or differential diagnosis, for the patient's left leg problem is established, and a good feel for the level of patient concern has been achieved. Tests to confirm the diagnosis often need to be arranged before the diagnosis is finally established. Careful explanation of the differential diagnosis, and careful explanation of the tests to the patient, often with another family member present, is important. Diagnostic certainty may be achieved nowadays as a result of sophisticated scanning, neurophysiological tests and laboratory investigations, but some patients are apprehensive about such investigations and others are very apprehensive about what diagnosis may emerge as a result of them. The need for excellent communication and patient explanation reaches its height when the final diagnosis and management plan are discussed with the patient (and family member). Plenty of opportunity should be given for the patient and family to express their feelings at this stage.

The following five points are helpful from the communication point of view. The doctor should show in an open and friendly way, that:

1. there is always enough time;
2. there is always enough concern;
3. enough privacy is always available for the patient to speak freely and openly;
4. there is always an opportunity to talk to the patient's family;
5. he can talk to the patient and family in language they can easily understand.

Investment of such time and effort with a patient who has a neurological illness is always worthwhile. The more the patient and family trust, like and respect the doctor, the greater will be their confidence in the diagnosis and their compliance with the management. It is clearly a shame if a bright doctor has established the correct explanation of our patient's left leg problem, but communicates very poorly and establishes little rapport with the patient. The patient may be far from satisfied, and seek help elsewhere.

Patience with patients
Time
Concern
Privacy
Relatives
Language

Some typical case histories

Let's create a few different neurological scenarios which might develop from a patient presenting with a malfunctioning left leg, to show the range of different outcomes.

A semi-retired builder of 68 years, smoker, has noticed gradually progressive weakness in the left leg for 6–8 weeks. Both he and his wife are worried, mainly because they have an imminent 4-week trip to visit their son and family in Australia.

General examination is normal.

Neurological examination reveals mild UMN signs in the left arm and major UMN signs in the left leg.

A chest X-ray shows a mass at the right hilum and a CT brain scan shows two mass lesions, one (apparently producing no problem) in the left frontal region, and one in the region of the precentral motor cortex high up in the right fronto-parietal region. Bronchoscopy confirms that the right hilar lesion is a bronchial carcinoma.

In discussion, it transpires that the patient had a strong notion that this was what was wrong from fairly early on, confirmed for him when he was asked to have a chest X-ray; that he would like to take advantage of the transient improvement produced by large-dose steroids, reducing the oedema around the brain lesions; and that, although not rich, he could afford hospital care or urgent flights home from Australia if required. They would continue with their planned visit, and cope as best they could when the inevitable worsening of his condition occurred, hopefully when they have returned home.

A widow of 63 years, who has been on treatment for high blood pressure for some years, developed sudden weakness of the left leg whilst washing up at 9 a.m. She fell over and had to call the doctor by shuffling across the floor of the house to the telephone. Now, 3 days later, there has been moderate recovery so that she can walk but she feels far from safe.

Her father had hypertension and died after a stroke.

General examination reveals a BP of 200/100, a right carotid arterial bruit, a right femoral arterial bruit and hypertensive retinopathy.

Neurological examination reveals mild UMN signs in the left arm and major UMN signs in the left leg.

Chest X-ray and ECG both confirm left ventricular hypertrophy.

Blood tests are all normal.

CT brain scan shows no definite abnormality.

Carotid doppler studies show critical stenosis of the lower end of the right internal carotid artery.

A small stroke, from which she seems to be recovering satisfactorily, is the diagnosis discussed with her. The patient is happy to see the physiotherapist to help recovery. She is worried about the degree of recovery from the point of view of driving, which isn't safe in her present car (which has a manual gear shift). She understands she is predisposed to future strokes because of her hypertension and carotid artery disease. She is prepared to take preventative drug treatment in the form of aspirin, blood pressure pills and a statin. She doesn't smoke. She wants to have a good talk to her doctor son before submitting herself to carotid endarterectomy, although she understands the prophylactic value of this operation to her.

A golf course groundsman of 58 years gives a history of lack of proper movement of the left leg, making his walking slower. It has been present for 6 months and has perhaps worsened slightly. Most of his work is on a tractor so the left leg problem hasn't really affected him at work. He feels he must have a nerve pinched in his left leg somewhere.

General examination is normal.

Neurological examination reveals a rather fixed facial expression, tremor of the lightly closed eyes, a little cogwheel rigidity in the left arm with slow fine movements in the left fingers. In the left leg there is a slight rest tremor and moderate rigidity. He walks in a posture of mild flexion, with reduced arm swinging on the left and shuffling of the left leg. His walking is a little slow.

He is profoundly disappointed to hear that he has Parkinson's disease. He has never had any previous illness, and somebody in his village has very severe Parkinson's disease indeed.

Several consultations are required to explain the nature of Parkinson's disease, the fact that some people have it mildly and some severely, that effective treatment exists in the form of tablets, and that a very pessimistic viewpoint isn't appropriate or helpful to him.

Gradually he's coming round to the idea and becoming more optimistic. Levodopa therapy is producing significant improvement. Literature produced by the Parkinson's Disease Society has helped his understanding of the illness.

A woman of 24 years presents with a 3-week history of heaviness and dragging of the left leg. She has had to stop driving because of left leg weakness and clumsiness. For a week she hasn't been able to tell the temperature of the bath water with the right leg, though she can with the weak leg. She has developed a little bladder frequency and urgency. She has had to stop her job as a riding school instructor.

Three years ago she lost the vision in her left eye for a few weeks, but it recovered well. Doctors whom she saw at the time talked about inflammation of the optic nerve.

She is engaged to be married in a few month's time.

General examination is normal.

Neurological examination reveals no abnormalities in the cranial nerves or arms. She has moderate UMN signs in the left leg, loss of sense of position in the left foot and toes, and spinothalamic sensory loss (pain and temperature) throughout the right leg. She drags her left leg as she walks.

She understands that she now, almost certainly, has another episode of inflammation, this time on the left hand side of her spinal cord, similar in nature to the optic nerve affair 3 years ago.

She accepts the offer of treatment with high-dose steroids for 3 days, to help to resolve the inflammation. She is keen to return to work.

The neurologist knows that he has got quite a lot more work to do for this girl. He has to arrange for the investigations to confirm his clinical opinion that she has multiple sclerosis. He will then have to see her (and her fiancé, if she would like it) and explain that multiple sclerosis is the underlying explanation for the symptoms. He will have to do his best to help her to have an appropriate reaction to this information. Both she and her fiancé will need information and support.

A man of 46 years, scaffold-erector, knows that his left foot is weak. It has been present for a few months. He has lost spring at the ankle, and the left foot is weak when taking all his weight on ladders and scaffold. He's had back pain, on and off, for many years like a lot of his work mates. He doesn't get paid if he's not working.

General examination is normal except for some restriction of forward flexion of the lumbar spine.

Neurological examination reveals wasting and weakness of the left posterior calf muscles (i.e. foot and toe plantar-flexors), an absent left ankle jerk, and impaired cutaneous sensation on the sole and lateral aspect of the left foot.

Scanning confirms the presence of a large prolapsed intervertebral disc compressing the left S1 nerve root.

He is offered referral to a neurosurgeon.

His concerns are:
- Will the operation work (i.e. restore better function to the left leg)?
  Yes — more likely than not, but only over several months, even up to a year.
- How much time off work?
  Probable minimum of 6–8 weeks and then light duties for a further 6–8 weeks.
- Should he be thinking of changing his job?
  Not essential, but an excellent idea if a good opportunity turned up.

A 38-year-old unkempt alcoholic presents with a left foot drop so that he cannot lift up the foot against gravity, and as he walks there is a double strike as his left foot hits the ground, first with the toe and then with the heel. He's very frequently intoxicated, and he can't remember how, or precisely when, the foot became like this.

General examination reveals alcohol in his breath, multiple bruises and minor injuries all over his body, no liver enlargement, but generally poor nutritional state.

Neurological examination reveals weakness of the left foot dorsiflexion, left foot eversion, left toe dorsiflexion and some altered cutaneous sensation down the lower anterolateral calf and dorsal aspect of the foot on the left.

A left common peroneal nerve palsy, secondary either to compression (when intoxicated) or to trauma, at the neck of the left fibula, is explained as the most probable diagnosis. Arrangements are made for a surgical appliance officer to provide a foot-support, the physiotherapists to assess him, and for neurophysiological confirmation of the diagnosis.

The patient defaults on all these and further appointments.

2

CHAPTER 2

Stroke

Introduction

Stroke causes sudden loss of neurological function by disrupting the blood supply to the brain. It is the biggest cause of physical disability in developed countries, and a leading cause of death. It is also common in many developing countries.

The great majority of strokes come on without warning. This means that for most patients the aims of management are to limit the damage to the brain, optimize recovery and prevent recurrence. Strategies to prevent strokes are clearly important. They concentrate on treating the vascular risk factors that predispose to stroke, such as hypertension, hyperlipidaemia, diabetes and smoking.

The two principal pathological processes that give rise to stroke are occlusion of arteries, causing cerebral ischaemia or infarction, and rupture of arteries, causing intracranial haemorrhage (Fig. 2.1). Haemorrhage tends to be much more destructive and dangerous than ischaemic stroke, with higher mortality rates and a higher incidence of severe neurological disability in survivors. Ischaemic stroke is much more common, and has a much wider range of outcomes.

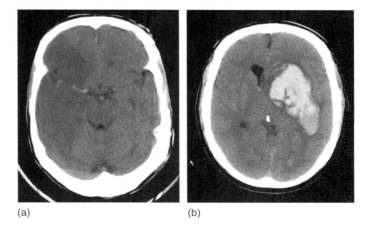

Fig. 2.1 (a) CT scan showing a right middle cerebral artery occlusion as a large wedge of low density; the blocked artery itself is bright. (b) CT scan showing a large left internal capsule haemorrhage.

(a)   (b)

Cerebral ischaemia and infarction

Reduction in the flow of blood to any part of the brain first causes ischaemia, a reversible loss of function, and then, if the reduction is severe or prolonged, infarction with irreversible cell death. The blood supply to the anterior parts of the brain (and to the eyes) comes from the two carotid arteries, which branch in the neck to give rise to the internal carotid arteries; these branch again in the head to give rise to the anterior and middle cerebral arteries. The posterior parts of the brain are supplied by the two vertebral arteries, which join within the head to form the basilar artery, which in turn gives rise to the posterior cerebral arteries (Figs 2.2 and 2.3).

The internal carotid and basilar arteries connect at the base of the brain through the circle of Willis. This anastomosis allows some cross-flow if one of the supply arteries is occluded, but the extent of this varies enormously from patient to patient. Beyond the circle of Willis, the cerebral arteries are best thought of as end-arteries. Restoration of normal perfusion in tissue made ischaemic by occlusion of one of these end-arteries cannot rely on blood reaching the ischaemic area through anastomotic channels. Recovery of function in the ischaemic tissue depends much more upon lysis or fragmentation of the occluding thrombo-embolic material.

The usual cause of occlusion of one of the cerebral arteries is acute thrombus formation at the site of an atheromatous plaque. The thrombus can occlude the vessel locally or throw off emboli which block more distal arteries. This process is particularly common at the origin of the internal carotid artery, but can occur anywhere from the aorta to the cerebral artery itself. A less common cause of occlusion is embolism from the heart. In younger patients, dissection of the carotid or vertebral artery (in which a split forms between the layers of the artery wall, often after

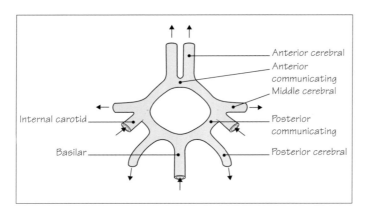

Fig. 2.2 Circle of Willis.

minor neck trauma) can either occlude the vessel or allow a thrombus to form and embolize distally (Fig. 2.3).

Patients with hypertension or diabetes may occlude smaller arteries within the brain through a pathological process which may have more to do with degeneration in the artery wall than atheroma and thrombosis. This *small vessel disease* may cause infarcts a few millimeters in diameter, termed lacunar strokes, or a more insidious illness with dementia and gait disturbance.

If complete recovery from an ischaemic event takes place within minutes or hours, it is termed a transient ischaemic attack (TIA). Where recovery takes longer than 24 hours the diagnosis is stroke. The pathophysiology of the two conditions, and the implications for investigation and treatment, are the same. In both situations, the history and examination help to establish the cause (with a view to secondary prevention) and assess the extent of the damage (to plan rehabilitation).

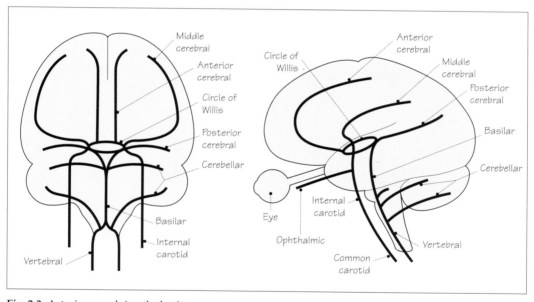

Fig. 2.3 Arteries supplying the brain.

Symptoms and signs of the cause of cerebral ischaemia and infarction

The common conditions which give rise to cerebral ischaemia and infarction are listed below.

1. *Atheroma* in either the large neck arteries or the cerebral arteries close to the brain. There may be a history of other atheromatous disease:

- previous angina pectoris or heart attack;
- intermittent claudication of the legs;
- previous TIA or stroke.

There may be a history of vascular risk factors:

- hypertension;
- diabetes;
- hyperlipidaemia;
- family history of atheromatous disease;
- smoking.

Examination may reveal evidence of these risk factors or evidence of atheroma, with bruits over the carotid, subclavian or femoral arteries, or absent leg pulses.

2. *Cardiac disease* associated with embolization:

- atrial fibrillation;
- mural thrombus after myocardial infarction;
- aortic or mitral valve disease;
- bacterial endocarditis.

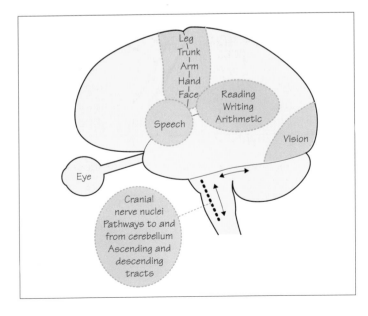

Less common conditions associated with cerebral ischaemia or infarction

Non-atheromatous arterial disease
- carotid or vertebral artery dissection
- arteritis
- subarachnoid haemorrhage

Unusual cardiac conditions giving rise to emboli
- non-bacterial endocarditis
- atrial myxoma
- paradoxical embolism (via a patent foramen ovale)

Unusual embolic material
- fat
- air

Increased blood viscosity or coagulability
- polycythaemia
- antiphospholipid antibodies
- perhaps other thrombophilic disorders

Venous infarction (where there is impaired perfusion of brain tissue drained by thrombosed or infected veins)
- sagittal sinus thrombosis
- cortical thrombophlebitis

Fig. 2.4 Localization of function within the brain.

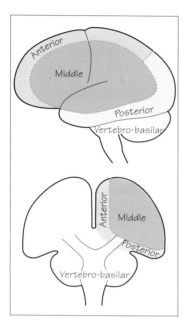

Neurological symptoms and signs of cerebral ischaemia and infarction

The loss of function that the patient notices, and which may be apparent on examination, depends on the area of brain tissue involved in the ischaemic process (Fig. 2.4).

The follow suggest *middle cerebral artery* ischaemia:
- loss of use of the contralateral face and arm;
- loss of feeling in the contralateral face and arm;
- dysphasia;
- dyslexia, dysgraphia, dyscalculia.

The following suggests *anterior cerebral artery* ischaemia:
- loss of use and / or feeling in the contralateral leg.

The following suggests *posterior cerebral artery* ischaemia:
- contralateral homonymous hemianopia.

Involvement of face, arm and leg with or without a homonymous hemianopia suggests:
- *internal carotid artery* occlusion.

The ophthalmic artery arises from the internal carotid artery just below the circle of Willis (see Fig. 2.3). The following suggests *ophthalmic artery* ischaemia:
- monocular loss of vision.

Combinations of the following suggest *vertebrobasilar artery* ischaemia:
- double vision (cranial nerves 3, 4 and 6 and connections);
- facial numbness (cranial nerve 5);
- facial weakness (cranial nerve 7);
- vertigo (cranial nerve 8);
- dysphagia (cranial nerves 9 and 10);
- dysarthria;
- ataxia;
- loss of use or feeling in *both* arms or legs.

The following suggest a small but crucially located *lacunar* stroke due to *small vessel* ischaemia:
- pure loss of use in contralateral arm and leg;
- pure loss of feeling in contralateral arm and leg.

Management of cerebral ischaemia and infarction

There are three aspects of management, which are carried out simultaneously.

Confirmation of diagnosis

A CT brain scan is usually required to exclude with certainty the alternative diagnosis of intracerebral haemorrhage.

Optimization of recovery

Thrombolytic therapy, for example with tissue plasminogen activator, has been shown to improve outcome if given within 3 hours of symptom onset. The great majority of patients come to hospital later than this, and studies to determine the role of thrombolysis in this group are under way. Acute aspirin treatment is of modest but definite benefit, probably because of its effect on platelet stickiness.

There is also good evidence that outcome is also improved by management in a dedicated stroke unit. This effect is probably attributable to a range of factors, including:

- careful explanation to the patient and his relatives;
- systematic assessment of swallowing, to prevent choking and aspiration pneumonia, with percutaneous gastrostomy feeding if necessary;
- early mobilization to prevent the secondary problems of pneumonia, deep vein thrombosis, pulmonary embolism, pressure sores, frozen shoulder and contractures;
- early socialization to help to prevent depression, and help the acceptance of any disability; and treatment of depression when this occurs;
- management of blood pressure, avoiding over-enthusiastic treatment of hypertension in the first 2 weeks or so (when cerebral perfusion of the ischaemic area is dependent upon blood pressure because of impaired autoregulation), moving towards active treatment to achieve normal blood pressure thereafter;
- early involvement of physiotherapists, speech therapists and occupational therapists with a multidisciplinary team approach;
- good liaison with local services for continuing rehabilitation, including attention to the occupational and financial consequences of the event with the help of a social worker.

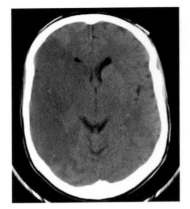

Large, wedge-shaped, low density area representing tissue infarction by a right middle cerebral artery occlusion.

Recovery from stroke

- ? Thrombolysis
- Aspirin
- Stroke unit
- Attention to swallowing
- Explanation
- Mobilization
- Socialization
- Careful BP management
- Paramedical therapists
- Rehabilitation

Prevention of further similar episodes

This means the identification and treatment of the aetiological factors already mentioned. The risk of further stroke is significantly diminished by blood pressure reduction, with a thiazide diuretic and an angiotensin-converting enzyme (ACE) inhibitor, even in patients with normal blood pressure, and also by statin therapy even if the cholesterol level lies within the normal range.

Investigations should include a full blood count, ESR (if elevated consider vasculitis, endocarditis, atrial myxoma or secondary infection), fasting glucose and lipids, and a search for cardiac sources of emboli. This starts with a careful cardiac examination, ECG and chest X-ray, supplemented by transthoracic or transoesophageal echocardiography if there is any suspicion of a cardiac source.

If the stroke is in the carotid territory, and especially if the patient has made a reasonable recovery and is otherwise healthy, further investigation should be undertaken to see if the patient might benefit from carotid endarterectomy. The patients who benefit most from such surgery are those with localized atheroma at the origin of the internal carotid artery in the neck, producing significant (over 70%) stenosis of the arterial lumen. The severity of stenosis can be established non-invasively by Doppler ultrasound or MR angiography, supplemented if necessary by catheter angiography. The presence or absence of a carotid bruit is not a reliable guide to the degree of stenosis. Well-selected patients in first-class surgical hands achieve a definite reduction in the incidence of subsequent ipsilateral stroke.

Antiplatelet drugs (e.g. aspirin) reduce the risk of further strokes (and myocardial infarction). Anticoagulation with warfarin is of particular benefit in atrial fibrillation and where a cardiac source of embolization has been found.

Despite all this, some patients continue to have strokes and may develop complex disability. Patients with predominantly small vessel disease may go on to suffer cognitive impairment (so-called multi-infarct dementia, described on p. 231) or gait disturbance with the *marche à petits pas* (walking by means of small shuffling steps, which may be out of proportion to the relatively minor abnormalities to be found in the legs on neurological examination). Patients with multiple infarcts arising from large vessels tend to accumulate physical deficits affecting vision, speech, limb movement and balance. Some degree of pseudobulbar palsy (with slurred speech, brisk jaw-jerk and emotional lability) is common in such cases due to the bilateral cerebral hemisphere involvement, affecting upper motor neurone innervation of the lower cranial nerve nuclei (see p. 134).

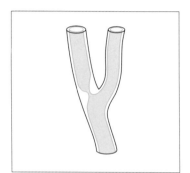

Significant stenosis by atheroma at the origin of the internal carotid artery.

Stroke prevention

- Lower blood pressure with thiazide ± ACE inhibitor
- Statin
- Aspirin
- Warfarin for those with a cardiac source of emboli
- Carotid endarterectomy for ideally selected patients
- Identify and treat ischaemic heart disease and diabetes
- Discourage smoking

Subarachnoid haemorrhage and intracerebral haemorrhage

Anatomy and pathology

The pathological process here is the sudden release of arterial blood, either into the subarachnoid space around the brain, or directly into the substance of the brain. In subarachnoid haemorrhage the bleeding usually comes from a berry aneurysm arising from one of the arteries at the base of the brain, around the circle of Willis (Fig. 2.5, left). In middle-aged, hypertensive patients, intracerebral haemorrhage tends to occur in the internal capsule or the pons, because of the rupture of long thin penetrating arteries (Fig. 2.5, right). In older patients, intracerebral haemorrhages occur more superficially in the cerebral cortex as a result of cerebral amyloid angiopathy. Arteriovenous malformations of the brain are a rare cause of either subarachnoid or intracerebral haemorrhage.

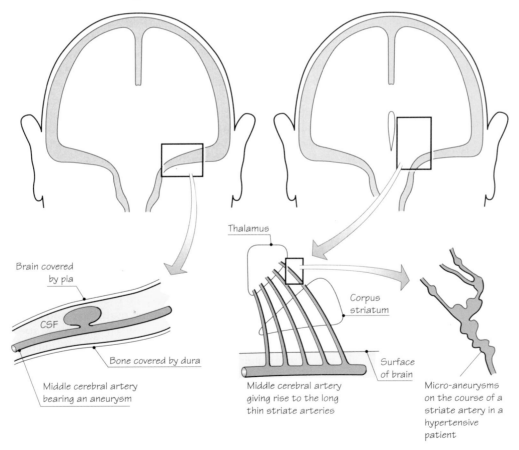

Thalamus

Brain covered by pia

CSF

Bone covered by dura

Middle cerebral artery bearing an aneurysm

Corpus striatum

Surface of brain

Middle cerebral artery giving rise to the long thin striate arteries

Micro-aneurysms on the course of a striate artery in a hypertensive patient

Fig. 2.5 *Left*: Berry aneurysm, the common cause of subarachnoid haemorrhage. *Right*: Micro-aneurysms, the common cause of intracerebral haemorrhage.

Neurological symptoms and signs

The range of consequences of subarachnoid and intracranial haemorrhage is illustrated in Figs 2.6 and 2.7. Both cause a sudden rise in intracranial pressure, with headache, vomiting and a decrease in conscious level, which may be followed by the development of papilloedema.

In *subarachnoid haemorrhage* the bleeding irritates the meninges. This causes the characteristic sudden severe headache ('like being hit on the head with a baseball bat') and neck stiffness; there is often a brief loss of consciousness at the moment of the bleed. It is the suddenness of onset which helps to differentiate subarachnoid haemorrhage from the headache and neck stiffness of infective meningitis, which come on over a few hours rather than seconds. Migraine can sometimes produce severe headache abruptly but without the severe neck stiffness of subarachnoid haemorrhage.

An *intracerebral bleed* in the region of the internal capsule will cause sudden severe motor, sensory and visual problems on the contralateral side of the body (hemiplegia, hemianaesthesia and homonymous hemianopia). In the pons, sudden loss of motor and sensory functions in all four limbs, associated with disordered brainstem function, accounts for the extremely high mortality of haemorrhage in this area.

Bleeding into the ventricular system, whether the initial bleed is subarachnoid or intracerebral, is of grave prognostic significance. It is frequently found in patients dying within hours of the bleed.

High blood pressure readings may be found in patients shortly after subarachnoid or intracerebral haemorrhage, either as a response to the bleed or because of pre-existing hypertension. Over-enthusiastic lowering of the blood pressure is not indicated because the damaged brain will have lost its ability to autoregulate. Low blood pressure therefore leads to reduced perfusion of the damaged brain tissue.

Subarachnoid haemorrhage

- Sudden, very severe headache
- Neck stiffness/rigidity
  ± vomiting
      loss of consciousness
      papilloedema
      neurological deficit

Intracerebral haemorrhage

- Sudden, severe neurological deficit
- Headache
  ± vomiting
      papilloedema

Common to all cases of **subarachnoid haemorrhage**

1 Blood throughout the subarachnoid space, therefore headache and neck stiffness

2 Raised intracranial pressure, therefore the possibility of depressed conscious level, headache, vomiting, papilloedema

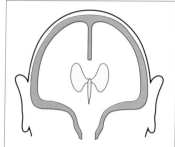

No brain damage, so no focal neurological deficit

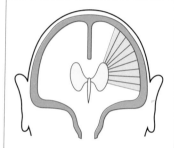

Spasm of a cerebral artery has occurred in the vicinity of an aneurysm, usually a few days after the initial bleed, causing focal ischaemia and neurological deficit

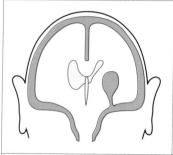

The aneurysm has also bled directly into adjacent brain tissue, forming a haematoma and causing immediate focal neurological deficit

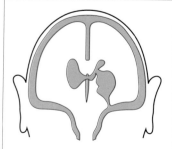

The aneurysm has bled into adjacent brain tissue, and the haematoma has burst into the ventricles. Focal neurological deficit and coma likely

Fig. 2.6 Diagram to show the clinical features of subarachnoid haemorrhage.

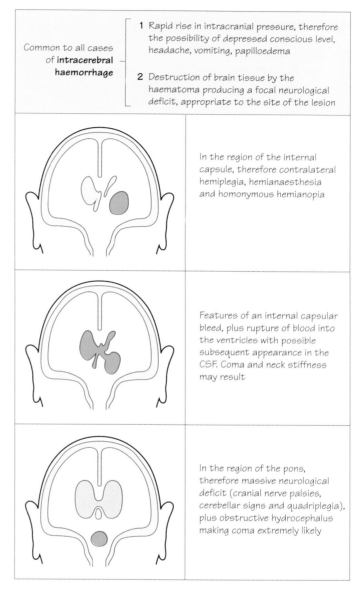

Common to all cases of **intracerebral haemorrhage**

1 Rapid rise in intracranial pressure, therefore the possibility of depressed conscious level, headache, vomiting, papilloedema

2 Destruction of brain tissue by the haematoma producing a focal neurological deficit, appropriate to the site of the lesion

In the region of the internal capsule, therefore contralateral hemiplegia, hemianaesthesia and homonymous hemianopia

Features of an internal capsular bleed, plus rupture of blood into the ventricles with possible subsequent appearance in the CSF. Coma and neck stiffness may result

In the region of the pons, therefore massive neurological deficit (cranial nerve palsies, cerebellar signs and quadriplegia), plus obstructive hydrocephalus making coma extremely likely

Fig. 2.7 Diagram to show the clinical features of intracerebral haemorrhage.

Management of subarachnoid haemorrhage

Establish the diagnosis

The first investigation for suspected subarachnoid haemorrhage is an urgent CT brain scan. This will confirm the presence of subarachnoid blood in the great majority of cases. If the scan is normal, a lumbar puncture should be performed to look for blood or xanthochromia (degraded blood) in the CSF. The CSF may be normal if the lumbar puncture is performed within a few hours or more than 2 weeks after the bleed. A lumbar puncture should not be performed if the subarachnoid haemorrhage has been complicated by the development of an intracerebral haematoma, since it may lead to coning (see pp. 42–4).

CT scan showing high density in the sulci over the right cerebral hemisphere due to subarachnoid blood.

Prevent spasm and minimize infarction

The calcium channel blocker nimodipine reduces cerebral infarction and improves outcome after subarachnoid haemorrhage. Disturbances of sodium homeostasis are common, and the electrolytes should be monitored regularly.

Prevent re-bleeding

Specialist neurosurgical advice should be sought. Patients who have withstood their first bleed well are offered carotid and vertebral angiography within a few days to establish whether or not a treatable aneurysm is present. Treatment usually involves either surgically placing a clip over the neck of the aneurysm to exclude it from the circulation, or packing of the aneurysm with metal coils, delivered by arterial catheter under radiological guidance, to cause it to thrombose.

Patients with subarachnoid haemorrhages confined to the area in front of the upper brainstem (so-called perimesencephalic haemorrhages) rarely have an underlying aneurysm and have an excellent prognosis without treatment.

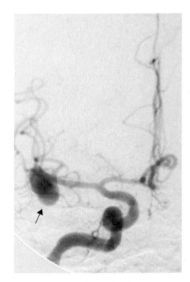

Rehabilitation

Many patients who survive subarachnoid haemorrhage (and its treatment) have significant brain damage. A proportion, often young, will not be able to return to normal activities. They will need support from relatives, nurses, physiotherapists, speech therapists, occupational therapists, psychologists and social workers, ideally in specialist rehabilitation units.

This has come from the large middle cerebral aneurysm arrowed.

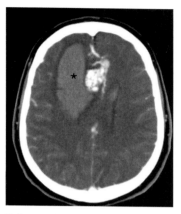

Enhanced CT scan showing high signal in an arteriovenous malformation, with bleeding into the adjacent brain (asterisk) and subarachnoid space.

Management of intracerebral haemorrhage

Establish the diagnosis
A CT brain scan will confirm the diagnosis and steer you away from thrombolytic therapy which would make the bleeding worse. The location and extent of the bleeding may give a clue to the cause and will determine management.

Lesions in the internal capsule
1. The optimal initial treatment is still a matter of research. It may sometimes be helpful to reduce intracranial pressure, for example with mannitol or by removing the haematoma.
2. Hypertension should be treated gently at first, and more vigorously after a few weeks.
3. Rehabilitation: a major and persistent neurological deficit is to be expected, and all the agencies mentioned under rehabilitation of patients with subarachnoid haemorrhage are likely to be of value.

Lesions in the pons
The mortality and morbidity of lesions in the pons are such as to make active treatment of any sort of questionable medical or ethical merit.

Lesions in the cerebral cortex
If there is a single cortical bleed, especially in a younger patient, then consideration should be given to a search for an underlying arteriovenous vascular malformation. This can be done with MR imaging once the haematoma has resolved. Multiple cortical bleeds in the elderly are usually due to cerebral amyloid angiopathy and are best treated conservatively. There is a high risk of both recurrence and subsequent dementia in this latter group of patients.

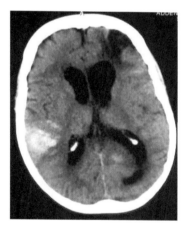

CT scan showing a recent right parietal haemorrhage and low density from a previous left frontal bleed, due to amyloid angiopathy.

The ideal treatment of intracerebral haemorrhage is prophylactic. Intracerebral haemorrhage is one of the major complications of untreated hypertension. There is good evidence to show that conscientious treatment of high blood pressure reduces the incidence of intracerebral haemorrhage in hypertensive patients.

CASE HISTORIES

Case 1

A 42-year-old teacher has to retire from the classroom abruptly on account of the most sudden and severe headache she has ever had in her life. She has to sit down in the staffroom and summon help on the phone. The school secretary calls for an ambulance as soon as she sees the patient, who is normally very robust and is clearly in extreme pain.

On arrival in the hospital A & E department, the patient is still in severe pain. Her BP is 160/100 and she shows marked neck stiffness but no other abnormalities on general or neurological examination. A clinical diagnosis of subarachnoid haemorrhage is made. She is admitted to the medical ward.

a. What investigations would you arrange?
b. How would you proceed now?

Case 2

A 55-year-old publican's wife is known to suffer from significant hypertension. She is receiving medication from her GP for this, but is not at all compliant. She smokes, and partakes of a drink. She is very overweight.

She suddenly collapses in the kitchen. She is unrousable except by painful stimuli, is retching and vomiting, and does not move her left limbs at all.

a. What is the most likely diagnosis?

She is taken to hospital by ambulance. Her physical signs in A & E are:

- obese;
- BP 240/140;
- no neck stiffness;
- no response to verbal command, and no speech;
- eyes closed, and deviated to the right when the eyelids are elevated;
- no movement of left limbs to painful stimuli;
- withdrawal of right limbs from painful stimuli;
- extensor left plantar response.

b. What is the most likely diagnosis?
c. What investigations would you arrange?
d. What would you tell her husband?

(For answers, see p. 255.)

Brain tumour

Introduction

Like malignant neoplasms anywhere else in the body, histolog-ically malignant brain tumours carry a poor prognosis. Histo-logically benign brain tumours are often difficult to remove. This may be the result of a lack of clear boundary between tumour tissue and normal brain substance, e.g. in a low-grade cerebral astrocytoma, or because the tumour lies very close to a part of the brain with important functions, e.g. an acoustic neuroma lying beside the brainstem.

Brain tumours therefore have an unfavourable reputation. It is frustrating that the improvements in our ability to diagnose brain tumours (with better imaging and less invasive biopsy techniques) are only just starting to be accompanied by improvements in our ability to treat them.

Intracranial compartments

Many of the problems caused by brain tumours arise because the brain lies within a rigid compartmentalized box (Fig. 3.1). The falx cerebri runs vertically from the front to the back of the head. The two compartments on either side each contain a cere-bral hemisphere. These are joined together below the front of the falx by the corpus callosum. At the back of the falx, the tento-rium cerebelli runs from side to side. Below it is the third com-partment, the posterior fossa. This contains the brainstem and the cerebellum. The top of the brainstem (i.e. the midbrain) is continuous with the cerebral hemispheres through a hole in the tentorium, the tentorial hiatus. The bottom of the brainstem (i.e. the medulla) leads to the spinal cord through a hole in the floor of the skull, the foramen magnum.

Figure 3.1 also shows the ventricular system. Cerebrospinal fluid is produced by the choroid plexus in each of the ventricles. It passes down through the ventricular system, leaving the fourth ventricles via the foramina of Luschka and Magendie to enter the subarachnoid space. It then circulates over the surface of the brain and spinal cord before being resorbed.

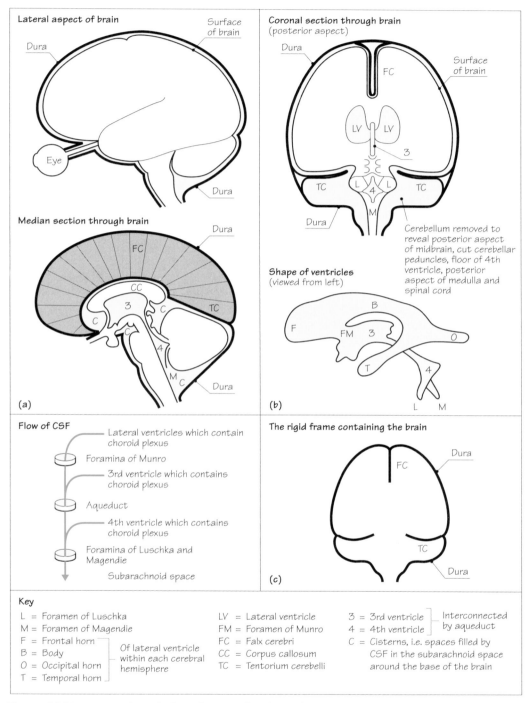

Fig. 3.1 (a) Diagrams to show the lateral aspect of, and a median section through, the brain. (b) Diagrams to show a coronal section through the brain (posterior aspect) and the shape of the ventricles as viewed from the left. (c) Diagram to show the rigid frame containing the brain.

Tentorial herniation, coning and shift

Figure 3.2 shows the influence of mass lesions situated in different parts of the compartmentalized space within the skull. When a mass lesion is making one cerebral hemisphere too large for its compartment (Fig. 3.2a):

- the supratentorial midline structures (corpus callosum and 3rd ventricle) are pushed towards the opposite side of the skull below the falx;
- the infero-medial part of the cerebral hemisphere is pushed through the tentorial hiatus (compressing the midbrain);
- the whole brainstem is pushed downwards so that the lowermost parts of the cerebellum and medulla oblongata become impacted in the foramen magnum.

The movement at the tentorial hiatus is known as *tentorial herniation*, and the impaction at the foramen magnum is known as *coning of the medulla*. They commonly occur simultaneously. The effects on the patient are:

- depression in conscious level (distortion of the reticular formation lying throughout the whole of the brainstem);
- an impairment of ipsilateral 3rd nerve function and dilatation of the pupil (tentorial herniation compressing the midbrain);
- interference with the vital functions of respiration and circulation (compression of the medulla oblongata).

A mass lesion situated in the midline (Fig. 3.2b) causes obstruction to the downward flow of CSF through the ventricular system. Under such circumstances, the ventricles above the site of obstruction dilate, and both cerebral hemispheres become too large for their compartments. Bilateral tentorial herniation and coning are likely to occur with the same dangerous clinical consequences.

In the presence of a unilateral posterior fossa mass lesion (Fig. 3.2c), there is movement of the midline posterior fossa structures to one side. This may compress the 4th ventricle sufficiently to block the downward flow of CSF, resulting in ventricular dilatation above the site of obstruction. There will be downward movement and compression at the level of the foramen magnum. At the tentorium cerebelli, there may be upward movement and compression of the midbrain or, if the supratentorial ventricular dilatation becomes very marked there may be downward herniation bilaterally. Depression of conscious level, dilated pupils and impaired vital functions may all result from such a lesion.

Coning

Cause:
- usually downward movement of brainstem

Effects:
- ↓ conscious level
- ↓ pupils' reaction to light
- ↓ vital functions including breathing

Aggravated:
- by lumbar puncture

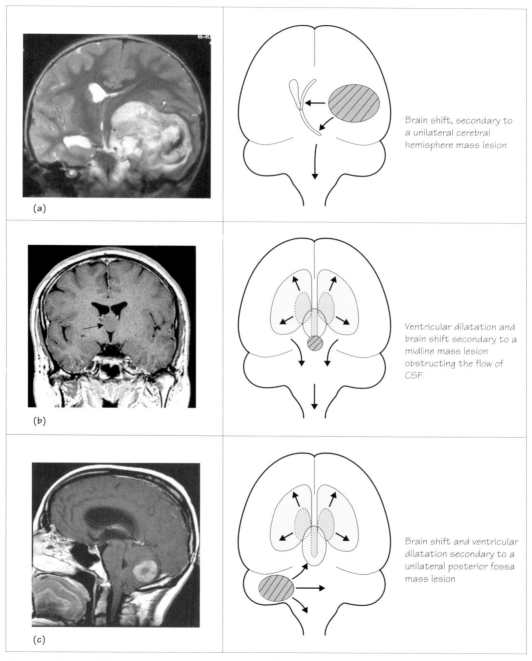

Fig. 3.2 (a) Brain shift secondary to a unilateral cerebral hemisphere mass lesion. (b) Ventricular dilatation and brain shift secondary to a midline mass lesion obstructing the flow of CSF. (c) Brain shift and ventricular dilatation secondary to a unilateral posterior fossa mass lesion.

Lethal lumbar puncture

Lumbar puncture is dangerous if intracranial pressure is raised due to a mass lesion. It reduces the CSF pressure below the foramen magnum. This can encourage downward brain shifts with tentorial herniation and coning of the medulla. This in turn causes progressive loss of consciousness and impaired control of breathing, which may be ultimately fatal. Lumbar puncture should not, therefore, be performed where there is known to be a mass lesion of sufficient size to cause raised intracranial pressure, or in situations where the possibility of one exists. Examples of these situations include patients with focal deficit (such as a hemiparesis), patients with papilloedema, and patients who are in a coma of unknown cause. In all these situations, the cause should be clarified with brain imaging before a lumbar puncture is contemplated.

On the other hand, where headache and papilloedema are due to a general elevation of intracranial pressure without any mass lesion, e.g. in meningitis and uncomplicated subarachnoid haemorrhage, lumbar puncture is safe and may relieve symptoms.

False localizing signs

We have seen that a mass lesion in one compartment of the brain can induce shift and compression in parts of the brain remote from the primary lesion. Brain tumours that are causing raised intracranial pressure are known to produce *false localizing signs*, which are no more than clinical evidence of these secondary movements of brain tissue:

• the descent of the brainstem may stretch the 6th cranial nerve to produce a non-localizing lateral rectus palsy:
• the ventricular dilatation above midline CSF obstructive lesions (Fig. 3.2b), or above posterior fossa lesions (Fig. 3.2c), may produce:
  —intellectual and behavioural changes suggestive of primary frontal pathology;
  —an interference with vertical eye movements (which are programmed in the upper midbrain) because of the dilatation of the posterior part of the 3rd ventricle and aqueduct;
• the impairment of conscious level, pupillary dilatation and depression of vital functions, mentioned already in this chapter, are the most pressing false localizing signs and demand immediate action by doctors in charge of the case.

Practical tip

1. Always measure the CSF pressure at the start of a lumbar puncture
2. Make sure the patient is relaxed and not too tightly curled
3. If the pressure is unexpectedly elevated (>25 cm of CSF):
• collect the sample in the manometer
• take out the LP needle
• secure IV access in case you need to give mannitol
• start neurological observations at 15-minute intervals
• arrange an urgent brain scan
• consider obtaining neurosurgical advice

False localizing sings

• Sixth nerve palsy
• 'Frontal' signs
• Impaired up-gaze
• Signs of coning

Clinical features

There are three groups of symptoms and signs resulting from brain tumours: raised intracranial pressure, epilepsy and an evolving focal neurological deficit.

Raised intracranial pressure

The cardinal features of raised intracranial pressure are:
- headache;
- vomiting;
- papulloedema;
- false localizing signs;
- depression of conscious level;
- signs of tentorial herniation and coning.

Only two further clinical points need to be made about these features.

1. The headaches of raised intracranial pressure tend not to be extremely severe, they do keep on troubling the patient, they are usually generalized throughout the head, and they tend to be worse in the mornings when the patient wakes. They sometimes wake the patient earlier than his normal waking time. They may be made worse by coughing, straining and bending. Unfortunately, like many things in clinical medicine, none of these features is absolutely specific.

2. Perfusion of the retina and optic disc may become critical in the presence of raised intracerebral pressure and papilloedema. The patient may report transient blurring or loss of vision. Such visual obscurations should stimulate urgent investigation and treatment.

Epilepsy

Focal epilepsy, focal epilepsy progressing on to a generalized tonic–clonic seizure, tonic–clonic seizures with post-ictal focal neurological signs, and tonic–clonic epilepsy without any apparent focal features may all indicate the presence of a tumour in the cerebrum. (Focal epilepsy is discussed in detail on pp. 196–8). Epilepsy is not a feature of posterior fossa tumours.

Epilepsy is not commonly caused by tumours, and less than 50% of cerebral tumours produce epilepsy, but the occurrence of epilepsy in adult life should prompt the possibility of a brain tumour in the doctor's mind.

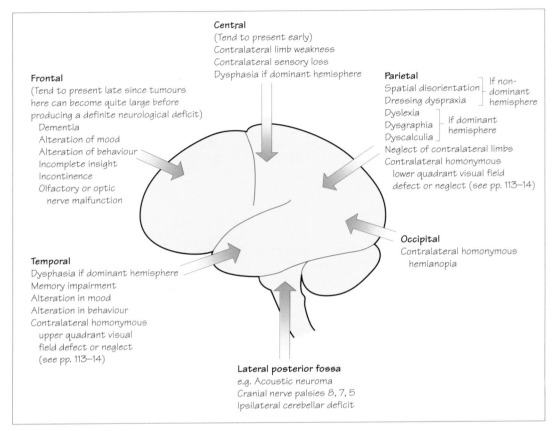

Central
(Tend to present early)
Contralateral limb weakness
Contralateral sensory loss
Dysphasia if dominant hemisphere

Frontal
(Tend to present late since tumours
here can become quite large before
producing a definite neurological deficit)
  Dementia
  Alteration of mood
  Alteration of behaviour
  Incomplete insight
  Incontinence
  Olfactory or optic
    nerve malfunction

Parietal
Spatial disorientation ⎤ If non-
Dressing dyspraxia   ⎦ dominant
                         hemisphere
Dyslexia   ⎤
Dysgraphia ⎬ If dominant
Dyscalculia ⎦ hemisphere
Neglect of contralateral limbs
Contralateral homonymous
  lower quadrant visual field
  defect or neglect (see pp. 113–14)

Occipital
Contralateral homonymous
  hemianopia

Temporal
Dysphasia if dominant hemisphere
Memory impairment
Alteration in mood
Alteration in behaviour
Contralateral homonymous
  upper quadrant visual
  field defect or neglect
  (see pp. 113–14)

Lateral posterior fossa
e.g. Acoustic neuroma
Cranial nerve palsies 8, 7, 5
Ipsilateral cerebellar deficit

Fig. 3.3 Lateral aspect of the brain, showing the neurological deficits produced by tumours at various sites.

An evolving focal neurological deficit

The presence of a tumour impairs the function of the part of the brain in which it resides. The nature of the evolving focal neurological deficit clearly depends on the site of the lesion. Figures 3.3 and 3.4 depict the principal neurological deficits produced by tumours situated in various parts of the brain. Tumours near the midline (Fig. 3.4) and in the posterior fossa may produce marked features of raised intracranial pressure before there are many localizing signs.

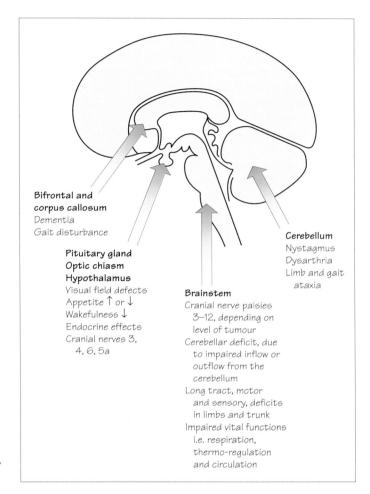

**Bifrontal and
corpus callosum**
Dementia
Gait disturbance

**Pituitary gland
Optic chiasm
Hypothalamus**
Visual field defects
Appetite ↑ or ↓
Wakefulness ↓
Endocrine effects
Cranial nerves 3,
  4, 6, 5a

Brainstem
Cranial nerve palsies
  3–12, depending on
  level of tumour
Cerebellar deficit, due
  to impaired inflow or
  outflow from the
  cerebellum
Long tract, motor
  and sensory, deficits
  in limbs and trunk
Impaired vital functions
  i.e. respiration,
  thermo-regulation
  and circulation

Cerebellum
Nystagmus
Dysarthria
Limb and gait
  ataxia

Fig. 3.4 Median section through the brain, showing the neurological deficits produced by tumours at various sites.

The length of history of any of the three main features of a brain tumour is a guide to the nature of the tumour, in terms of malignancy. This is not foolproof, however. Certainly a long history suggests a benign or low-grade malignancy tumour. A short progressive history obviously implies malignancy, but sometimes a benign tumour can be silent for years only to produce a short worrying history when the brain and the intracranial compartments finally become unable to absorb the presence of the enlarging mass lesion.

Common brain tumours

Gliomas are seen to appear in both the benign and malignant groups of tumours. Astrocytomas are by far the most common glial tumour; tumours derived from oligodendrocytes, ependyma, neurones, primitive neuroectodermal or other tissues are much rarer. Unless otherwise specified, the words 'primary brain tumour' or 'glioma' refer to an astrocytoma in clinical practice. Gliomas are classified histologically from grade 1 (benign) to grade 4 (the highly malignant glioblastoma multiforme). Benign gliomas are, unfortunately, much less common than malignant ones and have a tendency to become more malignant with time.

Meningiomas are nearly always benign. They may arise from any part of the meninges, over the surface of the brain, from the falx, or from the tentorium. There is a plane of cleavage between tumour and brain tissue which makes total removal a definite possibility, so long as the tumour is reasonably accessible and unattached to dural venous sinuses, e.g. the sagittal sinus.

Pituitary adenomas produce two principal sets of symptoms: space-occupying effects and endocrine disturbance. When the pituitary gland enlarges in the pituitary fossa, it most commonly expands upwards (suprasellar extension) to compress optic nerves/chiasm/tracts. The classical bitemporal hemianopia resulting from chiasmal compression occurs when the optic chiasm is right above a pituitary extension which is directly upwards. The exact position of the optic chiasm, and the direction of pituitary expansion, do, however, vary from one case to another, so monocular blindness due to optic nerve compression and homonymous hemianopia from optic tract compression are not uncommon in patients with pituitary adenomas. Lateral expansion of pituitary adenomas may compress structures on the lateral wall of the cavernous sinus (cranial nerves, 3, 4, 5a and 6), producing double vision and forehead numbness. Forward and downward expansion of the adenoma results in enormous expansion of the pituitary fossa and occasional erosion through bone into the sphenoidal air sinus.

The endocrine disturbances that accompany the development of a pituitary adenoma are *positive* if the tumour cells are secretory (prolactin, growth hormone, etc.), and *negative* if the tumour is preventing normal secretion by the rest of the pituitary gland (varying degrees of panhypopituitarism).

Benign

- Grade 1–2 gliomas
- Meningioma
- Pituitary adenoma
- Acoustic neuroma

Malignant

Primary
- grade 3–4 gliomas

Secondary
- metastatic carcinoma

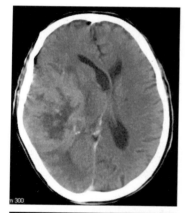

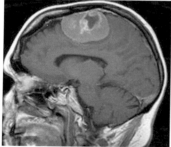

The glioma (top) is poorly differentiated from the surrounding brain, unlike the meningioma (bottom).

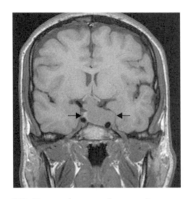

Pituitary adenoma (arrows).

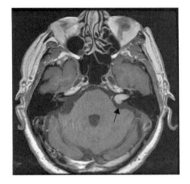

Acoustic neuroma (arrow).

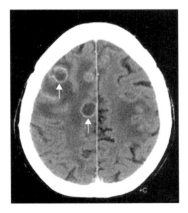

Metastases (arrows).

Acoustic neuromas are benign tumours of the Schwann cells along the course of the acoustic nerve, between the cerebello-pontine angle and the internal auditory meatus in the petrous temporal bone. First and foremost, they produce progressive unilateral nerve deafness, but by the time of recognition there may well be associated 5th and 7th nerve dysfunction, unilateral cerebellar signs and evidence of raised intracranial pressure. Early diagnosis is highly desirable since a small tumour can be treated with radiotherapy or surgery with fewer complications than a large one which has caused brainstem displacement and raised intracranial pressure.

Common malignant tumours in the brain are either *gliomas* or *metastases*, in particular malignant astrocytomas and metastatic carcinoma. Together these constitute well over 60% of all brain tumours. The history is usually short, of raised intracranial pressure, epilepsy or neurological deficit. Not uncommonly, all three groups of symptoms are present by the time of diagnosis. It is not uncommon for a primary carcinoma elsewhere in the body to present with metastatic disease in the brain. If the metastases are multiple, the differentiation from malignant glioma is not difficult, but solitary cerebral metastases are quite common.

Differential diagnosis

The common presenting symptoms of brain tumours are:
- raised intracranial pressure;
- epilepsy;
- a progressive focal neurological deficit.

Clearly, other mass lesions within the head may produce *all three features*. There may be difficulty in differentiating a malignant tumour from an intracerebral abscess when the history is a short one, and from subdural haematoma when the history is a little longer.

Other causes of raised intracranial pressure include severe arterial hypertension, chronic meningitis and so-called benign intracranial hypertension (BIH). BIH is probably due to reduced venous drainage of the brain, and mainly affects young obese women or patients with a predisposition to venous thrombosis.

Epilepsy and focal epilepsy are more usually caused by epileptogenic scars from previous intracranial disease.

The principal alternative cause of a progressive subacute focal neurological deficit is an ischaemic stroke, which occasionally, instead of developing with characteristic abruptness, comes on in a stuttering way.

Investigation

Brain imaging

Brain tumours can be detected using CT X-ray scanning or MR scanning. The choice of technique used will often depend upon local facilities. CT is cheaper, more widely available and (when used with contrast enhancement) capable of detecting the majority of tumours. MR scanning is superior in many ways, especially in detecting small tumours and tumours in the base of the skull and the posterior fossa. MR also allows the images to be presented in a range of planes, which helps with surgical planning.

Admission to hospital

If the clinical presentation and results of scanning suggest a brain tumour, admission to hospital for further investigation will be indicated in most cases, especially if there is progressive neurological deficit or evidence of raised intracranial pressure. This will be an extremely stressful experience for the patient and relatives. Reassurance, sympathy and encouragement together with adequate explanation are required.

Other tests

The brain imaging procedures mentioned above sometimes require the support of:
- radiological and other imaging techniques elsewhere in the body if metastatic disease seems likely;
- carotid or vertebral angiography if the neurosurgical team needs this information prior to surgery;
- haematological and biochemical investigation if cerebral abscess, granuloma, metastatic disease or pituitary pathology are under consideration.

(*NB* Lumbar puncture is contra-indicated in suspected cases of cerebral tumour.)

Management of brain tumours

- Admission to hospital
- Scanning
- No lumbar puncture
- Dexamethasone
- Surgery
- Radiotherapy
- Anticonvulsants

Management

If the patient shows marked features of raised intracranial pressure and scanning displays considerable cerebral oedema, dexamethasone may be used with significant benefit. The patient will be relieved of unpleasant, and sometimes dangerous, symptoms and signs, and the intracranial state made much safer if neurosurgical intervention is to be undertaken.

Surgical management

Complete removal

Meningiomas, pituitary tumours not susceptible to medical treatment, acoustic neuromas and some solitary metastases in accessible regions of the brain can all be removed completely. Sometimes, the neurosurgical operation required is long and difficult if the benign tumour is relatively inaccessible.

Partial removal

Gliomas in the frontal, occipital and temporal poles may be removed by fairly radical debulking operations. Sometimes, benign tumours cannot be removed in their entirety because of tumour position or patient frailty.

Biopsy

If at all possible, the histological nature of any mass lesion in the brain should be established. What looks like a glioma or metastasis from the clinical and radiological points of view occasionally turns out to be an abscess, a benign tumour or a granuloma. If the mass lesion is not in a part of the brain where partial removal can be attempted, biopsy by means of a needle through a burrhole usually establishes the histological diagnosis. The accuracy and safety of this procedure may be increased by use of stereotactic surgical techniques. Histological confirmation may not be mandatory where there is strong collateral evidence of metastatic disease.

Histological confirmation may be postponed in patients presenting with epilepsy only, in whom a rather small mass lesion in an inaccessible part of the brain is revealed by a scan. Sequential scanning, initially at short intervals, may be the most reasonable management plan in such patients.

Shunting and endoscopic surgery

Midline tumours causing ventricular dilatation are routinely treated by the insertion of a shunt into the dilated ventricular system. The shunt tubing is tunnelled under the skin to drain into the peritoneal cavity. This returns intracranial pressure to normal, and may completely relieve the patient's symptoms. Sometimes it is possible and desirable to remove the tumour or treat the hydrocephalus using intracranial endoscopic procedures instead.

Additional forms of treatment

Radiotherapy

Middle-grade gliomas, metastases and incompletely removed pituitary adenomas are the common intracranial tumours which are radiosensitive. The posterior fossa malignant tumours of childhood and lymphoma are also sensitive to radiotherapy. Radiotherapy commonly follows partial removal or biopsy of such lesions, and continues over a few weeks whilst the preoperative dose of dexamethasone is being gradually reduced.

Chemotherapy

Chemotherapy can be useful as primary treatment for lymphoma and as adjunctive therapy for oligodendroglioma and some high-grade astrocytomas.

Anticonvulsants

Control of epilepsy may be an important part of the management of a patient with a supratentorial brain tumour.

Dexamethasone

Taken in large and constant dosage, dexamethasone may be the most humane treatment of patients with highly malignant gliomas or metastatic disease. Used in this way, dexamethasone often allows significant symptomatic relief so that the patient can return home and enjoy a short period of dignified existence before the tumour once more shows its presence. At this point, dexamethasone can be withdrawn and opiates used as required.

Prognosis

The fact that the majority of brain tumours are either malignant gliomas or metastases, which obviously carry a very poor prognosis, hangs like a cloud over the outlook for patients with the common brain tumours.

The table below summarizes the outlook for patients with the common brain tumours. It can be seen that such pessimism is justified for malignant brain tumours, but not for the less common benign neoplasms.

Tumour	Treatment	Outcome
Meningioma	Surgical removal if possible and / or radiotherapy if not	Residual disability common Recurrence rate (1% per year)
Glioma		
Lower grades	Watch and wait *or* biopsy and radiotherapy *or* partial removal ± radiotherapy ± chemotherapy	Prolonged survival, usually with residual disability, but recurrence is very common and often higher grade
High grade	Partial removal and radiotherapy ± chemotherapy or palliative care	Few patients survive 1 year
Lymphoma	Biopsy and chemotherapy	Improving: median survival about 2 years
Pituitary adenoma	Medical therapy for prolactinoma *or* surgical removal ± radiotherapy	Excellent
Acoustic neuroma	Watch and wait *or* radiotherapy *or* surgical removal	Deafness ± facial weakness are common; survival is excellent

CASE HISTORIES

Case 1

A 65-year-old widow presents with a 6-month history of unsteadiness. She has started to veer to the left. She has been well prior to this, apart from a longstanding hearing problem and surgery for colon cancer 5 years ago. On examination she has an ataxic gait, slight leftwards nystagmus, an absent left corneal reflex and marked left-sided deafness. There is no papilloedema.

a. What do you think is the cause of her symptoms?

Case 2

A 45-year-old oil company executive returns from secondment in Nigeria because of ill health. Over the last 3 months he has become slow and erratic, making frequent mistakes at work and getting lost on his way home. His memory has become poor and he has had difficulty in finding his words. His appetite has faded and he has lost weight. In the last 2 weeks he has become unsteady on his feet and incontinent of urine.

On examination he is thin. He has no fever but his axillary and inguinal lymph nodes are slightly enlarged. He is drowsy. He had bilateral papilloedema. He has difficulty cooperating with a neurological examination and becomes increasingly irritated when you persist.

a. What do you think is the cause of his symptoms?

(For answers, see p. 256.)

CHAPTER 4

Head injury

The causes

Road traffic accidents involving car drivers, car passengers, motorcycle drivers and pillion-seat riders, cyclists, pedestrians and runners constitute the single greatest cause of head injury in Western society. Compulsory speed limits, car seat-belts, motorcycle and cycle helmets, stricter control over driving after drinking alcohol, and clothing to make cyclists and runners more visible have all proved helpful in preventing road accidents, yet road accidents are still responsible for more head injuries than any other source.

Accidents at work account for a significant number of head injuries, despite the greater use of protective headgear. Sport, especially boxing and horse riding, constitutes a further source for head injury, prevented to some extent by the increasing use of protective headgear. Accidents around the home account for an unfortunate number of head injuries, especially in young children who are unable to take proper precautions with open windows, ladders, stairs and bunk-beds. Child abuse has to be remembered as a possible cause of head injury.

It is a sad fact that head injury, trivial and severe, affects young people in significant numbers. Approximately 50% of patients admitted to hospital on account of head injury in the UK are under the age of 20 years. Accidents in the home, sports accidents, and accidents involving motorcycles, cars and alcohol, account for this emphasis on youth.

The outcome from head trauma depends upon the age and pre-existing health of the patient at the time of injury, and upon the type and severity of the primary injury to the brain. In the care of the individual patient, there is little that the doctor can do about these factors. They have had their influence by the time the patient is delivered into his hands. Outcome does also depend, however, upon minimizing the harm done by secondary insults to the brain after the injury. Prevention of secondary brain injury is the direct responsibility of those caring for the patient. It is one of the main messages of this chapter.

The effect in pathological terms

Primary brain injury

The brain is an organ of relatively soft consistency contained in a rigid, compartmentalized, unyielding box which has a rough and irregular bottom. Sudden acceleration, deceleration or rotation certainly allow movement of the brain within the skull. If sudden and massive enough, such movement will cause tearing of nerve fibres and petechial haemorrhages within the white matter, and contusions and lacerations of the cortex, especially over the base of the brain.

If the trauma has been severe, the diffuse damage to the brain described above may cause generalized brain swelling, just like the swelling that occurs with injury to any other organ. The brain, however, is contained within a rigid box, unlike other organs of the body. Diffuse brain swelling may result in the brain becoming too large in volume for the space allocated to it. As discussed in Chapter 3 (p. 42), this may lead to tentorial herniation, midbrain compression, impaction of the lower medulla and cerebellar hemispheres in the foramen magnum, secondary brainstem pathology and death (Fig. 4.1).

Severe rotational head injuries may cause primary brainstem injury, which may itself be fatal.

Secondary brain injury

In the circumstances of head injury, the diffusely damaged brain is extremely vulnerable to four other insults, all of which produce further brain swelling (Fig. 4.1). By causing further swelling, each of the four insults listed below tend to encourage the downward cascade towards brainstem failure and death:

1. Arterial hypotension—from blood loss at the time of injury, possibly from the scalp but more probably from an associated injury elsewhere in the body. Hypotension and hypoxia, in isolation but especially in combination, will cause hypoxic-ischaemic brain damage with swelling.

2. Arterial hypoxia—because of airway obstruction, associated chest injury or an epileptic fit.

3. Infection—head injuries in which skull fracture has occurred may allow organisms to enter the skull via an open wound, or from the ear or nose. Infection causes inflammatory oedema.

4. Intracranial haematoma—the force of injury may have torn a blood vessel inside the skull (either in the brain substance or in the meninges) so that a haematoma forms. This causes further compression of the brain by taking up volume within the rigid skull.

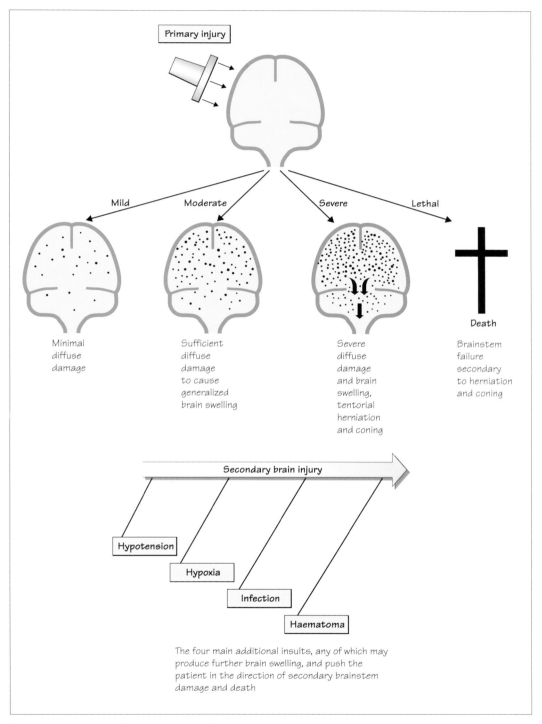

Fig. 4.1 A summary of the pathological effects that may occur as a consequence of head injury.

The effect in clinical terms

The clinical instrument that is used to monitor the effects of head injury on patients requiring admission to hospital is the neurological observation chart created by competent, trained nursing staff.

This chart includes the patient's responsiveness using the Glasgow Coma Scale (GCS), recording the patient's best eye, verbal and motor responses, together with his vital signs of pupil size and reactivity, blood pressure, pulse, respiratory rate and temperature. The observations are made at intervals appropriate to the patient's clinical condition—every 15 minutes in critically ill patients.

The Glasgow Coma Scale is described and illustrated in Chapter 11 (p. 184, Fig. 11.3). The changes in the charted observations of best eye, verbal and motor responses are used to signal changes in the patient's brain condition with great sensitivity. The vital signs of pupil size and reactivity, blood pressure, pulse, respiratory rate and temperature are, essentially, indicators of brainstem function.

Figure 4.2 shows the clinical states that accompany mild, moderate and severe degrees of diffuse cerebral damage after head injury. The adverse influence of hypotension, hypoxia, infection and intracranial haematoma will become apparent in the patient's chart observations, possibly accompanied by an epileptic fit. (An epileptic fit may be the cause or effect of a deteriorating intracranial situation, undesirable because of the associated anoxia and effects on intracranial pressure.) The appearance of abnormal brainstem signs indicates that the additional insult is adversely affecting the brain very seriously.

Figure 4.2 also shows the clinical clues, and definite signs, that confirm the presence of one or more of the four additional insults. Ideally, the clues should make the doctor so alert to the possibility of the insult becoming operational that the problem is rectified before the patient starts to decline significantly in his Glasgow Coma Scale observations, and certainly before evidence of impaired brainstem function appears. This is what is meant by the prevention of secondary brain injury.

Primary injury

Mild

Concussion,
or concussion
plus some
retrograde
and post-
traumatic
amnesia

Moderate

Persistent
coma after
the accident
with fairly
good scores
on the
Glasgow
Coma Scale,
and no signs
of brainstem
malfunction

Severe

Persistent coma
after the
accident, poor
scores on the
Glasgow Coma
Scale, and
evidence of
failing brainstem
function

Secondary brain injury

The four additional insults will show their adverse influence
on the brain by :
• declining performance in Glasgow Coma Scale observations
• an epileptic fit
• impaired brainstem function observations

Hypotension	Hypoxia	Infection	Haematoma
Clinical clues			
• Large scalp laceration i.e. external blood loss	• Patient found face down, unconscious	• Open scalp wound over skull fracture	• Factors known to be associated with the development of an intracranial haematoma, whether extradural, subdural or intracerebral :
• Associated major injury to chest, abdomen, pelvis, limbs, i.e. external and internal blood loss	• Upper airways obstruction whilst unconscious	• Leakage of CSF from scalp wound, nose or ear	• Skull fracture
• History that the patient was propped upright after injury with known blood loss and probable hypotension	• Severe associated facial injury	• Inadequate inspection, cleaning, or debridement of open scalp wound over fracture site	• Impaired conscious level (even disorientation) i.e. a fully orientated patient with no skull fracture is very unlikely to develop a haematoma
	• Aspiration of blood or vomit into trachea	• Skull fracture found on CT scan in region of wound, nose or ear	
	• Prolonged epileptic fit	• Intracranial air seen on CT scan	
	• Associated injury to chest wall or lungs		
	• Respiratory depression by alcohol or drugs		
Clinical evidence			
• Development of shock Low blood pressure Rapid pulse Sweating	• Noisy obstructed breathing	• Purulent discharge from scalp wound	• CT scan
	• Abnormal chest movement	• Proved infection of CSF	
	• Abnormal respiratory rate		
	• Abnormal chest X-ray		
	• Abnormal blood gases		

Fig. 4.2 A summary of the clinical effects of head injury.

Management

The first question, near or at the site of the head injury, is whether there is any indication for assessment in the hospital emergency department.

Indications for hospital assessment after head injury

- Any loss of consciousness, amnesia or fall in the Glasgow Coma Scale at any time.
- Any focal neurological symptom or sign.
- Suspicion of skull fracture or penetrating injury.
- Seizure, vomiting or persistent headache.
- Current drug or alcohol intoxication (making assessment unreliable).
- High-energy head injury (e.g. pedestrian struck by car; thrown from moving vehicle; fall downstairs; fall of 1 metre or more onto head).
- Coagulopathy (history of bleeding or clotting disorder or anticoagulated).
- Previous neurosurgery.
- Suspicion of non-accidental injury.
- Age 65 years or more.

Once in hospital, patients may require management in the emergency department, in the trauma ward of the district general hospital, or in a neurosurgical centre (Fig. 4.3). In all these places, and during transfer from one to another, management is directed towards prevention and treatment of the four serious insults causing secondary brain injury (see Fig. 4.2).

In the emergency department the patient must be assessed, Glasgow Coma Scale observations initiated (see p. 184), and if necessary the patient must be resuscitated. Then it has to be established whether there is any indication for a CT brain scan and/or neurosurgical advice.

Indications for CT brain scan after head injury

- GCS less than 13 at any time, or 13–14 at 2 hours after injury.
- Suspected skull fracture or penetrating head injury (see box).
- Post-traumatic epileptic seizure.
- Focal neurological deficit.
- More than one episode of vomiting (except perhaps in children).
- Amnesia for more than 30 minutes of events prior to impact.
- Any loss of consciousness or amnesia if also:
  —aged 65 years or older;
  —coagulopathy;
  —high-energy head injury.

A Airway
Clear airway, with cervical spine control until cervical injury is confidently excluded

B Breathing
Assess ventilation and chest movement. Arterial blood gases

C Circulation
Assess likelihood of blood loss. Monitor BP and P frequently. Establish IV line

D Dysfunction of CNS
Assess by Glasgow Coma Scale at frequent intervals

E Exposure
Identify all injuries, head to toe, front and back

Reasons to suspect a skull fracture or penetrating head injury

- Clear fluid (CSF) running from nose
- Blood or clear fluid running from ear(s)
- Bruising around eye(s) with no eye trauma (panda eyes)
- Bruising behind ear(s) (Battle's sign)
- New unilateral deafness
- Significant visible scalp or skull wound

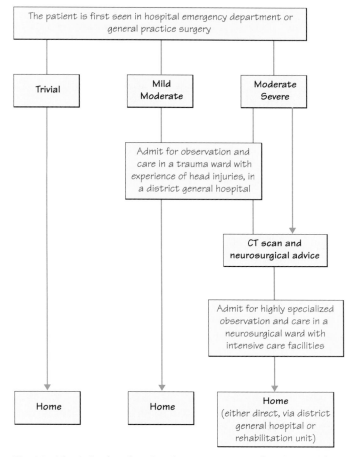

Fig. 4.3 A logistic plan showing the management of patients with head injury.

Reasons to talk to a neurosurgeon

- New and potentially significant abnormality on CT brain scan.
- Persisting coma (GCS of 8 or less) after initial resuscitation.
- Unexplained confusion (for more than 4 hours).
- Falling GCS (especially falling motor score).
- Progressive focal neurological deficit.
- Epileptic seizure without full recovery.
- Penetrating injury.
- CSF leak.

Whether in the emergency department, the CT scan suite, the trauma ward of the district general hospital, the ambulance or the neurosurgical centre, the same vigilant care of the patient with respect to GCS observations, blood pressure, oxygenation and avoidance of infection must be maintained.

It is important to:

- continue regular competent *neurological observations* at intervals appropriate to the patient's condition (half-hourly, hourly, 2-hourly, 4-hourly);
- remember the head injury may be *non-accidental*, especially if there is any uncertainty about its mechanism (see box);
- remember that there are *pharmacological dangers*. If the patient smells of alcohol, the doctor may recognize that this could be a contributory factor towards the patient's depressed state of consciousness, but he will be unwise to attribute the whole clinical picture to alcohol if a head injury is present, especially if a skull fracture is present. Do not complicate the state of consciousness, or the assessment of it, by the use of strong, CNS depressant, analgesics; by the overuse of intravenous, CNS depressant, drugs to control an individual epileptic fit; by permitting any procedures requiring general anaesthesia, which can possibly wait for 2 or 3 days; or by the use of mydriatic drugs to look at the fundi;
- continue to anticipate, prevent, detect early, and treat energetically any of the *four serious insults* which may further damage the brain and cause further brain swelling (see Fig. 4.2, p. 59).

If the patient requires admission to the neurosurgical centre great attention should be paid to the maintenance of normal intracranial pressure and perfusion of the brain. This often involves the use of intracranial pressure monitors, intermittent intravenous administration of mannitol and neurosurgery (e.g. to evacuate an extradural haematoma). The routine care of the unconscious patient (see Chapter 11, p. 187) is established.

> **Head injury may result from:**
>
> - stroke
> - cerebral haemorrhage
> - epilepsy
> - cardiac dysrhythmia
> - alcoholic intoxication
> - non-accidental injury to children

After-care

In all but the most trivial head injuries, the patient will benefit from some after-care. This may not amount to more than simple explanation and reassurance regarding a period of amnesia, headaches, uncertainty about a skull fracture, timing of return to work, etc. Without the opportunity to discuss such matters, unnecessary apprehensions may persist in the mind of the patient and his family.

At the other end of the scale, somebody recovering from a major head injury (often associated with other injuries) may need a great deal of further medical and paramedical care for months after the head injury. This may mean a considerable period in hospital or in a rehabilitation unit whilst recovery from the intellectual, psychological, neurological and orthopaedic deficits gradually occurs.

Initial features:
- level of consciousness
- skull fracture
- focal neurological signs

Secondary features:
- epilepsy
- intracranial haematoma
- meningitis

Duration:
- of coma
- of post-traumatic amnesia
- of stay in hospital

Persisting deficits:
- intellectual
- psychological
- focal neurological

The consequences

How severe a head injury was it, doctor?

Several factors, shown in the adjacent margin, must be borne in mind when formulating a reply to this enquiry.

With regard to the duration of coma and post-traumatic amnesia, confusion may arise. The duration of post-traumatic amnesia refers to the period after the accident until the time that the patient regains ongoing memory. The patient often describes the latter as the time he woke up after the accident. He means the time he recovered his memory, not the time he recovered consciousness. The time *he* says he woke up is often long after the time that observers have noted return of consciousness (eyes open and paying attention, speaking and using his limbs purposefully).

The duration of hospital stay must also be clarified. If there was associated (orthopaedic) injury, the patient may have been hospitalized long after the time for discharge purely on head injury grounds.

Post-concussion syndrome

Headache

Dizziness

Impaired concentration

Impaired memory

Fatigue

Anxiety

Depression

Irritability

Indecisiveness

Impaired self-confidence

Lack of drive

Impaired libido

This usually follows minor concussive head injury or less, with post-traumatic amnesic periods lasting a few minutes, rather than major head injury. It consists of a remarkably stereotyped set of symptoms, as shown alongside, unaccompanied by abnormal neurological signs.

Controversy exists as to the cause of the post-concussion syndrome. On the one hand, it is accepted that concussive head injury can produce diffuse minor brain damage. (If repeated, this may accumulate to the punch-drunk state, known as post-traumatic encephalopathy, seen in some boxers towards the end of their careers.) On the other hand, the syndrome can be seen in some patients suffering head injuries at work, where the evidence of concussion or amnesia is very minimal and where litigation and financial compensation are paramount.

The syndrome can be very disabling for months, even years, after a minor head injury. Despite our lack of understanding of its precise nature, the syndrome has to be recognized as a definite entity responsible for considerable morbidity after head injury in some patients.

Post-traumatic epilepsy

Patients surviving head injury may have developed an epileptogenic scar in the brain, which may subsequently give rise to focal or secondarily generalized epileptic attacks. Post-traumatic epilepsy shows its presence within a year of the accident in about 50% of patients who are going to develop this late complication of their head injury. In the rest, it may not occur for several years.

There are certain features of the head injury which make post-traumatic epilepsy more likely:
- post-traumatic amnesia lasting more than 24 hours;
- focal neurological signs during the week after the head injury;
- epilepsy during the week after the head injury;
- depressed skull fracture;
- dural tear;
- intracranial haematoma.

These risk factors enable fairly accurate prediction of the risk of epilepsy in a patient after head injury, and are valuable when advising patients about prophylactic anticonvulsants and driving.

Chronic subdural haematoma

In elderly patients who have suffered trivial head injury, sometimes so trivial that it is not clearly remembered, blood may start to collect in the subdural space. This is not sudden, severe arterial bleeding, but a process that evolves over several weeks, a gradual accumulation and liquefaction of blood. The blood accumulates over the convexity of the brain, with gradual elevation of intracranial pressure, shift of midline structures and eventual tentorial herniation and coning.

The clinical picture is of subacute fluctuating drowsiness and confusion, often associated with headache, in which focal neurological signs appear late. Any elderly patient presenting in this way is a candidate for a chronic subdural haematoma, with or without a history of head injury. Chronic alcoholics and patients on anticoagulants have an increased risk of chronic subdural haematoma.

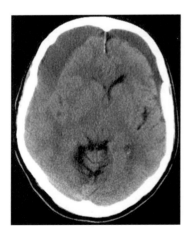

Bilateral subdural haematomas.

Chronic subdural haematomas may occur bilaterally, and may be hard to visualize on conventional CT scans if the altered blood is isodense with brain tissue. They are treated by evacuation of the blood through burrholes, with good results.

Outcome from severe head injury

- 50% mortality
- Disability common in survivors
- Often young people

Outcome from severe head injury

Mortality from severe head injury (coma lasting more than 6 hours) is of the order of 50%. Those who survive are likely to have deficits in some or all of the following areas, depending on which parts of the brain have been most damaged:
- intellectual function;
- mood, behaviour, personality;
- speech and communication;
- vision;
- motor and sensory function in the limbs;
- post-traumatic epilepsy.

Most of a patient's recovery will have occurred within 6 months of the injury, though further slower improvement may occur in the next 12–18 months.

Patients displaying deficits in all areas constitute what the general public recognize as a brain-damaged person, often unable to live independently. Commonly, the patients are young at the time of their accident, and many years of life may lie ahead of them. In general, provision for such patients is inadequate in terms of chronic young sick units, where their ongoing care may be successfully managed in some sort of shared care system with the patient's relatives.

Compensation and medico-legal aspects

Because road traffic accidents and accidents at work cause a large percentage of head injuries, compensation for suffering, disability, loss of earnings, restriction in recreational pursuits, etc. is very commonly sought in the months and years after the accident. This occurs after both minor and major injuries, and it is unusual for a case to be settled before 2 years have elapsed after the accident.

Though this activity is entirely reasonable, it is unsettling for the patient and his family. It tends to perpetuate the accident and its effects in their minds longer than would otherwise be the case.

CASE HISTORIES

Case 1

A 12-year-old boy has been involved in an accident whilst riding his bicycle. All the details are not clear, but the accident happened at traffic lights, the boy was not wearing a helmet, he was struck by a car and he lost consciousness transiently though he was subsequently able to talk reasonably coherently. He was not able to walk into the ambulance which brought him to the emergency department.

On examination he is orientated in person but not in time or place. There is some bruising and swelling above his left ear, though no scalp laceration. There are no focal neurological signs. There are no signs of injury to any other part of his body.

a. What management would you arrange?

Ninety minutes later, some 3 hours after the accident, the neurological observations start to show deterioration. He will only open his eyes to strong painful stimuli and his speech is reduced to mumbled incomprehensible sounds. His limb responses are variable but he can localize painful stimuli with each hand. Vital functions and pupil reactions remain normal.

b. What is your management now?

Case 2

A dishevelled middle-aged man is brought to the emergency department by ambulance. He has been found unconscious on the pavement outside a public house. He smells strongly of alcohol. He is bleeding from a large left-sided scalp wound. He is deeply unconscious with a Glasgow Coma Scale of 8 (E2 V2 M4) but no focal neurological deficit.

a. What are the possible reasons for his state?

(For answers, see pp. 256–7.)

CHAPTER 5

Parkinsonism, involuntary movements and ataxia

Introduction

An elderly man comes to see you to report a 6-month history of progressive dragging of his left leg and difficulty using his left hand for fiddly tasks. He is worried that he has a brain tumour. You find no weakness or spasticity but note that he stoops and shuffles a little when he walks and cannot wiggle the left fingers or open and close the left hand rapidly. You are able to tell him that he has the entirely happier diagnosis of Parkinson's disease.

What this case emphasizes is the principle outlined in Chapter 1 that normal, smooth, well-coordinated movements rely not just on the integrity of the primary motor pathway (upper motor neurone–lower motor neurone–neuromuscular junction–muscle). They also require normal inputs to this pathway from the basal ganglia, cerebellum and sensory pathways, as shown in Fig. 5.1. It also illustrates the fact that many of the disorders of movement and coordination that we will discuss in this chapter can be diagnosed by history-taking and examination, without sophisticated investigations.

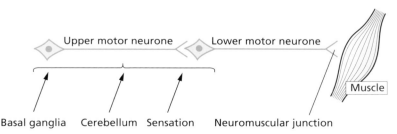

Fig. 5.1 Diagram to show the basic components of the nervous system required for normal movement.

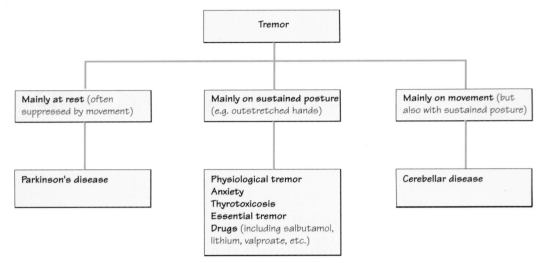

Fig. 5.2 Classification of tremor.

Tremor

Tremor is a rhythmic (or fairly rhythmic) to and fro movement of a part of the body. It can range in severity from something that the patient can feel but you cannot see, through to something that causes wild involuntary movements that prevent any useful limb function. A classification of the common forms of tremor is shown in Fig. 5.2.

The important differentiating feature of Parkinson's disease tremor is the fact that it is most evident at rest. It is reduced or abolished by voluntary movement. Other core features of Parkinson's disease, such as bradykinesia and rigidity, are usually also present to some degree and point to the correct diagnosis.

Patients with disease in the cerebellum and its brainstem connections commonly have clumsy, uncoordinated movements of their limbs. The incoordination is present throughout the proximal and distal limb muscles, leading to large-amplitude, chaotic shaking of the limb. This is most marked on attempted movement, and is therefore termed kinetic tremor, although it is almost always also present on sustained posture. Much the most common cause of severe kinetic tremor is multiple sclerosis.

Patients with cerebellar degenerations may have a milder kinetic tremor, where the involuntary of oscillations appear as the limb approaches its intended target, a phenomenon sometimes referred to as intention tremor.

In both situations, there are likely to be additional signs of cerebellar or brainstem dysfunction, such as dysarthria, gait ataxia, limb ataxia with past pointing and dysdiadochokinesia, and nystagmus.

Examining for tremor

Look for tremor at rest:
- hands in lap
- patient distracted ('Close your eyes and count backwards')

Look for postural tremor:
- arms outstretched
- hands slowly brought in towards the face

Look for kinetic tremor:
- 'Touch my finger, then your chin'

If you cannot see the tremor:
- listen to the affect muscles with a stethoscope

We all have some degree of tremor on sustained posture, termed physiological tremor. This is faster than parkinsonian or cerebellar tremor, absent at rest, and most evident in the hands. Most of the predominantly postural tremors are due to an exaggeration of this phenomenon.

Postural tremors are made more obvious when circulating catecholamines are increased, for example by anxiety, and by sympathomimetic drugs like salbutamol. Conversely, they are suppressed to some extent by beta-adrenergic blockade and sometimes by alcohol. The mechanisms of these effects are not understood. They are often exploited by people who require a steady hand, such as surgeons, snooker players or musicians, who may take propranolol or alcohol on important occasions. Reliance on alcohol to treat tremor can lead to dependency and liver disease.

The most disabling postural tremor is familial essential tremor, which tends to be dominantly inherited. A more jerky, asymmetrical variant of essential tremor is seen in patients with a personal or family history of dystonia, and is referred to as dystonic tremor; it is less responsive to beta-blockers or alcohol.

Parkinson's disease

Parkinson's disease is rare before the age of 40, but becomes increasing common with age, and affects 1–2% of people over 65 years old. Several genes causing familial Parkinson's disease have been identified, and other genes probably contribute to the risk of developing the disease in those with no family history. Environmental factors that increase the risk of developing Parkinson's disease include working with pesticides; drinking coffee and smoking cigarettes both reduce the risk.

The symptoms and signs of Parkinson's disease reflect a highly selective pattern of degeneration in the brain. The worst damage occurs in the dopamine-producing neurones of the substantia nigra, and this accounts for many of the abnormalities of movement, referred to as 'parkinsonism'. These neurones project to the corpus striatum via the nigrostriatal pathway. The consequence of loss of neurones in the substantia nigra is dopamine deficiency in the corpus striatum. This may be unilateral, asymmetrical or symmetrical.

The noradrenaline- and 5HT-producing neurones in the brainstem are also affected, and this may explain the high incidence of depression in Parkinson's disease. The neurones that deliver acetylcholine to the cerebral cortex are affected as well; this, together with involvement of the cortial neurones themselves, contributes to cognitive symptoms. In all these locations the neurones degenerate in a characteristic way, forming clumps of protein called Lewy bodies.

The speed and extent of this process vary considerably between individuals. Some patients become disabled by impaired movement and then dementia within a few years. Others have a barely progressive tremor that may require little or no treatment for a decade or more. Most patients fall between these extremes, with symptoms that become slightly more troublesome (and require increasingly complex treatment) with each passing year. With treatment, people with Parkinson's disease now have a normal life expectancy, unless they go on to develop dementia. This is much harder to treat and still shortens life.

Features of Parkinson's disease

There is often a delay in diagnosing Parkinson's disease. The early symptoms of Parkinson's disease can be vague (see box). The signs are usually asymmetrical, leading to confusion with strokes and tumours.

The core features of Parkinson's disease are bradykinesia and rigidity. Bradykinesia is a lack of spontaneous movements (often most noticeable as reduced blinking, lack of facial expression and reduced arm swing when walking), and a slowing of movements, especially fine repetitive ones. Rigidity is an increase in tone throughout the full range of movement, unlike spasticity which builds up and then gives way. Rigidity may have a constant resistance (like bending a *lead pipe*) or a juddering feel (like turning a *cogwheel* against a ratchet).

The rest tremor of Parkinson's disease (in the limbs, the jaw or the lightly closed eyes) is highly characteristic, but 50% of patients do not have it at presentation and 20% never get it. Gait disturbance is usually mild in the first few years. Patients may then develop difficulty in starting to walk or in stopping (festination) or may abruptly freeze in doorways or crowds. Eventually most patients have falls. The falling is partly a consequence of slow, stiff muscles or freezing, but partly also due to a failure of more complex postural righting reflexes or orthostatic hypotension. It has a very bad effect on quality of life.

Non-motor symptoms are often equally distressing, especially depression, dementia and disturbed sleep. Depression has a prevalence of 30% and should be actively sought and treated. Dementia is unusual before 70 years but affects many patients thereafter. Losing the thread of sentences and memory loss are followed by periods of confusion, often accompanied by visual hallucinations (see p. 230). Sleep may be disrupted for several reasons. The most worrying is REM sleep behavioural disturbance, in which patients act out their vivid dreams.

Early symptoms of Parkinson's disease

Commonly non-specific at first:
- aches and pains
- disturbed sleep
- anxiety and depression
- slower dressing
- slower walking

Later more specific:
- tremor
- difficulty turning in bed
- stooping or shuffling
- softer speech
- spidery handwriting

Main signs of Parkinson's disease

- Rigidity
- Bradykinesia
- Tremor
- Gait disturbance
- Stooped posture

Causes of reduced facial expression

- Parkinsonism
- Depression
- Severe facial weakness
- Severe hypothyroidism

Management of patients with Parkinson's disease

The management of patients with Parkinson's disease requires patience and persistence. The patient's concerns and expectations may be very different from yours. It may take time to reach a shared understanding and objectives. Specialist nurses and patient groups like the Parkinson's Disease Society are a huge help with this. Non-drug treatments should be sought where possible, and advice from speech therapists, physiotherapists, occupational therapists and dieticians is often required.

Drug schedules should be altered gradually. Side-effects from the drugs are common, making regular consultations important. As the illness evolves, drug schedules can become quite complicated, needing clear explanation and written confirmation.

The mainstay of drug treatment is to boost dopaminergic activity in the nigrostriatal pathway, either by giving levodopa which can be turned into dopamine within the remaining neurones in the substantia nigra or by giving dopamine agonists which mimic the effect of dopamine in the striatum (Fig. 5.3). Less potent benefits can be obtained from drugs which inhibit the metabolism of dopamine by monoamine oxidase type B and catechol-O-methyl transferase, and from drugs that modify other neurotransmitters in the striatum such as amantadine and anticholinergics.

Levodopa treatment was developed in the 1960s and remains the most powerful treatment for Parkinson's disease. Levodopa

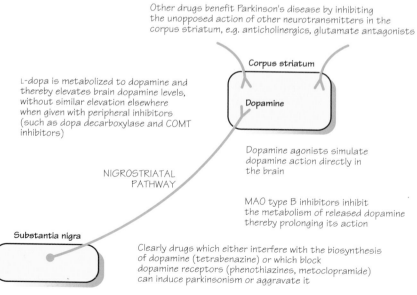

Other drugs benefit Parkinson's disease by inhibiting the unopposed action of other neurotransmitters in the corpus striatum, e.g. anticholinergics, glutamate antagonists

Corpus striatum

L-dopa is metabolized to dopamine and thereby elevates brain dopamine levels, without similar elevation elsewhere when given with peripheral inhibitors (such as dopa decarboxylase and COMT inhibitors)

Dopamine

Dopamine agonists simulate dopamine action directly in the brain

NIGROSTRIATAL PATHWAY

MAO type B inhibitors inhibit the metabolism of released dopamine thereby prolonging its action

Substantia nigra

Clearly drugs which either interfere with the biosynthesis of dopamine (tetrabenazine) or which block dopamine receptors (phenothiazines, metoclopramide) can induce parkinsonism or aggravate it

Fig. 5.3 Diagram to show the substantia nigra in the midbrain, and the nigrostriatal pathway.

is absorbed from the gut, crosses the blood–brain barrier and is converted into dopamine by the enzyme dopa-decarboxylase. It is given with a dopa-decarboxylase inhibitor which does not cross into the brain. This prevents the levodopa from being converted into dopamine in the body (where it would cause nausea and vomiting) without interfering with the production of dopamine in the brain.

Most patients initially respond brilliantly to levodopa therapy. There are three subsequent problems:
- *Wearing off*: the response becomes shorter and less marked.
- *Dyskinesia*: each dose produces involuntary chorea movements.
- *On–off effect*: the transition between lack of response (off) and response (on) becomes rapid.

The oral dopamine agonists are not as potent as levodopa in alleviating parkinsonism, but are less prone to cause dyskinesia and fluctuation. Young and mildly affected patients are sometimes started therefore on a dopamine agonist initially, in the hope of postponing levodopa therapy and its complications for a while. Alternatively the agonist drugs can be introduced later, to reduce the patient's reliance on levodopa after these complications have begun. It is not clear whether one strategy is better than the other. Dopamine agonists often cause their own adverse effects in older patients, especially hallucinations.

Selegiline and entacapone prolong the duration of action of levodopa, and have a limited role in smoothing fluctuations. Amantadine can be very helpful in suppressing dyskinesia.

There are two strategies for very refractory fluctuation or dyskinesia:
- *Apomorphine infusion*: this parenteral dopamine agonist can be infused subcutaneously to achieve stable control. This is tricky and requires specialist medical and nursing input.
- *Surgical treatments*: these are aimed at inhibiting overactive parts of the basal ganglia circuitry, either with a stereotactic lesion or by implanting an electrode with an impulse generator. Targets for these operations include the internal globus pallidus within the striatum (to reduce dyskinesia) and the tiny subthalamic nucleus (to reduce the parkinsonism itself). Procedures to graft the striatum with fetal substantia nigra cells or stem cells remain experimental.

Anticholinergic drugs are useful for treating tremor, but have much less effect on the other aspects of parkinsonism, and often seriously aggravate memory problems and hallucinations. Conversely, memory problems and hallucinations often respond to cholinergic therapy with drugs like donepezil and rivastigmine. These inhibit the cholinesterase enzyme that beaks down acetylcholine. They do not aggravate the parkinsonism. An alternative way of suppressing hallucinations (but not

---

Drugs for Parkinson's disease

Levodopa with dopa decarboxylase inhibitor:
- cobeneldopa (Madopar)
- cocareldopa (Sinemet)

Dopamine agonists:
- cabergoline
- pergolide
- ropinirole
- premipexole
- bromocriptine
- apomorphine

MAO-B inhibitor:
- selegiline

COMT inhibitor:
- entacapone

Glutamate antagonist:
- amantadine

Anticholinergics

Cholinergics:
- rivastigmine
- donepezil

Atypical neuroleptics:
- quetiapine
- clozapine

Antidepressants

The main side-effects or overdose phenomena when enhancing the failing nigrostriatal pathway

↑ Dopamine in the gut:
- nausea
- vomiting

↑ Dopamine in the striatum:
- dyskinesia

↑ Dopamine elsewhere in the brain:
- postural hypotension
- confusion/hallucinations

memory problems) is to use atypical neuroleptic drugs such as quetiapine or clozapine. Conventional neuroleptics (such as haloperidol or chlorpromazine) cannot be used in Parkinson's disease because they exacerbate parkinsonism, occasionally to a fatal degree.

Other causes of parkinsonism

Parkinsonism can result from other problems in the nigrostriatal pathway (Fig. 5.4). The commonest is drug-induced parkinsonism, due to *drugs* which block striatal dopamine receptors, such as antipsychotics or antiemetics. *Vascular parkinsonism* is due to multiple small infarcts in the basal ganglia and often causes more trouble with walking than the upper limbs. Other neurodegenerative diseases can cause parkinsonism together with additional features. These include *multiple system atrophy* where there may be any combination of parkinsonism, cerebellar ataxia and autonomic failure, and *progressive supranuclear palsy* where there is usually a severe disturbance of vertical eye movements. Clinical pointers to these other causes include:

- symmetrical bradykinesia and rigidity, without tremor;
- lack of response to levodopa therapy;
- poor balance and falls in the first 2 years of the illness.

The substantia nigra, nigrostriatal pathway and corpus striatum may be involved in diffuse cerebral pathology:
- viral encephalitis
- cerebrovascular disease
- severe head injury
Parkinsonian signs may feature amongst other neurological deficits subsequently

There are rarer patterns of neuronal loss from the CNS which involve nigral and striatal neurones:
- progressive supranuclear palsy (Steele–Richardson syndrome)
- multisystem CNS degeneration with autonomic failure (Shy–Drager syndrome)

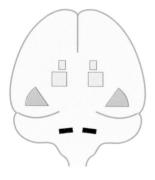

Drugs which interfere with dopamine synthesis and release by the pre-synaptic terminal of the nigrostriatal axon, **A**, or which block dopamine uptake by the receptors on the surface of the corpus striatal neurone, **B**, may induce parkinsonism

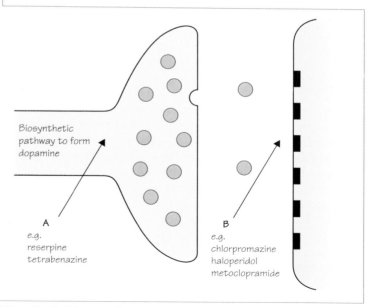

Biosynthetic pathway to form dopamine

A
e.g.
reserpine
tetrabenazine

B
e.g.
chlorpromazine
haloperidol
metoclopramide

Fig. 5.4 Parkinsonism other than idiopathic Parkinson's disease.

Involuntary movements

The main categories of involuntary movements are tremor, chorea and dystonia, tics, and myoclonus.

Chorea and dystonia

Chorea refers to fidgety momentary movements which flit randomly around the body. They resemble fragments of purposeful acts or gestures. If you find yourself responding to the movements then you are likely to be dealing with chorea. *Dystonia* refers to slower involuntary movements that give rise to repetitive twisting or fixed abnormal postures.

There is an overlap between the two movement disorders, in both their clinical manifestations and their causes. Both are due to dysfunction in the basal ganglia. Many patients will have mainly chorea with a little dystonia, or vice versa. The term *athetosis* refers to slow writhing movements that are halfway between chorea and dystonia, but is now largely reserved for a form of cerebral palsy where these movements predominate.

Hemichorea and hemiballismus

If chorea affects just one side of the body it is termed hemichorea, or hemiballismus if the movements are wild and large scale. This is usually due to a small infarct in the subthalamic nucleus on the opposite side of the brain. Although the movements usually subside within weeks, they can be exhausting and can be suppressed with dopamine-blocking drugs (like haloperidol).

Huntington's disease

The most serious cause of chorea is Huntington's disease. This is inherited as an autosomal dominant disorder, and is one of several neurodegenerative diseases that are due to an expansion in a run of repeated CAG nucleotide triplets within a gene. It typically starts with chorea, often accompanied by impulsive or erratic behaviour, and progresses relentlessly to cause dystonia and parkinsonism together with dementia. Depression and suicide are common, but most patients ultimately succumb to the complications of immobility. People who are at risk of developing Huntington's disease because of their family history can, if they wish, undergo predictive genetic testing. This process is surrounded by emotional issues and requires very careful genetic counselling.

Causes of chorea

Drugs:
- levodopa in Parkinson's patients
- oral contraceptive pill
- many psychiatric drugs

Vascular disease of the basal ganglia:
- atheroma
- systemic lupus erythematosus

Degenerative diseases:
- Huntington's disease

Post-infectious:
- Sydenham's chorea

Other causes:
- thyrotoxicosis

Trinucleotide repeat diseases

Many genes have stretches of DNA where the same three nucleotides are repeated over and over again (e.g. CAGCAGCAG etc.). Several neurological diseases are due to expansions of these sequences, with an excessive number of repeats. Examples include:

- Huntington's disease
- several dominantly inherited cerebellar ataxias
- Friedreich's ataxia
- one form of motor neurone disease
- myotonic dystrophy
- fragile X mental retardation

These expansions have unusual features. The expansions are unstable and can increase in size from one generation to the next, leading to an earlier age of onset (termed anticipation). This tendency may exclusively affect expansions transmitted by mothers or fathers. The ways in which the extra nucleotides cause disease is a matter of intense current research, but may involve changes in the expression of the gene and the folding of the protein product.

Sydenham's chorea

This used to be a common sequel to streptococcal infection in young people, along with rheumatic fever. It is now rare in developed countries but remains common elsewhere. Other post-streptococcal movement disorders are described in Chapter 15 (p. 253).

Drug-induced movement disorders

We have seen already how tremor and parkinsonism can be induced by drugs. Drugs can also cause all the other movement disorders, especially chorea and dystonia. Drugs which block dopamine receptors are the main culprit. They can cause acute dystonia (for example, when intravenous metoclopramide is given to a young person for nausea), with spasms of the face, neck and arms and a phenomenon called an oculogyric crisis where the eyes roll up involuntarily. Long-term use of these drugs (for example, when neuroleptic drugs are used for depression or schizophrenia) can cause complex involuntary chewing and grimacing movements in the face called tardive dyskinesia, which persist after the causative drug is withdrawn.

Focal dystonia

Dystonia can affect one localized area of the body. Common forms of focal dystonia include *blepharospasm*, where there are repetitive spasms of eye closure that can seriously interfere with vision; *torticollis*, where the head pulls painfully to one side and may also shake; and *writer's cramp*, where the forearm cramps up and causes the hand to take on a painful twisted posture when writing is attempted. These conditions can be treated by weakening the overactive muscles with regular botulinum toxin injections.

Other forms of dystonia

Dystonia can affect larger areas of the body, such as the neck and one arm, *segmental dystonia*, the trunk muscles, *axial dystonia*, or the whole of the body, *generalized dystonia*. Generalized dystonia usually begins in childhood and often has a genetic basis. It can be treated to a very limited extent with drugs. There is increasing interest in treatment with brain stimulator operations.

Wilson's disease

This is a very rare metabolic disorder characterized by the accumulation of copper in various organs of the body, especially the brain, liver and cornea. It is inherited in an autosomal recessive fashion, and is due to mutations in a gene for ATP-dependent copper-transporting protein.

It is a disease of children and young adults. In the brain, it chiefly affects basal ganglia function, giving rise to all sorts of movement disorders including tremor, chorea, dystonia and parkinsonism. It can also cause behavioural disturbance, psychosis or dementia. In the liver it may cause cirrhosis and failure. In the cornea it is visible (with a slit lamp) peripherally as a brownish Kayser–Fleischer ring. Looking for this and a low serum caeruloplasmin level are ways of screening for the disease.

The importance of Wilson's disease is that it can be treated with copper-chelating drugs (like penicillamine) if diagnosed early, when brain and liver changes are reversible.

Tics

Tics are stereotyped movements that can be momentary or more complex and prolonged. They differ from chorea in that they can be suppressed for a while by an effort of will. Simple tics, like blinking or grimacing or shrugging repeatedly, are very common in children, especially boys aged 7–10 years. In a small minority these persist into adult life. A wider range of tics, producing noises as well as movements, is suggestive of Gilles de la Tourette syndrome.

Gilles de la Tourette syndrome

Georges Gilles de la Tourette was a nineteenth-century French neurologist who came across the disorder while attempting to classify chorea. He went on to have a distinguished career, survived being shot by the husband of a patient, and died of neurosyphilis. Gilles de la Tourette syndrome begins in children and teenagers with:

- multiple motor tics, with a gradually evolving repertoire of movements;
- phonic tics, commonly sniffs and grunts, rarely repetitive speech (*echolalia*) or swearing (*coprolalia*);
- obsessive–compulsive disorder, such as repeated checking or complex rituals.

Mild forms are common in the general population, and very common in people with learning disability. The tics respond to dopamine-blocking drugs. The obsessive–compulsive disorder (which is often more disabling) may improve with selective serotonin reuptake inhibitors (like fluoxetine) or behavioural therapy. It is possible that some cases may be caused or exacerbated by autoimmune responses to streptococcal infection analogous to Sydenham's chorea.

Myoclonus

Myoclonus produces sudden, shock-like jerks. It is a normal phenomenon in most children and many adults as they are falling off to sleep. It also occurs in a wide range of disease states, and can be due to dysfunction in the cerebral cortex, basal ganglia, brainstem or spinal cord.

Myoclonus as part of general medicine:
- hepatic encephalopathy ('liver flap');
- renal failure;
- carbon dioxide retention.

Myoclonus as part of degenerations of the cerebral cortex:
- Alzheimer's disease;
- Lewy body dementia;
- Creutzfeldt–Jakob disease.

Myoclonus as part of epilepsy:
- juvenile myoclonic epilepsy (where there are jerks in the morning: 'messy breakfast syndrome');
- severe infantile epilepsies.

Myoclonus due to basal ganglia disease:
- jerking on attempted movement ('action myoclonus') after anoxia due to cardiorespiratory arrest or carbon monoxide poisoning.

Myoclonus due to brainstem disease:
- exaggerated jerks in response to sudden noise ('startle myoclonus') in rare metabolic and degenerative disorders.

Cerebellar ataxia

Figure 5.5 is a grossly oversimplified representation of the cerebellum. The function of the cerebellum is to coordinate agonist, antagonist and synergist muscle activity in the performance of learned movements, and to maintain body equilibrium whilst such movements are being executed. Using a massive amount of input from proprioceptors throughout the body, from the inner ear and from the cerebral hemispheres, a complex subconscious computation occurs within the cerebellum. The product of this process largely re-enters the CNS through the superior peduncle and ensures a smooth and orderly sequence of muscular contraction, characteristic of voluntary skilled movement.

In man, the function of the cerebellum is seen at its best in athletes, sportsmen, gymnasts and ballet dancers, and at its worst during states of alcoholic intoxication when all the features of cerebellar malfunction appear. A concern of patients with organic cerebellar disease is that people will think they are drunk.

Localization of lesions

From Fig. 5.5 it is clear that patients may show defective cerebellar function if they have lesions in the cerebellum itself, in the cerebellar peduncles, or in the midbrain, pons or medulla. The rest of the CNS will lack the benefit of correct cerebellar function whether the pathology is in the cerebellum itself, or in its incoming and outflowing connections. Localization of the lesion may be possible on the basis of the clinical signs.

- *Midline cerebellar lesions* predominantly interfere with the maintenance of body equilibrium, producing gait and stance ataxia, without too much ataxia of limb movement.
- *Lesions in the superior cerebellar peduncle*, along the course of one of the chief outflow tracts from the dentate nucleus in the cerebellum to the red nucleus in the midbrain, classically produce a very marked kinetic tremor, as mentioned at the beginning of this chapter.
- *Lesions in the midbrain, pons and medulla*, which are causing cerebellar deficits by interfering with inflow or outflow pathways to or from the cerebellum, may also cause other brainstem signs, e.g. cranial nerve palsies, and/or long tract signs (upper motor neurone or sensory) in the limbs.

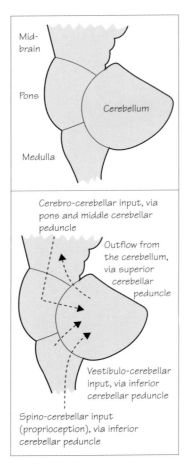

Fig. 5.5 Highly simplified diagrammatic representation of the brainstem and cerebellum as viewed from the left.

Clinical signs of cerebellar dysfunction

The common, important clinical signs of cerebellar dysfunction are listed below.

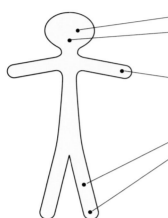

- *Nystagmus.*
- *Dysarthria*: the muscles of voice production and speech lack coordination so that sudden irregular changes in volume and timing occur, i.e. scanning or staccato speech.
- *Upper limbs: ataxia and intention tremor*, best seen in movement directed towards a restricted target, e.g. the finger–nose test; *dysdiadochokinesia*, i.e. slow, inaccurate, rapid alternating movements.
- *Lower limbs: ataxia*, best seen in the heel–knee–shin test.
- *Gait and stance ataxia*, especially if the patient is asked to walk heel to toe, or to stand still on one leg.
- *Hypotonia*, though a feature of cerebellar lesions, is not very useful in clinical practice.

Cerebellar representation is ipsilateral, so a left cerebellar hemisphere lesion will produce nystagmus which is of greater amplitude when the patient looks to the left, ataxia which is more evident in the left limbs, and a tendency to deviate or fall to the left when standing or walking.

To date, it has not been possible to improve defective cerebellar function pharmacologically.

Causes of cerebellar malfunction

The common causes of cerebellar malfunction are:
- cerebrovascular disease;
- multiple sclerosis;
- drugs, especially anticonvulsant intoxication;
- alcohol, acute intoxication.

Rarer cerebellar lesions include:
- posterior fossa tumours;
- cerebellar abscess, usually secondary to otitis media;
- cerebellar degeneration, either hereditary (e.g. Friedreich's ataxia and autosomal dominant cerebellar ataxia), alcohol induced, or paraneoplastic;
- Arnold–Chiari malformation (the cerebellum and medulla are unusually low in relation to the foramen magnum);
- hypothyroidism.

Sensory ataxia

Since proprioception is such an important input to the cerebellum for normal movement, it is not surprising that loss of proprioception may cause ataxia, and that this ataxia may resemble cerebellar ataxia.

Pronounced loss of touch sensation, particularly in the hands and feet, seriously interferes with fine manipulative skills in the hands, and with standing and walking in the case of the feet.

In the presence of such sensory loss, the patient compensates by using his eyes to monitor movement of the hands or feet. This may be partially successful. An important clue that a patient's impaired movement is due to sensory loss is that his clumsiness and unsteadiness are worse in the dark, or at other times when his eyes are closed, e.g. washing his face, having a shower, whilst putting clothes over his head in dressing.

Signs of sensory ataxia

In the hands
- Pseudoathetosis: the patient is unable to keep his fingers still in the outstretched position. Because of the lack of feedback on hand and finger position, curious postures develop in the outstretched fingers and hands when the eyes are closed.
- Clumsiness of finger movement, e.g. when turning over the pages of a book singly, and when manipulating small objects in the hands, made much worse by eye closure. Shirt and pyjama top buttons, which cannot be seen, present more difficulty than other buttons.
- Difficulty in recognizing objects placed in the hands when the patient's eyes are closed, and difficulty in selecting familiar articles from pockets and handbags without the use of the eyes.
- Loss of touch and joint position sense in the fingers.

In the legs
- Marked and unequivocal Rombergism. The patient immediately becomes hopelessly unsteady in the standing position when the eyes are closed.
- As the patient walks, he is obviously looking at the ground and at his feet.
- Loss of touch and joint position sense in the feet and toes.

Causes of sensory ataxia

These are shown in Fig. 5.6:

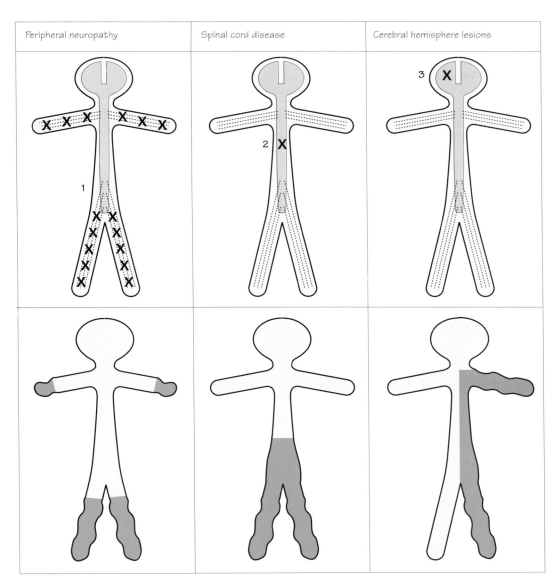

Fig. 5.6 Sensory deficits causing sensory ataxia.

Ataxia in vestibular disease

Again, because vestibular inputs are vital to cerebellar function, disorders of the vestibular system can produce ataxia, especially of gait. This cause of unsteadiness can usually be recognized by the presence of prominent vestibular symptoms and signs like vertigo and rotatory nystagmus (see pp. 126–8), and by the absence of other cerebellar, brainstem and sensory signs.

CASE HISTORIES

Case 1

A 75-year-old woman notices that she can no longer deal the cards at her bridge club because her hands have become clumsy and slow. Her handwriting has become spidery and small. She cannot roll over in bed. She shuffles when she walks.

She lives with her husband who is in good health. She has never smoked. Her parents both lived into their eighties without anything similar, and her sister is alive and well. She is on medication for hypertension and a hiatus hernia.

On examination she walks with a flexed posture, a shuffling gait and no arm swing. She has moderate bradykinesia and rigidity in both arms. There is no tremor or cerebellar deficit. Her eye movements are normal for her age. Her pulse and blood pressure are normal.

a. What part of the history would you most like to clarify?

Case 2

A 16-year-old boy comes to see you about his balance. He has avoided running and football for 2 years because of a slowly increasing tendency to fall, but now he topples over if he is jostled in the corridor and has to stay close to the wall for support. His speech is a little slurred, especially when he is tired. He has no headaches or weakness.

He has no past medical history or family history of similar problems. He is the oldest of four children. He does not consume alcohol or drugs.

On examination he walks on a broad base, lurching from side to side. He cannot walk heel to toe or stand with his feet together. He has mild finger–nose and heel–knee–shin ataxia and performs alternating movements slowly and awkwardly. His speech is slurred. There is no nystagmus. Both optic discs are pale. All of his reflexes are absent. His plantar responses are extensor. He cannot feel the vibration of a tuning fork in his feet.

a. Where in the nervous system does the problem lie?
b. What do you think is the cause of his problems?
c. What are the issues for his parents?

(For answers, see pp. 257–8.)

6

Paraplegia

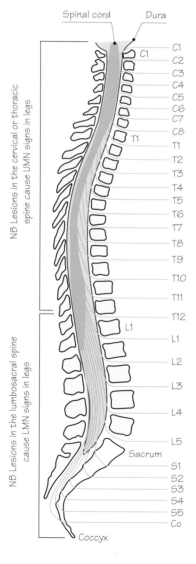

Fig. 6.1 Diagram to show the relationship of the spinal cord, dura and spinal nerves to the vertebrae. Co, coccygeal.

Anatomical considerations

Figure 6.1 shows the relationship of the spinal cord, dura, spinal nerves and vertebrae to each other. The important points to note are:

- the spinal cord terminates at the level of the L1 vertebra. Any disease process below the level of this vertebra may cause neurological problems, but it will do so by interfering with function in the cauda equina not in the spinal cord;
- because the vertebral column is so much longer than the spinal cord, there is a progressive slip in the numerical value of the vertebra with the numerical value of the spinal cord at that level, e.g.
  - C7 vertebra corresponds to T1 cord
  - T10 vertebra corresponds to T12 cord
  - L1 vertebra corresponds to S1 cord;
- the dural lining of the bony spinal canal runs right down to the sacrum, housing the cauda equina below the level of the spinal cord at L1;
- the vertebrae become progressively more massive because of the increasing weight-bearing load put upon them;
- any lesion of the spine in the cervical and thoracic region, as far down as the 10th thoracic vertebra, may result in upper motor neurone signs in the legs;
- lesions in the lumbosacral spine may result in lower motor neurone signs in the legs.

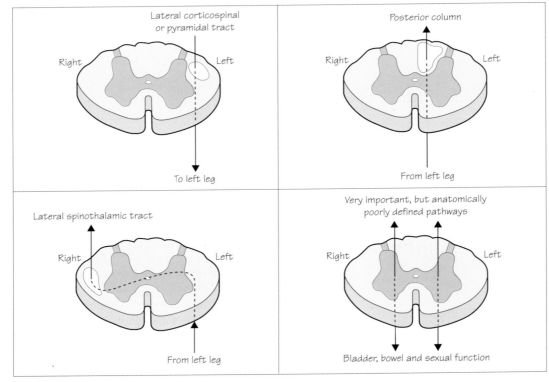

Fig. 6.2 Diagram to show the spinal cord, the important tracts and their relationship to the left leg.

Figure 6.2 shows those tracts in the spinal cord which are important from the clinical point of view:

- the UMN pathway or pyramidal tract from the right hemisphere crosses from right to left in the lower medulla and innervates lower motor neurones in the left ventral horn. Axons from these lower motor neurones in turn innervate muscles in the left arm, trunk and leg;
- the posterior column contains ascending sensory axons carrying proprioception and vibration sense from the left side of the body. These are axons of dorsal root ganglion cells situated beside the left-hand side of the spinal cord. After relay and crossing to the other side in the medulla, this pathway gains the right thalamus and right sensory cortex;
- the lateral spinothalamic tract consists of sensory axons carrying pain and temperature sense from the left side of the body. These are axons of neurones situated in the left posterior horn of the spinal cord, which cross to the right and ascend as the spinothalamic tract to gain the right thalamus and right sensory cortex;
- ascending and descending pathways subserving bladder, bowel and sexual function.

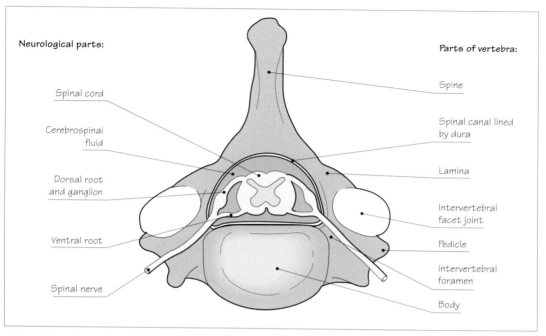

Neurological parts:

Spinal cord

Cerebrospinal
fluid

Dorsal root
and ganglion

Ventral root

Spinal nerve

Parts of vertebra:

Spine

Spinal canal lined
by dura

Lamina

Intervertebral
facet joint

Pedicle

Intervertebral
foramen

Body

Fig. 6.3 Superior aspect of a cervical vertebra, showing the spinal cord, the nerve roots and the spinal nerves.

Figure 6.3 shows the upper aspect of a cervical vertebra, noting the bony spinal canal, lined by dura, in which the spinal cord lies. Four points are important from the clinical point of view:

- some individuals have wide spinal canals, some have narrow spinal canals. People with constitutionally narrow canals are more vulnerable to cord compression by any mass lesion within the canal;
- the vulnerability of the spinal nerve, in or near the intervertebral foramen, (i) to the presence of a posterolateral intervertebral disc protrusion and (ii) to osteoarthritic enlargement of the intervertebral facet joint;
- the vulnerability of the spinal cord, in the spinal canal, to a large posterior intervertebral disc protrusion;
- below the first lumbar vertebra a constitutionally narrow canal will predispose to cauda equina compression (see Fig. 6.1).

Clinical considerations

The clinical picture of a patient presenting with a lesion in the spinal cord is a composite of tract signs and segmental signs, as shown in Fig. 6.4.

Tract signs

A complete lesion, affecting all parts of the cord at one level (Fig. 6.5), will give rise to:
- bilateral upper motor neurone paralysis of the part of the body below the level of the lesion;
- bilateral loss of all modalities of sensation below the level of the lesion;
- complete loss of all bladder, bowel and sexual function.

It is more frequent for lesions to be *incomplete*, however, and this may be in two ways.

1. The lesion may be affecting all parts of the spinal cord at one level (Fig. 6.5a), but not completely stopping all function in the descending and ascending tracts. In this case there is:
- bilateral weakness, but not complete paralysis, below the level of the lesion;
- impaired sensory function, but not complete loss;
- defective bladder, bowel and sexual function, rather than complete lack of function.

2. At the level of the lesion, function in one part of the cord may be more affected than elsewhere, for instance:
- just one side of the spinal cord may be affected at the site of the lesion (Fig. 6.5b), the so-called Brown-Séqard syndrome;
- the lesion may be interfering with function in the posterior columns, with little effect on other parts of the cord (Fig. 6.5c);
- the anterior and lateral parts of the cord may be damaged, with relative sparing of posterior column function (Fig. 6.5d).

The level of the lesion in the spinal cord may be deduced by finding the upper limit of the physical signs due to tract malfunction when examining the patient. For instance, in a patient with clear upper motor neurone signs in the legs, the presence of upper motor neurone signs in the arms is good evidence that the lesion is above C5. If the arms and hands are completely normal on examination, a spinal cord lesion below T1 is more likely.

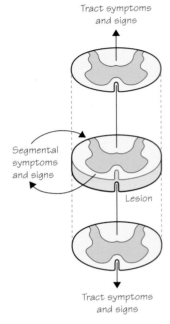

Tract symptoms and signs

Segmental symptoms and signs

Lesion

Tract symptoms and signs

Fig. 6.4 Diagram to show that the clinical phenomena generated by a spinal cord lesion are a composite of tract and segmental features.

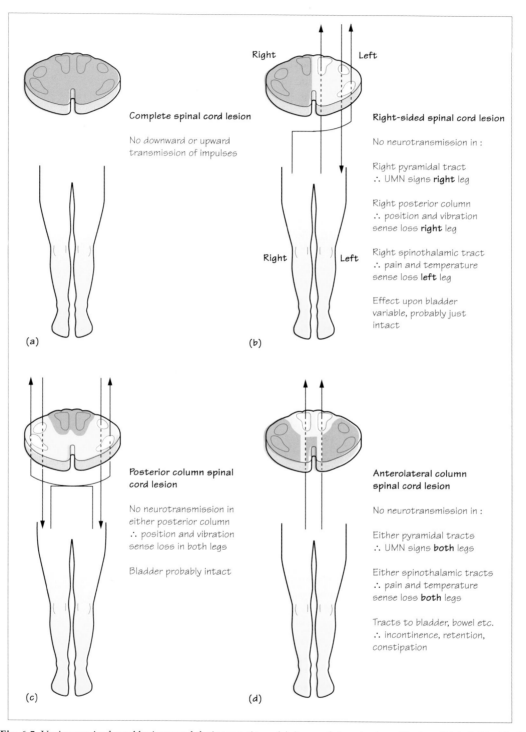

Fig. 6.5 Various spinal cord lesions and their tract signs. (a) A complete spinal cord lesion. (b) A right-sided spinal cord lesion. (c) A posterior spinal cord lesion. (d) An anterolateral spinal cord lesion.

Segmental signs

In addition to interfering with function in the ascending and descending tracts, a spinal cord lesion may disturb sensory input, reflex activity and lower motor neurone outflow at the level of the lesion. These segmental features may be unilateral or bilateral, depending on the nature of the causative pathology. Chief amongst the segmental symptoms and signs are:

- pain in the spine at the level of the lesion (caused by the pathological causative process);
- pain, paraesthesiae or sensory loss in the relevant dermatome (caused by involvement of the dorsal nerve root, or dorsal horn, in the lesion);
- lower motor neurone signs in the relevant myotome (caused by involvement of the ventral nerve root, or ventral horn, in the lesion);
- loss of deep tendon reflexes, if reflex arcs which can be assessed clinically are present at the relevant level. (A lesion at C5/6 may show itself in this way by loss of the biceps or supinator jerks. A lesion at C2/3 will not cause loss of deep tendon reflexes on clinical examination.)

A common example of the value of segmental symptoms and signs in assessing the level of a spinal cord lesion is shown in Fig. 6.6.

Knowledge of all dermatomes, myotomes and reflex arc segmental values is not essential to practise clinical neurology, but some are vital. The essential requirements are shown in Fig. 6.7.

Before proceeding to consider the causes of paraplegia in the next section, two further, rather obvious, points should be noted.

- Paraplegia is more common than tetraplegia. This is simply a reflection of the fact that there is a much greater length of spinal cord, vulnerable to various diseases, involved in leg innervation than in arm innervation, as shown in Fig. 6.1.
- At the beginning of this section, and in Fig. 6.4, it was stated that patients with spinal cord lesions present with a composite picture of tract and segmental signs. This is the truth, but not the whole truth. It would be more accurate to say that such patients present with the features of their spinal cord lesion (tract and segmental), and with the features of the cause of their spinal cord lesion. At the same time as we are assessing the site and severity of the spinal cord lesion in a patient, we should be looking for clinical clues of the cause of the lesion.

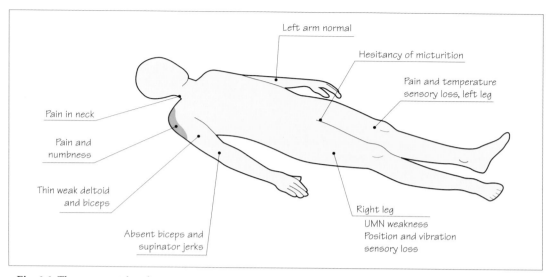

Fig. 6.6 The segmental and tract symptoms and signs of a right-sided C5/6 spinal cord lesion.

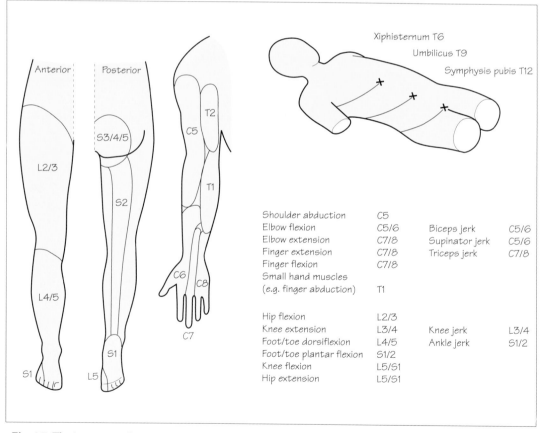

Fig. 6.7 The important dermatomes, myotomes and reflex arc segmental values, with which a student should be conversant.

Causes of paraplegia

The four common causes of spinal cord dysfunction are illustrated in Fig. 6.8: trauma, multiple sclerosis, malignant disease and spondylotic degenerative disease of the spine.

Trauma

Road traffic accidents involving motorcycles and cars are the commonest cause, followed by domestic falls, accidents at work and accidents in sport. The order of frequency of injury in terms of neurological level is cervical, then thoracic, then lumbar. Initial care at the site of the accident is vitally important, ensuring that neurological damage is not incurred or increased by clumsy inexperienced movement of the patient at this stage. Unless the life of the patient is in jeopardy by leaving him at the site of the accident, one person should not attempt to move the patient. He should await the arrival of four or five other people, hopefully with a medical or paramedical person in attendance. Movement of the patient suspected of spinal trauma should be slow and careful, with or without the aid of adequate machinery to 'cut' the patient out of distorted vehicles. It should be carried out by several people able to support different parts of the body, so that the patient is moved all in one piece.

Multiple sclerosis

An episode of paraplegia in a patient with multiple sclerosis usually evolves over the period of 1–2 weeks, and recovers in a couple of months, as with other episodes of demyelination elsewhere in the CNS. Occasionally, however, the paraplegia may evolve slowly and insidiously (see Chapter 7). Spinal cord lesions due to multiple sclerosis are usually asymmetrical and incomplete.

Malignant disease of the spine

Secondary deposits of carcinoma are the main type of trouble in this category: from prostate, lung, breast and kidney. Often, plain X-rays of the spine will show vertebral deposits within and beside the spine, but sometimes the tumour deposit is primarily meningeal with little bony change. Steroid treatment, surgical decompression, radiotherapy or chemotherapy can sometimes make a lot of difference to the disability suffered by such patients, even though their long-term prognosis is poor.

Causes of spinal cord disease

Common
Trauma
Multiple sclerosis
Malignant disease
Spondylosis

Rare
Infarction
Transverse myelitis
'Bends' in divers
Vitamin B_{12} deficiency
Syringomyelia
Motor neurone disease
Intrinsic cord glioma
Radiation myelopathy
Arteriovenous malformation
Extradural abscess
Prolapsed intervertebral
    thoracic disc
Neurofibroma
Meningioma
Atlanto-axial subluxation in
    rheumatoid arthritis

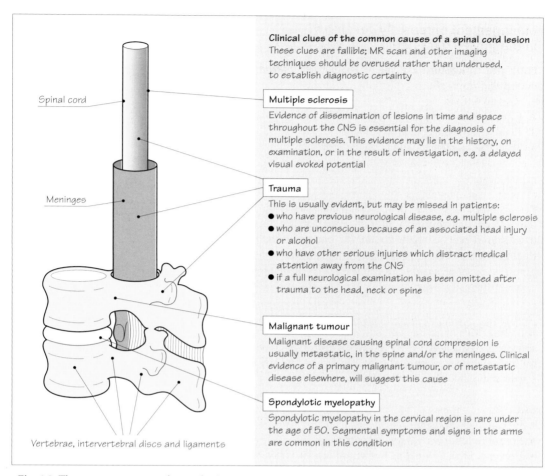

Clinical clues of the common causes of a spinal cord lesion
These clues are fallible; MR scan and other imaging techniques should be overused rather than underused, to establish diagnostic certainty

Multiple sclerosis

Evidence of dissemination of lesions in time and space throughout the CNS is essential for the diagnosis of multiple sclerosis. This evidence may lie in the history, on examination, or in the result of investigation, e.g. a delayed visual evoked potential

Trauma

This is usually evident, but may be missed in patients:
● who have previous neurological disease, e.g. multiple sclerosis
● who are unconscious because of an associated head injury or alcohol
● who have other serious injuries which distract medical attention away from the CNS
● if a full neurological examination has been omitted after trauma to the head, neck or spine

Malignant tumour

Malignant disease causing spinal cord compression is usually metastatic, in the spine and/or the meninges. Clinical evidence of a primary malignant tumour, or of metastatic disease elsewhere, will suggest this cause

Spondylotic myelopathy

Spondylotic myelopathy in the cervical region is rare under the age of 50. Segmental symptoms and signs in the arms are common in this condition

Spinal cord

Meninges

Vertebrae, intervertebral discs and ligaments

Fig. 6.8 The common causes of paraplegia.

Spondylotic myelopathy

Patients with central posterior intervertebral disc prolapse between C4 and T1, with or without consitutionally narrow canals, make up the majority of this group. The cord compression may be at more than one level. The myelopathy may be compressive or ischaemic in nature (the latter due to interference with arterial supply and venous drainage of the cord in the presence of multiple-level disc degenerative disease in the neck). Decompressive surgery is aimed at preventing further deterioration in the patient, rather than guaranteeing improvement.

Management of recently developed undiagnosed paraplegia

Four principles underly the management of patients with evolving paraplegia.
1. 'Get on with it!'
2. Care of the patient to prevent unnecessary complications.
3. Establish the diagnosis.
4. Treat the specific cause.

'Get on with it!'

Reversibility is not a conspicuous characteristic of damage to the CNS. It is important to try to establish the diagnosis and treat spinal cord disease whilst the clinical deficit is minor. Recovery from complete cord lesions is slow and imperfect. Hours may make a difference to the outcome of a patient with cord compression.

Care of the patient to prevent unnecessary complications

The parts of the body rendered weak, numb or functionless by the spinal cord lesion need care. Nurses and physiotherapists are the usual people to provide this.

Skin
• Frequent inspection.
• Frequent relief of pressure (by turning).
• Prevention and vigorous treatment of any damage.

Weak or paralysed limbs
• Frequent passive movement and stockings to prevent venous stagnation, thrombosis and pulmonary embolism.
• Frequent passive movement to prevent joint stiffness and contracture, without overstretching.
• Exercise of non-paralysed muscles.

Non-functioning bladder and bowels
• Catheterization.
• Adequate fluids.
• Dietary fibre regulation.
• Laxatives.
• Suppositories.
• Enemas.

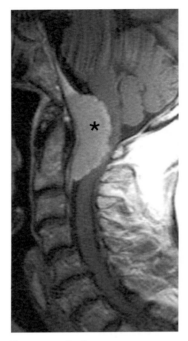

Tumour at the foramen magnum (asterisk) causing high spinal cord compression.

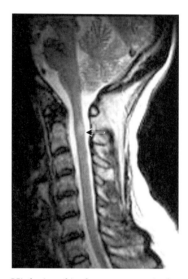

High signal in the upper cervical cord due to multiple sclerosis (arrow).

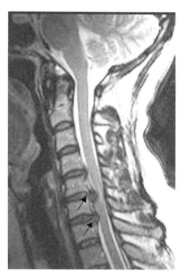

Low cervical cord compression due to prolapsed discs (arrows).

Establish the diagnosis

Foremost in establishing the diagnosis is an MR scan of the spine and sometimes other imaging techniques. These investigations will reveal cord-compressing pathology and the need for neurosurgical intervention. Areas of demyelination can also be visualized within the cord.

If no compressive or intrinsic cord lesion is demonstrated by scanning, other investigations may be helpful:

- CSF analysis, visual evoked potentials, MR scan of the brain — multiple sclerosis;
- EMG studies — motor neurone disease;
- haematological tests and serum vitamin B_{12} estimation — subacute combined degeneration of the cord.

Treat the specific cause

- *Trauma*: intravenous steroids, restoration of alignment and stabilization by operative and non-operative means.
- *Multiple sclerosis*: consider use of high dose methylprednisolone.
- *Malignant disease*: surgical decompression, steroids, radiotherapy, chemotherapy.
- *Spondylotic myelopathy*: surgical decompression.
- *Infarction*: nil.
- *Bends*: hyperbaric chamber.
- *Subacute combined degeneration of the cord*: vitamin B_{12} injections.
- *Syringomyelia*: consider surgery.
- *Motor neurone disease*: riluzole.
- *Benign spinal cord tumours*: consider surgery.
- *Radiation myelopathy*: nil.
- *Arteriovenous malformation*: embolization or surgery, which may be difficult.
- *Extradural abscess*: surgery and antibiotics.
- *Thoracic disc*: surgery, which may be difficult.
- *Spinal neurofibroma and meningioma*: surgery.
- *Atlanto-axial subluxation in rheumatoid arthritis*: consider surgery, which is difficult.

Management of chronic diagnosed paraplegia

From whatever cause, there is a group of patients who have become severely paraplegic, and will remain so on a long-term basis. Their mobility is going to rely heavily on a wheelchair. Multiple sclerosis accounts for the largest number of such patients in the UK, many of whom are young with much of their lives still ahead. Such patients benefit from education, encouragement and the expertise of nurses, physiotherapists, dietitians, social workers, occupational therapists, housing departments, industrial rehabilitation units, psychologists and doctors. They also need the emotional support of their family and friends. They have to come to terms with a major disability and believe in their value despite the loss of normal function in the lower half of their body.

There are lots of ways of helping patients with 'incurable paraplegia'

Attention should be given to the following:
1. *Patient education about the level of cord involvement*:
   • what does and does not work.
2. *The loss of motor function*:
   • wheelchair acceptance and wheelchair skills;
   • 'transfers' on and off the wheelchair;
   • physiotherapy: passive to prevent joint contractures; active to strengthen non-paralysed muscles;
   • drugs to reduce spasticity: baclofen, dantrolene, tizanidine.
3. *Sensory loss*:
   • care of skin;
   • guarding against hot, hard or sharp objects;
   • taking the weight of the body off the seat of the wheelchair routinely every 15 or 20 minutes.
4. *Bladder*:
   • reflex bladder emptying, condom drainage;
   • intermittent self-catheterization, indwelling catheter;
   • cholinergic or anticholinergic drugs as necessary;
   • alertness to urinary tract infection.
5. *Bowel*:
   • regularity of diet;
   • laxatives and suppositories.
6. *Sexual function*:
   • often an area of great disappointment;
   • normal sexual enjoyment, male ejaculation, orgasm, motor skills for intercourse, all lacking;
   • fertility often unimpaired in either sex, though seminal emission in males will require either vibrator stimulation of the fraenum of the penis or electro-ejaculation;
   • counselling of patient and spouse helps adjustment.

7. *Weight and calories*:
   - wheelchair life probably halves the patient's calorie requirements. It is very easy, and counterproductive, for paraplegic patients to gain weight. Eating and drinking are enjoyable activities still left open to them. Heaviness is difficult for their mobility, and bad for the weight-bearing pressure areas.

8. *Psychological aspects*:
   - disappointment, depression, shame, resentment, anger and a sense of an altered role in the family are some of the natural feelings that paraplegic patients experience.

9. *Family support*:
   - the presence or absence of this makes a very great difference to the ease of life of a paraplegic patient.

10. *Employment*:
    - the patient's self-esteem may be much higher if he can still continue his previous work, or if he can be retrained to obtain new work.

11. *House adaptation*:
    - this is almost inevitable and very helpful. Living on the ground floor, with modifications for a wheelchair life, is important.

12. *Car adaptation*:
    - conversion of the controls to arm and hand use may give a great deal of independence.

13. *Financial advice*:
    - this will often be needed, especially if the patient is not going to be able to work. Medical social workers are conversant with house conversion and attendance and mobility allowances.

14. *Recreational activity and holidays*:
    - should be actively pursued.

15. *Legal advice*:
    - this may be required if the paraplegia was the result of an accident, or if the patient's paraplegia leads to marriage disintegration, which sometimes happens.

16. *Respite care*:
    - this may be appropriate to help the patient and/or his relatives. It can be arranged in several different ways, for example:
      —admission to a young chronic sick unit for 1–2 weeks, on a planned, infrequent, regular basis;
      —a care attendant lives at the patient's home for 1–2 weeks, whilst the relatives take a holiday.

Syringomyelia

It is worth devoting a short section of this chapter to syringomyelia because the illness is a neurological 'classic'. It brings together much of what we have learnt about cord lesions, and is grossly over-represented in the clinical part of medical professional examinations. It is a rare condition.

The symptoms and signs are due to an intramedullary (within the spinal cord), fluid-filled cavity extending over several segments of the spinal cord (Fig. 6.9a). The cavity, or syrinx, is most evident in the cervical and upper thoracic cord. There may be an associated Arnold–Chiari malformation at the level of the foramen magnum, in which the medulla and the lowermost parts of the cerebellum are below the level of the foramen magnum. There may be an associated kyphoscoliosis. These associated congenital anomalies suggest that syringomyelia is itself the consequence of malformation of this part of the CNS.

The cavity, and consequent neurological deficit, tend to get larger, very slowly, with the passage of time. This deterioration may occur as sudden exacerbations, between which long stationary periods occur.

The symptoms and signs are the direct consequence of a lesion that extends over several segments within the substance of the cord. There is a combination of segmental and tract signs, as shown in Fig. 6.9b.

Over the length of the cord affected by the syrinx there are segmental symptoms and signs. These are found mainly in the upper limbs, since the syrinx is in the cervical and upper dorsal part of the cord.

- Pain sometimes, but usually transient at the time of an exacerbation.
- Sensory loss which affects pain and temperature, and often leaves the posterior column function intact. Burns and poorly healed sores over the skin of the arms are common because of the anaesthesia. The sensory loss of pain and temperature with preserved proprioceptive sense is known as dissociated sensory loss.
- Areflexia, due to the interruption of the monosynaptic stretch reflex within the cord.
- Lower motor neurone signs of wasting and weakness.

In the legs, below the level of the syrinx, there may be motor or sensory signs due to descending or ascending tract involvement by the syrinx. Most common of such signs are upper motor neurone weakness, with increased tone, increased reflexes and extensor plantar responses.

The only place where syringomyelia is common is in the clinical part of Finals, and other exams

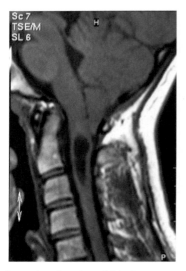

Low signal cavity within the upper cervical cord, with mild Arnold–Chiari malformation.

Spine
- Kyphoscoliosis

Arms
- Painless skin lesions
- Dissociated sensory loss
- Areflexia
- Weakness and wasting

Legs
- Spastic paraparesis

Plus or minus
- Brainstem signs
- Cerebellar signs
- Charcot joints

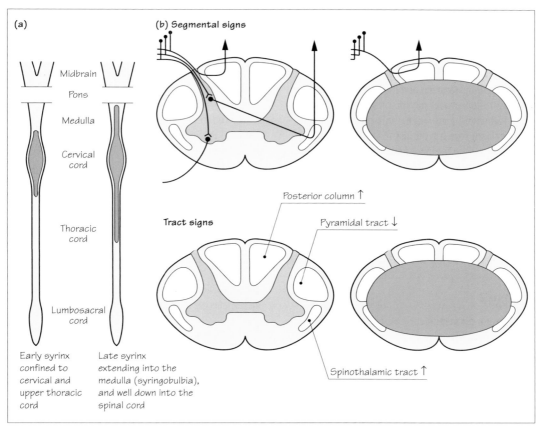

Fig. 6.9 Diagram to show the main features of syringomyelia. (a) The extent of the cavity in the early and late stages. (b) Segmental and tract signs.

Figure 6.9 is drawn symmetrically, but commonly the clinical expression of syringomyelia is asymmetrical.

Extension of the syrinx into the medulla (syringobulbia), or medullary compression due to the associated Arnold–Chiari malformation, may result in cerebellar and bulbar signs.

The loss of pain sensation in the arms may lead to the development of gross joint disorganization and osteo-arthritic change (described by Charcot) in the upper limbs.

There has been a good deal of theorizing about the mechanisms responsible for the cavity formation within the spinal cord in syringomyelia. No one hypothesis yet stands firm. Certainly, a hydrodynamic abnormality in the region of the foramen magnum may exist in those patients with an Arnold–Chiari malformation, and further deterioration may be prevented by surgical decompression of the lower medullary region by removal of the posterior margin of the foramen magnum.

CASE HISTORIES

Case 1

A 63-year-old farmer is admitted in the night with a 3-day history of back pain and weakness in both legs. The admitting doctor notes that weakness is particularly severe in the iliopsoas, hamstrings and tibialis anterior, the lower limb reflexes are normal and the plantar responses are extensor.

Your colleague arranges for the patient to have an MR scan of his lumbosacral spine early the next morning and goes off duty. You are telephoned by the radiologist who informs you that the scan is normal.

a. What should you do now?

Case 2

A 55-year-old instrument maker gradually develops numbness and tingling in the ulnar aspects of both hands, which worsens over several weeks. He reports that bending his head to look down at his lathe gives him a tingling sensation down both arms. He has started having to hurry to pass urine.

He is a recent ex-smoker with a past history of asthma. He takes an inhaler but no other medication.

On examination of the upper limbs he has normal muscle bulk, tone and power, the biceps and supinator reflexes are absent, the triceps reflexes are brisk, and there is diffuse impairment of light touch and pain appreciation in the hands. In the lower limbs there is increased tone, with no wasting or weakness but brisk jerks and extensor plantar responses.

a. Where in the nervous system does the problem lie?
b. What is the most likely cause?

(For answers, see pp. 258–9.)

7

Multiple sclerosis

General comments

Multiple sclerosis

- Common in UK
- Not usually severely disabling
- Sufficiently common to be responsible for a significant number of young chronically neurologically disabled people

After stroke, Parkinson's disease and multiple sclerosis are the two commonest physically disabling diseases of the CNS in the UK. Multiple sclerosis affects young people, however, usually presenting between the ages of 20 and 40 years, which is quite different from stroke and Parkinson's disease, which are unusual conditions in patients under 45.

Though potentially a very severe disease, multiple sclerosis does not inevitably lead to disability, wheelchair life, or worse. As with many crippling diseases, the common image of multiple sclerosis is worse than it usually proves to be in practice. This severe image of the disease is not helped by charities (some of which do noble work for research and welfare) who appeal to the public by presenting the illness as a 'crippler' in print, in illustration, or in person. A more correct image of the disease has resulted from a greater frankness between patients and neurologists, so that now it is not only patients who have the disease very severely who know their diagnosis. Nowadays, most patients who are suffering from multiple sclerosis know that this is what is wrong with them, and the majority of these patients will be ambulant, working and playing a full role in society. The poor image of the disease leads to considerable anxiety in young people who develop any visual or sensory symptoms from whatever cause, especially if they have some medical knowledge. Most neurologists will see one or more such patients a week, and will have the pleasure of being able to reassure the patients that their symptoms are not indicative of multiple sclerosis.

On the other hand, the disease is common, and enough patients have the disease severely to make multiple sclerosis one of the commonest causes of major neurological disability amongst people under the age of 50 years. Provision for young patients with major neurological disability is not good in this or many other developed countries. There is still plenty that can be done to help patients, and often this is best supervised and coordinated by their doctor.

The lesion

The classical lesion of multiple sclerosis is a plaque of demyelination in the CNS (Fig. 7.1). This means:

1. The lesion is in the CNS, not the peripheral nervous system, i.e. in the cerebrum, brainstem, cerebellum or spinal cord. It must be remembered that the optic nerve is an outgrowth from the CNS embryologically. This explains why multiple sclerosis frequently involves the optic nerves, whereas lesions in the other cranial nerves, spinal nerves and peripheral nerves in the limbs do not occur.

2. In the lesion the main insult is to the myelin sheaths with relative sparing of the axon. Saltatory conduction (from node to node along myelinated nerve fibres) requires healthy myelin sheaths. It cannot occur along the nerve fibres through a plaque of demyelination, and non-saltatory conduction is very slow and inefficient. Neurotransmission is accordingly impaired, depending upon the size of the lesion, for plaques vary considerably in size.

Clinically, the lesion evolves over a few days, lasts for a few days or weeks and gradually settles, as shown in Fig. 7.2. Vision in one eye may deteriorate and improve in this way, or the power in one leg may follow the same pattern. Clearly, the nature of the neurological deficit depends on the site of the plaque of demyelination (in the optic nerve or the pyramidal tract in the spinal cord, in the examples given here).

The evolving pathological lesion underlying the clinical episode is summarized in Fig. 7.2.

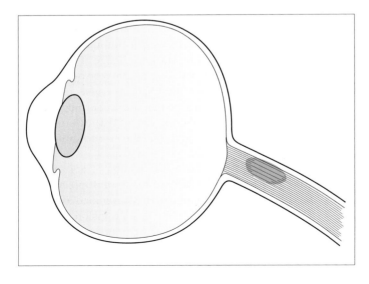

Fig. 7.1 An obvious established plaque of demyelination in the myelinated nerve fibres of an optic nerve.

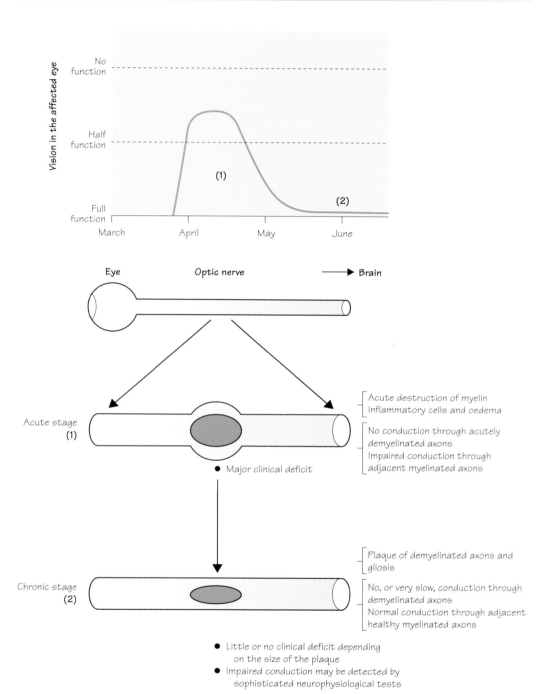

Fig. 7.2 Diagram to show an episode of demyelination. The optic nerve has been taken as an example in this instance.

Dissemination of lesions in time and place

Multiple sclerosis is caused by the occurrence of lesions just described in different parts of the CNS, occurring at different times in a person's life. This dissemination of lesions in time and place remains the classical and diagnostic characteristic of multiple sclerosis from the clinical point of view.

Lesions may occur anywhere in the CNS. Individual plaques vary in size. One way in which a permanent ongoing disability may evolve in a patient with multiple sclerosis is illustrated in Fig. 7.3, and the common sites of lesions which may occur irregularly during the patient's life are illustrated in Fig. 7.4.

Another cause for the development of a neurological deficit may be axonal damage occurring in the wake of the primary inflammatory myelin pathology. Evidence is accumulating to suggest that the axons do not escape completely unscathed in the CNS of patients with multiple sclerosis.

The number of lesions that show themselves as attacks or relapses in the clinical history of a patient with multiple sclerosis is much less than the number of lesions that can be found in the patient's CNS post mortem. This agrees with the fact that MR scanning of the brain and spinal cord at the time of the first clinical episode of demyelination frequently shows the presence of plaques elsewhere in the CNS, especially in the periventricular white matter. Furthermore, it is not uncommon to be able to detect lesions in optic, auditory, sensory and motor CNS pathways by electrical neurophysiological techniques in patients with multiple sclerosis. Often, there are no symptoms or signs accompanying such lesions, indicating unsuspected subclinical involvement of various parts of the CNS.

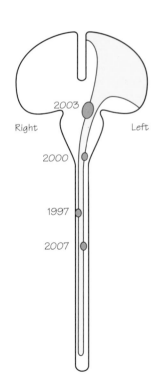

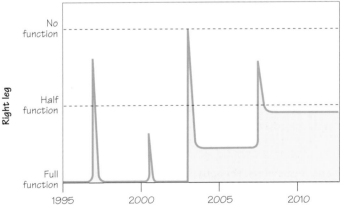

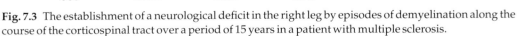

Fig. 7.3 The establishment of a neurological deficit in the right leg by episodes of demyelination along the course of the corticospinal tract over a period of 15 years in a patient with multiple sclerosis.

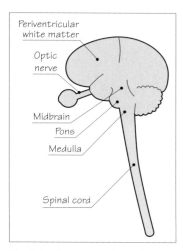

Fig. 7.4 Diagram to show the common sites at which plaques occur in the CNS of patients with multiple sclerosis.

Common clinical expressions of multiple sclerosis

This section describes what occurs during individual episodes of demyelination in different parts of the CNS. It also describes the common neurological deficits that characterize a patient who has multiple sclerosis moderately severely. Figure 7.4 shows the common sites for plaques of demyelination.

Periventricular white matter

Lesions are very common in this part of the brain. They are seen early in the disease in patients studied by MR brain scanning, and are always found post mortem. They do not give rise to definite symptomatology, however.

Optic nerve

Optic neuritis is a common and typical manifestation of multiple sclerosis. If the lesion is in the optic nerve between the globe of the eye and the optic chiasm, it is sometimes called retrobulbar (behind the globe of the eye) neuritis. If it is right at the front of the optic nerve, the lesion itself is visible with an ophthalmoscope, and is sometimes called papillitis (inflammation of the optic disc). The effect on vision is the same whether the lesion is anterior or posterior in the optic nerve. If anterior, the optic disc is visibly red and swollen, with exudates and haemorrhages. If posterior, the appearance of the optic disc is normal at the time of active neuritis. A section of the optic nerve is acutely inflamed in all instances of optic neuritis, so that pain in the orbit on eye movement is a common symptom.

The effect on vision in the affected eye is to reduce acuity, and cause blurring, and this most commonly affects central vision. The patient develops a central scotoma of variable size and density. Colour vision becomes faded, even to a point of fairly uniform greyness. In severe optic neuritis, vision may be lost except for a rim of preserved peripheral vision, or may be lost altogether. At this stage, there is a diminished pupil reaction to direct light with a normal consensual response (often called an afferent pupillary defect).

After days or weeks, recovery commences. Recovery from optic neuritis is characteristically very good, taking 4–8 weeks to occur. Five years later, the patient often has difficulty remembering which eye was affected. Occasionally, recovery is slow and incomplete.

Tell-tale signs of previous optic neuritis

- Slightly impaired acuity
- Slightly impaired colour vision
- Mild afferent pupillary defect
- Slightly pale optic disc
- Delay in the visual evoked potential

Midbrain, pons and medulla

Here episodes of demyelination may cause:

- double vision due to individual cranial nerve dysfunction within the midbrain or pons, or more commonly due to a lesion in the fibre pathways that maintain conjugate movement of the eyes. Lesions of the medial longitudinal fasciculus cause an internuclear ophthalmoplegia, in which there is failure of movement of the adducting eye with preserved movement of the abducting eye, on attempted conjugate deviation of the eyes to one side (see Chapter 8, p. 117);
- facial numbness (cranial nerve 5 within the pons);
- facial weakness (cranial nerve 7 within the pons);
- vertigo, nausea, vomiting, ataxia (cranial nerve 8 within the pons);
- dysarthria and occasional dysphagia (cranial nerves 9, 10 and 12 within the medulla);
- cerebellar dysfunction due to lesions on fibre pathways passing in and out of the cerebellum in the cerebellar peduncles, hence nystagmus, dysarthria, ataxia of limbs and gait;
- motor deficits of upper motor neurone type in any of the four limbs;
- sensory deficits, spinothalamic or posterior column in type, in any of the four limbs.

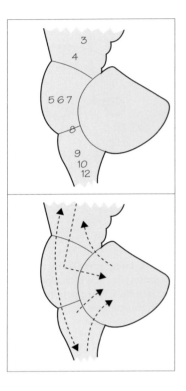

Spinal cord

Lower motor neurone and segmental signs are unusual in multiple sclerosis. Episodes of demyelination in the spinal cord cause fibre tract (upper motor neurone, posterior column, spinothalamic and autonomic) symptoms and signs below the level of the lesion. Since the length of the fibre tracts in the spinal cord are physically longer for leg function than for arm function, there is a greater likelihood of plaques in the spinal cord interfering with the legs than the arms. Episodes of spinal cord demyelination may cause:

- heaviness, dragging or weakness of the arms, trunk or legs;
- loss of pain and temperature sensation in the arms, trunk or legs;
- tingling, numbness, sense of coldness, sense of skin wetness, sense of skin tightness, or a sensation like that which follows a local anaesthetic or a nettle-sting, in the arms, trunk or legs;
- clumsiness of a hand due to loss of position sense and stereognosis;
- bladder, bowel or sexual malfunction.

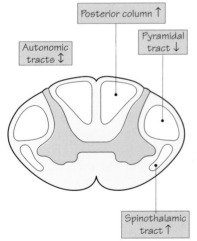

In *a patient with established multiple sclerosis*, who has suffered multiple episodes of demyelination throughout the CNS (Fig. 7.5), the accumulated ongoing neurological deficit is likely to consist of:

- asymmetrical optic pallor without a major defect in visual acuity;
- a cerebellar deficit causing nystagmus, dysarthria and arm ataxia;
- an upper motor neurone deficit, mild in the arms, moderate in the trunk and most evident in the legs. The weakness of the legs often does not allow ataxia to reveal itself in leg movement and walking;
- impaired sexual, bladder and bowel function;
- a variable amount and variety of sensory loss, more evident in the legs and lower trunk than in the arms.

Doctors probably tend to overfocus on the specific neurological disabilities in a patient with multiple sclerosis. The orientation of the patient and family may be less specific, and more concerned with general lack of mobility and vitality, less robust physical health, and the patient's limited social roles.

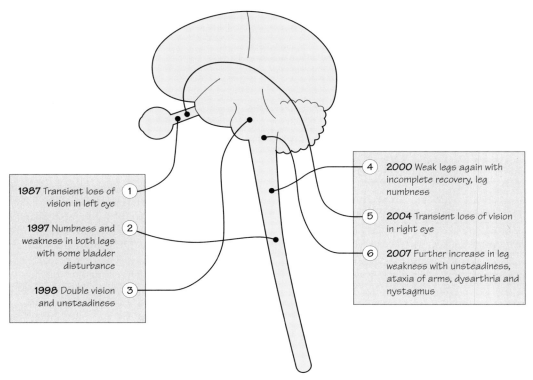

Fig. 7.5 Diagram to show the classical dissemination of lesions in time and space, and the accumulation of a neurological deficit, in a patient who has multiple sclerosis moderately severely.

1987 Transient loss of vision in left eye ①

1997 Numbness and weakness in both legs with some bladder disturbance ②

1998 Double vision and unsteadiness ③

④ **2000** Weak legs again with incomplete recovery, leg numbness

⑤ **2004** Transient loss of vision in right eye

⑥ **2007** Further increase in leg weakness with unsteadiness, ataxia of arms, dysarthria and nystagmus

Diagnosis

There is no specific laboratory test that confirms the presence of multiple sclerosis. The diagnosis is a clinical one, based upon the occurrence of lesions in the CNS which are disseminated in time and place. The presence of subclinical lesions in the CNS may be detected by:

- various clinical neurophysiological techniques. Such techniques essentially measure conduction in a CNS pathway, detecting any delay in neurotransmission by comparison with normal control data. The visual evoked potential is the one most commonly used;
- imaging techniques. Frequently MR brain scanning reveals multiple lesions, especially in the periventricular regions.

The inflammatory nature of the demyelinating lesion may result in an elevated lymphocyte count and globulin content in the CSF. These changes also lack specificity. Immunoelectrophoretic demonstration of oligoclonal bands in the CSF globulin has come closest to becoming a diagnostic feature of multiple sclerosis, but it is not specific, producing both false-positive and false-negative results (Fig. 7.6).

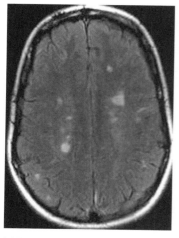

MR scan showing multiple areas of high signal in the white matter due to multiple sclerosis.

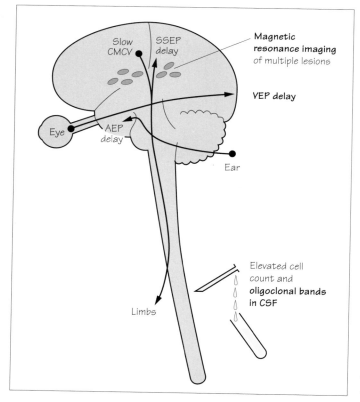

Fig. 7.6 Diagram to show the abnormal investigations in patients with multiple sclerosis. None is specific. MR scanning is used. CSF abnormalities are found, especially the presence of oligoclonal bands in the CSF globulin. AEP, auditory evoked potential from ear to temporal cortex; CMCV, central motor conduction velocity from motor cortex to limbs; SSEP, somatosensory evoked potential from limbs to sensory cortex; VEP, visual evoked potential from eye to occipital cortex.

Aetiology

The cause of multiple sclerosis remains unknown. There appears to be an interaction of environmental factors with some form of genetically determined patient susceptibility.

The evidence for *genetic susceptibility* is as follows:
- multiple sclerosis is more common in females than males, ratio 1.5 : 1;
- there is a firm association of multiple sclerosis with certain HLA types, particularly DR2;
- there is an increased incidence of multiple sclerosis in close relatives;
- in multiple sclerosis patients who have a twin, identical co-twins are more likely to develop it than non-identical twins.

The evidence for an *environmental factor* is as follows:
- multiple sclerosis is more common in temperate than in equatorial parts of the world. Migrants moving from high-risk to low-risk areas (e.g. from northern Europe to Israel) under the age of puberty acquire low risk, and vice versa;
- IgG levels are higher in the CSF of patients with multiple sclerosis. Antibodies to measles virus, and to some other viruses, are higher in the CSF of patients with multiple sclerosis.

Management

Mild or early cases

1. Inform the patient and family of the diagnosis.
2. Educate the patient and family about multiple sclerosis.
3. Dispel the concept of inevitable progression to major disability. Make explanatory literature available.
4. Encourage normal attitudes to life, and normal activities. (This advice should be given initially by the consultant neurologist, and two interviews at an interval will nearly always be needed. Subsequent counselling and support by a specialist nurse or the family doctor may be very valuable, depending on the patient's reaction to the problem.)

More serious cases

1. Continued education about the nature of multiple sclerosis.
2. Continued support over the disappointment and uncertainty of having multiple sclerosis.
3. Attention to individual symptoms:
- *vision*, rarely a major problem. Low visual acuity aids may prove helpful in the minority of patients who need them;
- *cerebellar deficit*, difficult to help pharmacologically;
- *paraplegia*—all the problems attendant upon chronic paraplegia (see Chapter 6, pp. 94 and 95) may occur, and require attention;
- *pain*—may arise from faulty transmission of sensation and may respond to antidepressants (e.g. amitriptyline) or anticonvulsants (e.g. gabapentin);
- *fatigue*—common and hard to treat, but may respond to antidepressants (e.g. fluoxetine) or yoga.

4. Help from nurses, physiotherapists, occupational therapists, speech therapists and medical social workers, as required.
5. Attention to psychological reactions occurring in the patient or family. Encourage all activities which the patient enjoys and are still possible.
6. Respite care arrangements, as required.

All cases of multiple sclerosis

1. Several immunomodulatory drugs (azathioprine, beta-interferon, copaxone, mitoxantrone, etc.) reduce the incidence of relapses somewhat in ambulatory patients with relapsing and remitting multiple sclerosis. They have a much more questionable effect on the development of disability.
2. Corticosteroids, often in the form of high-dose intravenous methyl-prednisolone over 3 days, reduce the duration and severity of individual episodes of demyelination, without influencing the final outcome.
3. Dietary exclusions and most supplements are of no proven advantage. Fish oil supplements may be of benefit. The main dietary requirement is the avoidance of obesity in the enforced sedentary state.

CASE HISTORIES

Case 1

A 37-year-old man presents with double vision, right facial numbness and a clumsy right arm. His symptoms began over the course of a weekend and are starting to improve 3 weeks later. He had an episode of the same symptoms 4 years ago which took 2 months to clear up. His sister has MS.

Examination reveals a right internuclear ophthalmoplegia (i.e. when he looks to the left, the right eye does not adduct and the left eye shows nystagmus), right trigeminal numbness and right-sided limb ataxia.

a. What is the most likely diagnosis?
b. What treatment should he have?

Case 2

A 48-year-old woman has had clinically definite MS for more than 20 years. She had about ten relapses in the first 15 years, beginning with left optic neuritis. Over the last 5 years her disability has steadily progressed. She is now wheelchair-bound and catheterized. She takes baclofen for leg cramps.

She comes to see you because she is very worried about the slowly increasing tingling and weakness in her hands, which is making it difficult for her to do up buttons or hold a pen. She says that losing the use of her hands would be the final straw. Examination reveals wasting and weakness of the first dorsal interosseus, lumbrical and adductor digiti minimi muscles; the rest of her hand and forearm muscles are reasonably strong. Her reflexes are all brisk.

a. What is the cause of this problem?
b. What would you advise?

(For answers, see p. 260.)

Cranial nerve disorders

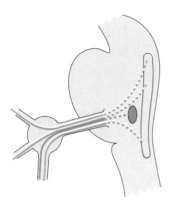

Nuclei, intermedullary nerve fibre pathways, cranial nerve, sensory ganglion and the three main branches of the trigeminal nerve (motor in dark grey; sensory in green)

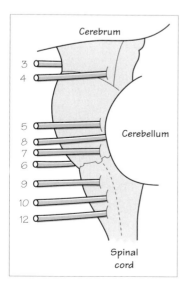

Introduction

Disorders of the cranial nerves usually produce clear abnormalities, apparent to both patient and doctor alike. The specialists who become involved in the management of patients with cranial nerve problems are neurologists, neurosurgeons, ophthalmologists (cranial nerves 2–4, 6), dentists (cranial nerve 5) and ENT surgeons (cranial nerves 1, 5, 7–10, 12).

Cranial nerves 1, 2 and 11 are a little different from the others. Nerves 1 and 2 are highly specialized extensions of the brain, for smell and sight, in the anterior cranial fossa and suprasellar region. Nerve 11 largely originates from the cervical spinal cord, rises into the posterior fossa only to exit it again very quickly, to supply muscles of the neck and shoulder.

It is useful to remember that the other cranial nerves (3–10 and 12; Fig. 8.1) can be damaged at three different points along their paths. The lesion may affect the nucleus of the cranial nerve within the brainstem, where its cell bodies lie. Alternatively, the lesion may damage the axons travelling to or from the nucleus but still within the brainstem. In both these situations there is commonly damage to nearby pathways running through the brainstem, so that in addition to the cranial nerve palsy, the patient will often have weakness, sensory loss or ataxia in the limbs. Finally the lesion may affect the nerve itself outside the brainstem as it passes to or from the structure which it supplies. This causes either an isolated cranial nerve palsy, or a cluster of palsies arising from adjacent nerves. Examples of these clusters include malfunction of 5, 7 and 8 caused by an acoustic neuroma in the cerebellopontine angle, or malfunction of 9, 10 and 11 due to malignancy infiltrating the skull base.

Fig. 8.1 Lateral aspect of the brainstem, and cranial nerves 3–10 and 12 (*seen from the left*).

Olfactory (1) nerve (Fig. 8.2)

Patients who have impaired olfactory function complain that they are unable to smell and that all their food tastes the same. This reflects the fact that appreciation of the subtleties of flavour (beyond the simple sweet, salt, acid, meaty and bitter tastes) is achieved by aromatic stimulation of the olfactory nerves in the nose. This is why wine tasters sniff and slurp.

The commonest cause of this loss is nasal obstruction by infective or allergic oedema of the nasal mucosa. Olfactory nerve function declines with age and with some neurodegenerative diseases. Olfactory nerve lesions are not common. They may result from head injury, either involving fracture in the anterior fossa floor, or as a result of damage to the nerves on the anterior fossa floor at the time of impact of the head injury. Sometimes, the olfactory nerves stop working on a permanent basis for no apparent reason, i.e. idiopathic anosmia. Very occasionally, a tumour arising from the floor of the anterior fossa (e.g. meningioma) may cause unilateral or bilateral loss of olfactory function.

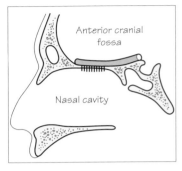

Fig. 8.2 Olfactory nerve and bulb on the floor of the anterior cranial fossa, and olfactory nerve bundles penetrating the thin cribiform plate to innervate the mucosa in the roof of the nasal cavity.

Optic (2) nerve, chiasm and radiation (Fig. 8.3)

Figure 8.3 shows the anatomical basis of the three common neurological patterns of visual loss: monocular blindness, bitemporal hemianopia and homonymous hemianopia.

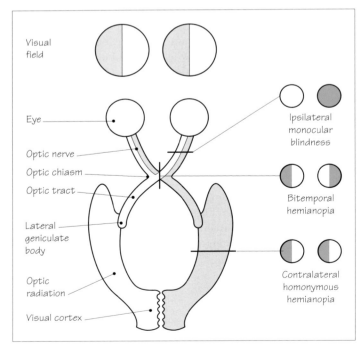

Fig. 8.3 The anatomy of the visual pathways, and the three common types of lesion occurring therein.

When recording visual field defects, the convention is to show the field from the left eye on the left, and the right eye on the right, as if the fields were projecting out of the patient's eyes and down onto the page

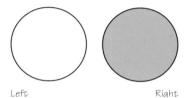

Left   Right

Left   Right

Monocular blindness

Monocular visual disturbances occur transiently in the prodromal phase of migraine (see pp. 214–15), or as a consequence of thrombo-embolism in the ophthalmic artery, as a result of ipsilateral carotid artery atheromatous disease or embolism from the heart. Transient visual loss due to embolization often commences 'like a curtain descending over the vision'. Infarction of the optic nerve or retina, with permanent monocular visual loss, is relatively uncommon in patients with thrombo-embolic disease, though common in untreated patients with giant cell arteritis (see p. 218). Monocular visual loss occurs in patients with optic neuritis as part of multiple sclerosis (see p. 103).

Rarely, impairment of vision in both eyes occurs as a result of bilateral simultaneous optic nerve disease:

- bilateral optic neuritis due to multiple sclerosis;
- methanol poisoning;
- Leber's hereditary optic neuropathy;
- tobacco–alcohol amblyopia;
- longstanding papilloedema due to untreated intracranial hypertension.

Bitemporal hemianopia

Bitemporal hemianopia due to optic chiasm compression by a pituitary adenoma growing upwards out of the pituitary fossa is the most classical situation to be considered here (Chapter 3, see pp. 47–8). Like most 'classical' syndromes, it is rather unusual in every typical detail because:

- the pituitary tumour does not always grow directly upwards in the midline, so that asymmetrical compression of one optic nerve or one optic tract may occur;
- the precise relationship of pituitary gland and optic chiasm varies from person to person. If the optic chiasm is posteriorly situated, pituitary adenomas are more likely to compress the optic nerves. If the optic chiasm is well forward, optic tract compression is more likely;
- not all suprasellar lesions compressing the optic chiasm are pituitary adenomas. Craniopharyngiomas, meningiomas and large internal carotid artery aneurysms are alternative, rare, slowly evolving lesions in this vicinity.

Homonymous hemianopia

Homonymous hemianopia, for example due to posterior cerebral artery occlusion, may or may not be noticed by the patient. If central vision is spared, the patient may become aware of the field defect only by bumping into things on the affected side, either with his body, or occasionally with his car! If the homonymous field defect involves central vision on the affected side, the patient usually complains that he can see only half of what he is looking at, which is very noticeable when reading.

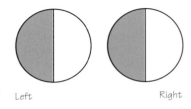

Left   Right

Though posterior cerebral artery occlusion and infarction of the occipital cortex is the commonest cerebral hemisphere lesion causing permanent visual loss, other hemisphere lesions do cause visual problems:

• an infarct or haematoma in the region of the internal capsule may cause a contralateral homonymous hemianopia, due to involvement of optic tract fibres in the posterior limb of the internal capsule. Contralateral hemiplegia and hemianaesthesia are commonly associated with the visual field defect in patients with lesions in this site;

• vascular lesions, abscesses and tumours situated in the posterior half of the cerebral hemisphere, affecting the optic radiation (between internal capsule and occipital cortex), may cause incomplete or partial homonymous hemianopia. Lesions in the temporal region, affecting the lower parts of the optic radiation, cause homonymous visual field loss in the contralateral upper quadrant. Similarly, by disturbing function in the upper parts of the optic radiation, lesions in the parietal region tend to cause contralateral homonymous lower quadrant field defects.

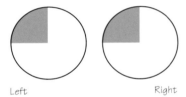

Left   Right

More subtle dysfunction in the visual pathways may cause difficulty in attending to stimuli in one half of the visual field, effectively a lesser form of contralateral homonymous hemianopia. In this situation the patient can actually see in each half of the visual field when it is tested on its own. When both half-fields are tested simultaneously, for example by the examiner wiggling her fingers to either side of a patient who has both eyes open, the patient consistently notices the finger movements on the normal side and ignores the movements on the affected side. This phenomenon, which is common after strokes, is referred to as visual inattention or visual neglect.

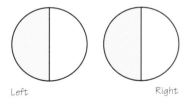

Left   Right

Third, fourth and sixth cranial nerves

Some modification of the primary motor pathway for voluntary movement (Fig. 8.4) is necessary in the case of eye movement to enable simultaneous movement of the two eyes together, i.e. conjugate movement. This is shown in Fig. 8.5. The centres and pathways which integrate 3rd, 4th and 6th nerve function lie in the midbrain and pons.

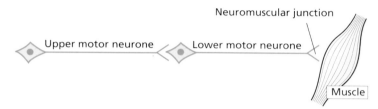

Fig. 8.4 Diagram to show the primary motor pathway.

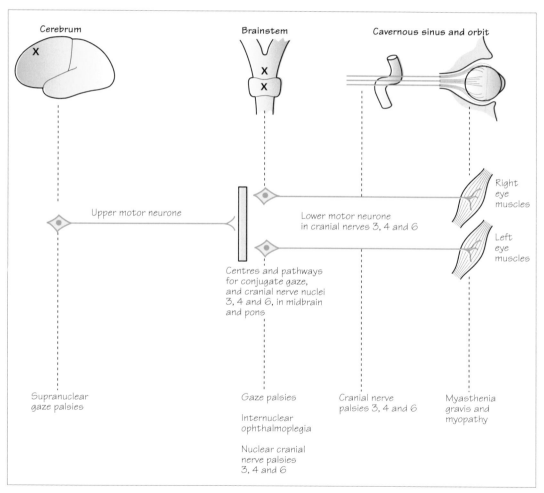

Fig. 8.5 Diagram to show the parts of the nervous system involved in eye movement, and the type of eye movement disorder that results from lesions in each part.

Supranuclear gaze palsy

- Site of lesion: cerebral hemisphere.
- Common.
- Common causes:
  massive stroke;
  severe head injury.
- Movement of the eyes to the left is initiated by the right cerebral hemisphere, just like all motor, sensory and visual functions involving the left-hand side of the body. Each cerebral hemisphere has a 'centre' in the frontal region, involved in conjugate deviation of the eyes to the opposite side. Patients with an acute major cerebral hemisphere lesion are unable to deviate their eyes towards the contralateral side. This is the commonest form of supranuclear gaze palsy (right cerebral hemisphere lesion, and paralysis of conjugate gaze to the left in the diagram).
- The centres for conjugate gaze in the brainstem and the cranial nerves are intact. If the brainstem is stimulated reflexly to induce conjugate eye movement, either by caloric stimulation of the ears, or by rapid doll's head movement of the head from side to side, perfectly normal responses will occur. Paralysis of voluntary conjugate gaze, with preserved reflex conjugate eye movement, is the hallmark of supranuclear gaze palsy.
- Supranuclear vertical gaze palsy, i.e. loss of the ability to look up or down voluntarily, is occasionally seen in neurodegenerative diseases.

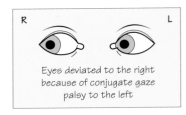

Eyes deviated to the right
because of conjugate gaze
palsy to the left

Gaze palsy

At the midbrain level

- Uncommon.
- The programming of the 3rd and 4th cranial nerve nuclei for conjugate vertical eye movement, and for convergence of the two eyes, occurs in centres in the midbrain. The paralysis of voluntary and reflex eye movement which occurs with lesions in this region is known as Parinaud's syndrome.

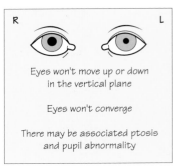

Eyes won't move up or down
in the vertical plane

Eyes won't converge

There may be associated ptosis
and pupil abnormality

At the pontine level

- Uncommon.
- Conjugation of the two eyes in horizontal eye movements is achieved by an ipsilateral pontine gaze centre, as shown in Fig. 8.6. A lesion in the lateral pontine region (on the right in the diagram) will cause voluntary and reflex paralysis of conjugate gaze towards the side of the lesion.

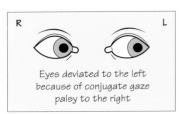

Eyes deviated to the left
because of conjugate gaze
palsy to the right

Fig. 8.6 Brainstem centres and pathways for conjugate horizontal movement. Voluntary gaze to the left is initiated in the right cerebral hemisphere. A descending pathway from the right cerebral hemisphere innervates the left pontine gaze centre. From there, impulses pass directly to the left 6th nerve nucleus to abduct the left eye, and (via the medial longitudinal fasciculus) to the right 3rd nerve nucleus to adduct the right eye.

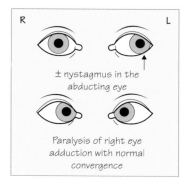

± nystagmus in the abducting eye

Paralysis of right eye adduction with normal convergence

Internuclear ophthalmoplegia

- Site of lesion: midbrain/pons (Fig. 8.6).
- Common.
- Common cause: multiple sclerosis.

A lesion between the 3rd nerve nucleus in the midbrain and the 6th nerve nucleus in the pons—an internuclear lesion—on the course of the medial longitudinal fasciculus (on the right side in the diagram):

- does not interfere with activation of the left 6th nerve nucleus in the pons from the left pontine gaze centre, so that abduction of the left eye is normal (except for some nystagmus which is difficult to explain);
- does interfere with activation of the right 3rd nerve nucleus in the midbrain from the left pontine gaze centre, so that adduction of the right eye may be slow, incomplete or paralysed;
- does not interfere with activation of either 3rd nerve nucleus by the midbrain convergence coordinating centres, so that convergence of the eyes is normal.

Before considering 3rd, 4th and 6th nerve palsies in detail, it is worth remembering the individual action of each of the eye muscles, and their innervation (Fig. 8.7).

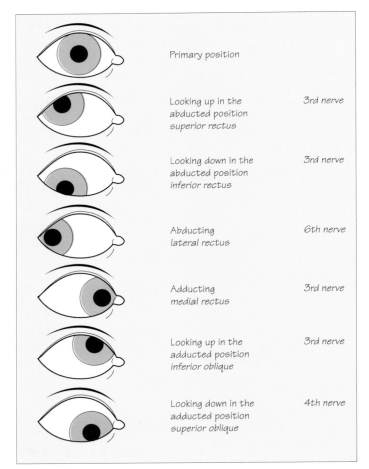

Primary position

Looking up in the   3rd nerve
abducted position
superior rectus

Looking down in the   3rd nerve
abducted position
inferior rectus

Abducting   6th nerve
lateral rectus

Adducting   3rd nerve
medial rectus

Looking up in the   3rd nerve
adducted position
inferior oblique

Looking down in the   4th nerve
adducted position
superior oblique

Fig. 8.7 Normal eye movements in terms of which muscle and which nerve effect them. Diagram shows the right eye viewed from the front.

Furthermore, we have to remember that:
- the eyelid is kept up by levator palpebrae superioris which has two sources of innervation, minor from the sympathetic nervous system, major from the 3rd cranial nerve;
- pupillary dilatation is activated by the sympathetic nervous system, and is adrenergic;
- pupillary constriction is mediated through the parasympathetic component of the 3rd cranial nerve, and is cholinergic.

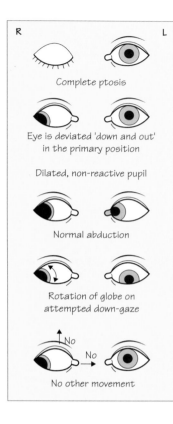

Complete ptosis

Eye is deviated 'down and out' in the primary position

Dilated, non-reactive pupil

Normal abduction

Rotation of globe on attempted down-gaze

No other movement

Third nerve palsy

- Common.
- Common causes:
  posterior communicating artery aneurysm (painful);
  mononeuritis in diabetes (pupil usually normal);
  pathology beside the cavernous sinus, in the superior orbital fissure or in the orbit (adjacent nerves commonly involved, e.g. 4, 6, 5a, and 2 if in the orbit).
- The parasympathetic innervation of the eye is supplied by the 3rd nerve.
- The diagram shows a complete right 3rd nerve palsy. The lesion can be incomplete of course, in terms of ptosis, pupil dilatation or weakness of eye movement.

Fourth nerve palsy

- Uncommon.
- Common cause; trauma affecting the orbit.

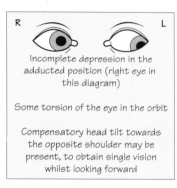

Incomplete depression in the adducted position (right eye in this diagram)

Some torsion of the eye in the orbit

Compensatory head tilt towards the opposite shoulder may be present, to obtain single vision whilst looking forward

Sixth nerve palsy

- Common.
- Common causes:
  as a false localizing sign in patients with raised intracranial pressure;
  multiple sclerosis and small cerebrovascular lesions within the pons;
  pathology beside the cavernous sinus, in the superior orbital fissure or orbit (adjacent nerves commonly involved, e.g. 3, 4, 5a, and 2 if in the orbit).

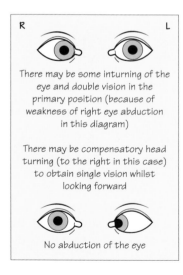

There may be some inturning of the eye and double vision in the primary position (because of weakness of right eye abduction in this diagram)

There may be compensatory head turning (to the right in this case) to obtain single vision whilst looking forward

No abduction of the eye

Myasthenia gravis

- Uncommon.
- Ocular involvement common in myasthenia gravis.
- Myasthenia should be considered in any unexplained ophthalmoplegia, even if it looks like a 4th, 6th or partial 3rd nerve palsy (see pp. 119 and 164–6).

Ptosis

Eye movement abnormality which doesn't necessarily match gaze palsy, internuclear ophthalmoplegia, or cranial nerve palsy

Variability

Fatiguability

Normal pupils

Myopathy

- Graves' disease is the only common myopathy to involve eye muscles.
- The patient may be hyperthyroid, euthyroid or hypothyroid.
- Inflammatory swelling of the external ocular muscles within the orbit, often leading to fibrosis, is responsible.
- Involvement of the external ocular muscles in other forms of myopathy occurs, but is exceedingly rare.

Often asymmetrical
Sometimes unilateral
Proptosis
Lid retraction
Lid lag
Ophthalmoplegia in any direction
Normal pupils

Concomitant squint

- Very common.
- Caused by dissimilar visual acuity and refractive properties in the two eyes from an early age.
- Proper binocular fixation has never been established.
- Known as amblyopia.
- Fixation is by the better-seeing eye; the image from the amblyopic eye is suppressed, so there is no complaint of double vision.

Non-paralytic, each eye possessing a full range of movement when tested individually with the other eye covered

When one eye is covered, the other fixes. Alternate covering of each eye shows a refixation movement in each eye very clearly

Horner's syndrome

- Uncommon.
- Caused by loss of sympathetic innervation to the eye.
- The sympathetic supply to the face and eye is derived from the hypothalamic region, descends ipsilaterally through the brainstem and cervical cord, and reaches the sympathetic chain via the motor root of T1. From the superior cervical sympathetic ganglion, the fibres pass along the outer sheath of the common carotid artery. Fibres to the eye travel via the internal carotid artery and its ophthalmic branch. Fibres to the face travel with the external carotid artery.

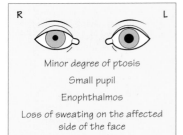

Minor degree of ptosis

Small pupil

Enophthalmos

Loss of sweating on the affected side of the face

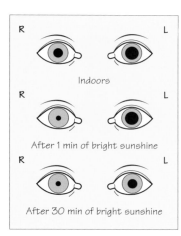

Indoors

After 1 min of bright sunshine

After 30 min of bright sunshine

Holmes–Adie syndrome

- Uncommon.
- Often unilateral.
- An interesting curiosity of no sinister significance.
- Very slow pupillary reaction to light, myotonic pupil (left eye in diagram).
- Absent deep tendon reflexes in the limbs is a common accompaniment, especially knee and ankle jerks.
- Site of pathology uncertain.

Argyll–Robertson pupil

- Very uncommon.
- A sign of tertiary syphilis.
- Site of pathology uncertain.

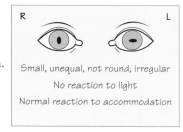

Small, unequal, not round, irregular
No reaction to light
Normal reaction to accommodation

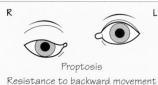

Proptosis
Resistance to backward movement of the globe in the orbit
Palpable orbital mass
Globe displacement in the orbit by the mass
Distortion of the eyelid
Mechanical limitation of eye movement in the orbit
Possible impairment of vision in the affected eye

Orbital mass lesions

- Uncommon.
- Causes:
  benign tumours;
  malignant tumours, primary or secondary;
  extension of inflammatory pathology from the paranasal sinuses;
  non-neoplastic inflammatory infiltrate at the back of the orbit, so-called 'pseudotumour'.
- CT scanning of the orbits is the most helpful investigation.

Trigeminal (5) nerve

Sensory loss in the face is very noticeable, as a visit to the dentist which requires a local anaesthetic will remind us. Sensory loss affecting the cornea can lead unwittingly to serious corneal damage. Pain in the face is very intrusive.

Figures 8.8 and 8.9 demonstrate the relevant clinical anatomical features of the trigeminal nerve. The following points are worth noting:

- the upper border of sensory loss in a trigeminal nerve lesion lies between the ear and the vertex, and the lower border is above the angle of the jaw. Patients with non-organic sensory loss on the face tend to have the junction of forehead and scalp as the upper border, and the angle of the jaw as the lower border;
- the corneal reflex requires corneal, not scleral, stimulation, and the response (mediated through the 7th cranial nerve) is to blink bilaterally. It can therefore be tested in the presence of an ipsilateral 7th nerve lesion;
- the jaw-jerk, like any other stretch reflex, is exaggerated in the presence of an upper motor neurone lesion. In the case of the jaw-jerk, the lesion must be above the level of the trigeminal motor nucleus in the pons. In patients with upper motor neurone signs in all four limbs, an exaggerated jaw-jerk is sometimes helpful in suggesting that the lesion is above the pons, rather than between the pons and the mid-cervical region of the spinal cord;
- pathology in the cavernous sinus affects only the ophthalmic and maxillary branches of the trigeminal nerve, as the mandibular branch has dived through the foramen ovale, behind the cavernous sinus. Similarly, orbital pathology affects only the ophthalmic branch, since the maxillary branch has exited the skull through the foramen rotundum posterior to the orbit.

Figure 8.9 gives information about the diseases that may affect the trigeminal nerve. There are really only two common ones: trigeminal neuralgia and herpes zoster.

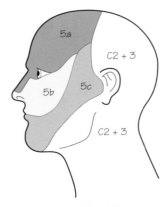

Fig. 8.8 Areas of the skin supplied by each branch of the trigeminal nerve and the 2nd and 3rd cervical dermatomes.

Trigeminal neuralgia is described in Chapter 13 (see p. 219), and is the most common disease affecting the trigeminal nerve. It can be caused by irritation of the nerve as it enters the brainstem (for example by an adjacent blood vessel) or within the brainstem itself (rarely; for example by multiple sclerosis). Presumably abnormal paroxysmal discharges within the nerve give rise to the lancinating pain.

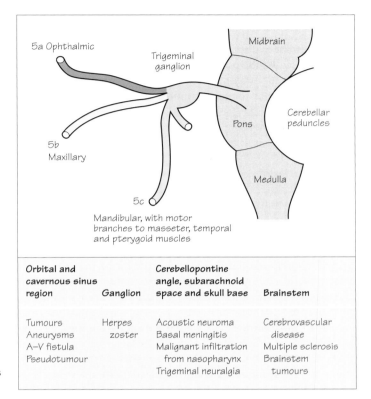

Fig. 8.9 Diagram to show the trigeminal nerve, and the diseases that may affect it.

Orbital and cavernous sinus region	Ganglion	Cerebellopontine angle, subarachnoid space and skull base	Brainstem
Tumours	Herpes	Acoustic neuroma	Cerebrovascular
Aneurysms	zoster	Basal meningitis	disease
A–V fistula		Malignant infiltration	Multiple sclerosis
Pseudotumour		from nasopharynx	Brainstem
		Trigeminal neuralgia	tumours

Herpes zoster (shingles) affecting the trigeminal nerve is also mentioned in Chapter 13 (see p. 220) and in Chapter 15 (see p. 239). Though the virus is in the trigeminal ganglion, clinical involvement is most usually confined to the skin and cornea supplied by the ophthalmic branch. The painful vesicular rash, sometimes preceded by pain for a few days and sometimes followed by pain for ever, is similar to shingles elsewhere in the body. The involvement of the cornea, however, makes urgent ophthalmic referral essential, and the use of local, oral, or parenteral antiviral agents (like aciclovir) important. Parenteral administration is especially likely if there is any evidence of immunosuppression in the patient.

Facial (7) nerve

Figure 8.10 shows the peripheral distribution of the facial nerve. The nerve leaves the pons in the cerebellopontine angle. It provides autonomic efferent fibres to lacrimal and salivary glands, collects afferent taste fibres from the anterior two-thirds of the tongue, and provides the innervation of the stapedius muscle in the ear, before emerging from the stylomastoid foramen behind and below the ear to innervate the facial muscles as shown in Fig. 8.10.

Proximal lesions of the facial nerve produce, therefore, in addition to weakness of all the ipsilateral facial muscles, an alteration of secretion in the ipsilateral lacrimal and salivary glands, impairment of taste perception on the anterior two-thirds of the tongue, and hyperacusis (sounds heard abnormally loudly) in the ear on the side of the lesion. If the lesion has been complete, with Wallerian axonal degeneration distal to the site of the lesion, recovery is rarely complete and re-innervation is often incorrect. Axons, which used to supply the lower part of the face, may regrow along Schwann tubes which lead to the upper part of the face, and vice versa. Patients in whom this has happened are unable to contract part of their facial muscles in isolation. When they close their eyes vigorously, there is retraction of the corner of the mouth on the affected side. When they contract mouth muscles as in whistling, there is eye muscle contraction and possible closure on the side of the lesion. Sometimes, axons that used to supply the salivary glands find their way to the lacrimal glands. In such patients, tears may form excessively in the eye of the affected side at mealtimes.

Bell's palsy

The common disease of the facial nerve is Bell's palsy. The cause of this condition is not certain, although there is some evidence to suggest inflammation due to reactivation of herpes simplex virus within the nerve ganglion in many cases. The lesion is usually proximal enough to have effects on taste and hearing. After some aching around the ear, the facial weakness develops quite quickly within 24 hours. It affects all the facial muscles including the forehead, which distinguishes it from supranuclear facial weakness (for example due to a stroke) where the forehead is spared. The patient is usually very concerned by the facial appearance. Drainage of tears from the eye may be disturbed on the affected side because the eyelids lose close apposition with the globe of the eye, so the eye waters. The cornea may be vulnerable because of impaired eye closure. Speaking, eating and drinking may be difficult because of the weakness around the mouth.

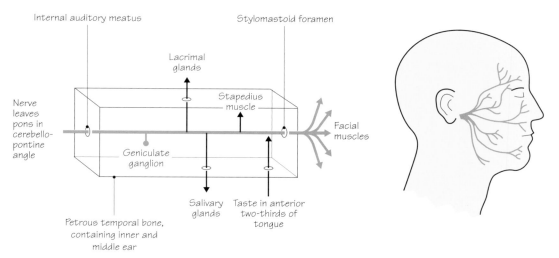

Fig. 8.10 The peripheral distribution of the facial nerve to the muscles of the face, and a highly diagrammatic representation of the proximal part of the facial nerve within the petrous temporal bone.

The risk of poor recovery is increased if the facial paralysis is complete, if there is hyperacusis or loss of taste, if the patient is pregnant or elderly, and if the nerve is electrically inexcitable (if neurophysiological studies are done).

Care of the eye, encouragement and facial exercises in the mirror are all that can be offered in the way of treatment in the acute stage, unless the patient is seen within 72 hours of onset when a short course of steroids may improve the patient's prospects for recovery.

Rarer causes of facial palsy

- *Herpes zoster* affecting the geniculate ganglion, which lies on the course of the facial nerve. Vesicles may appear in the external auditory meatus or soft palate to indicate this cause of the facial palsy. This is known as the Ramsay–Hunt syndrome and behaves like an idiopathic Bell's palsy from the point of view of recovery.
- *Trauma*, fractures involving the petrous temporal bone.
- *Middle ear infection*, acute or chronic.
- *Diabetes mellitus*.
- *Sarcoidosis*.
- *Acoustic neuroma*, either before or after its removal from the cerebellopontine angle.
- *Surgery* in the ear and parotid gland region.
- *Lyme disease*.
- *Pregnancy* increases the risk of Bell's palsy (as Bell himself recognized).

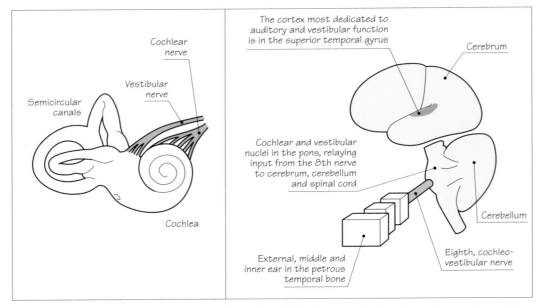

Fig. 8.11 The left-hand side of the diagram shows detail of the inner ear in the petrous temporal bone. The right-hand side of the diagram shows the central connections of the 8th nerve.

Cochleo-vestibular (8) nerve

Figure 8.11 reminds us of the extremely delicate structure of the cochlea and labyrinth within the petrous temporal bone, of the radiation of incoming information from the inner ear throughout the CNS, and of the localization of auditory and vestibular functions in the posterior part of the superior temporal gyrus in the cerebral hemisphere.

The common symptoms and signs found in patients with cochleo-vestibular disorders, and the common tests used to evaluate them, appear below.

Symptoms	Signs	Tests
• Deafness	• Deafness of sensorineural type	• Audiometry
• Tinnitus	• Nystagmus	• Auditory evoked potentials
• Vertigo	• Positional nystagmus	• Caloric responses
• Loss of balance	• Ataxia of gait	• Electronystagmography

Common causes of deafness and loss of balance

The top section of Fig. 8.12 demonstrates that the common causes of deafness are in the external, middle or inner ear.

Acoustic neuroma is an occasional cause of slowly progressive unilateral nerve deafness. Ideally, it should be diagnosed and treated at this stage, before it has caused other evidence of a cerebellopontine space-occupying lesion (i.e. 5th and 7th cranial nerve palsy, ipsilateral cerebellar signs, and raised intracranial pressure). The tumour is a benign one, derived from the Schwann cells on the 8th nerve.

Fig. 8.12 The main diseases affecting hearing, balance, or both.

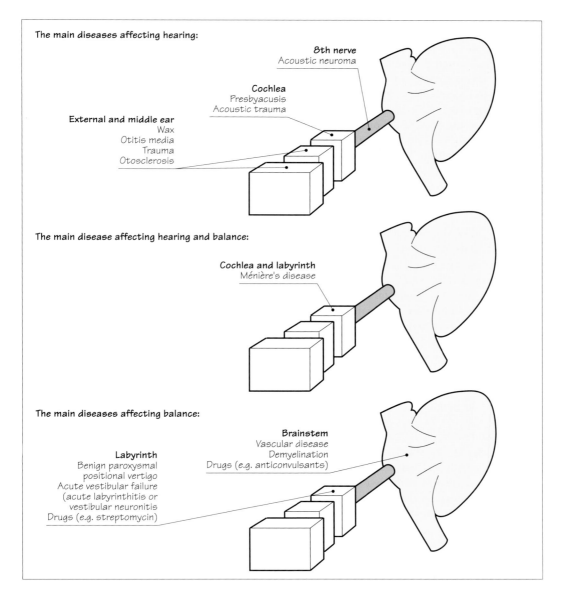

The main diseases affecting hearing:

8th nerve
Acoustic neuroma

Cochlea
Presbyacusis
Acoustic trauma

External and middle ear
Wax
Otitis media
Trauma
Otosclerosis

The main disease affecting hearing and balance:

Cochlea and labyrinth
Ménière's disease

The main diseases affecting balance:

Brainstem
Vascular disease
Demyelination
Drugs (e.g. anticonvulsants)

Labyrinth
Benign paroxysmal
positional vertigo
Acute vestibular failure
(acute labyrinthitis or
vestibular neuronitis)
Drugs (e.g. streptomycin)

Ménière's disease is depicted in the central section of Fig. 8.12. It is probably due to a lesion in the endolymph in both the cochlea and the labyrinth. It therefore causes auditory and vestibular symptoms. The typical patient is middle-aged with a history of unilateral deafness and tinnitus, followed by episodes of very severe vertigo, vomiting and ataxia lasting hours. It is not easy to treat.

The common diseases to affect balance without hearing loss are shown in the lower part of Fig. 8.12. It can be seen that the lesion is likely to be central in the brainstem, or peripheral in the labyrinth.

Episodes of *ischaemia* or *infarction* in the brainstem, or episodes of *demyelination* in patients with multiple sclerosis, are the common structural lesions in the brainstem to disturb balance. Such lesions commonly produce other neurological signs (cranial nerve, cerebellar or long tract in the limbs).

The diagnosis of *benign paroxysmal positional vertigo* is suggested by the occurrence of intermittent transient vertigo lasting less than 30 seconds strongly related to putting the head into a specific position. Turning over in bed, lying down in bed and looking upwards are common precipitants. No abnormalities are found on examination except for definite positional nystagmus. Spontaneous resolution of the problem occurs after a few months.

Perhaps the commonest type of severe vertigo is due to *sudden vestibular failure*. This denotes the sudden occurrence of rotatory vertigo, gait ataxia, vomiting and the need to stay in bed. Lateralized nystagmus and gait ataxia are the two abnormal physical signs. The incapacity lasts very severely for a few days and then gradually resolves over 4–6 weeks. Head movement aggravates the symptoms so the patient keeps still in bed in the acute stage, and walks with his head rather set on his shoulders in the convalescent stage. The underlying pathology is not certain. The problem may follow an upper respiratory infection and occasionally occurs in epidemics, hence the use of the diagnostic terms *acute labyrinthitis* or *vestibular neuronitis*.

Drugs that impair balance include:
- amino-glycoside antibiotics, such as streptomycin and gentamicin, which may permanently impair vestibular function if toxic blood levels are allowed to accumulate;
- anticonvulsants, barbiturates and alcohol which impair the function of the brainstem/cerebellum whilst blood levels are too high.

Spinal accessory (11) nerve

This nerve arises from the upper segments of the cervical spinal cord, ascends into the skull through the foramen magnum, only to exit the skull again with the 9th and 10th cranial nerves through the jugular foramen. The nerve then travels down the side of the neck to supply the sternomastoid muscle, and then crosses the posterior triangle of the neck quite superficially to supply the upper parts of the trapezius muscle.

Lesions of this nerve are uncommon. It is very vulnerable to surgical trauma in the posterior triangle of the neck. Loss of function in the upper part of the trapezius muscle produces a significant disability in the shoulder region. The scapula and shoulder sag downwards and outwards in the resting position. Arm elevation is impaired because of poor scapular stability and rotation, as illustrated in Fig. 8.13.

(a) (b) (c)

A patient, seen from behind, with a right-sided accessory nerve palsy: (a) at rest, (b) attempting to lift his arms to the horizontal position, and (c) attempting to lift his arms as high as possible (the scapulae are shown in green)

The first half of the shoulder abduction requires good scapula stabilization by the trapezius (and other muscles), so that deltoid muscle contraction can take the arm to the horizontal position

The second half of the shoulder abduction requires elevation of the shoulder and scapula rotation through almost 90° by the trapezius (and other muscles)

Fig. 8.13 The importance of the trapezius muscle in arm elevation.

Glossopharyngeal (9), vagus (10) and hypoglossal (12) nerves

These three lower cranial nerves are considered in one section of this chapter for two reasons.

1. Together they innervate the mouth and throat for normal speech and swallowing.

2. They are commonly involved in disease processes together, to give rise to the clinical picture of bulbar palsy.

More specifically, the glossopharyngeal nerve supplies the palate and pharynx, the vagus nerve supplies the pharynx and larynx, and the hypoglossal nerve supplies the tongue. Taste perception in the posterior third of the tongue is a function of the glossopharyngeal nerve. Both the glossopharyngeal and vagus nerves (especially the latter) have an enormous autonomic function, as shown in Fig. 8.14. Innervation of the vocal cords by the long, thin, recurrent laryngeal nerves (from the vagus) exposes them to possible damage as far down as the subclavian artery on the right, and the arch of the aorta on the left.

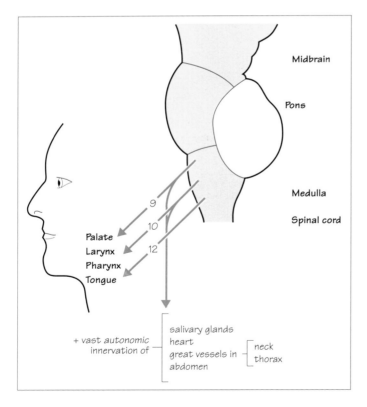

Fig. 8.14 Highly diagrammatic representation of cranial nerves 9, 10 and 12.

Bulbar palsy

When there is bilateral impairment of function in the 9th, 10th and 12th cranial nerves, the clinical syndrome of bulbar palsy evolves. The features of bulbar palsy are:

- *dysarthria*;
- *dysphagia*, often with choking episodes and/or nasal regurgitation of fluids;
- *dysphonia* and *poor cough*, because of weak vocal cords;
- *susceptibility to aspiration pneumonia*.

Even though the vagus nerve has a vast and important autonomic role, it is uncommon for autonomic abnormalities to feature in the diseases discussed in this section.

Common conditions affecting 9th, 10th and 12th nerve function

Figure 8.15 illustrates the common conditions which affect 9th, 10th and 12th nerve function. The use of the word 'common' is relative, since none of the conditions are very common.

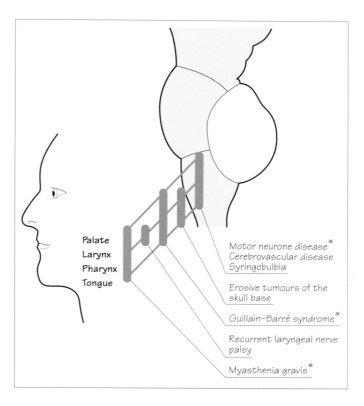

Palate
Larynx
Pharynx
Tongue

Motor neurone disease[*]
Cerebrovascular disease
Syringobulbia

Erosive tumours of the skull base

Guillain–Barré syndrome[*]

Recurrent laryngeal nerve palsy

Myasthenia gravis[*]

Fig. 8.15 Common conditions that affect cranial nerves 9, 10, and 12. *Because these conditions involve 9th, 10th and 12th nerve function bilaterally, they are the common causes of bulbar palsy.

Motor neurone disease

When motor neurone disease is causing loss of motor neurones from the lower cranial motor nuclei in the medulla, the bulbar palsy can eventually lead to extreme difficulty in speech (anarthria) and swallowing. Inanition and aspiration pneumonia are commonly responsible for such patients' deaths. The tongue is small, weak or immobile, and fasciculating (Chapter 10, see pp. 155–7).

Infarction of the lateral medulla

Infarction of the lateral medulla, following posterior inferior cerebellar artery occlusion, is one of the most dramatic cerebrovascular syndromes to involve speech and swallowing. Ipsilateral trigeminal, vestibular, glossopharyngeal and vagal nuclei may be involved, along with cerebellar and spinothalamic fibre tracts in the lateral medulla.

Guillain–Barré syndrome

Patients with Guillain–Barré syndrome, acute, post-infectious polyneuropathy (Chapter 10, see p. 163), may need ventilation via an endotracheal tube or cuffed tracheostomy tube. This may be necessary either because of neuropathic weakness of the chest wall and diaphragm, or because of bulbar palsy secondary to lower cranial nerve involvement in the neuropathy.

Recurrent laryngeal nerve palsy

The recurrent laryngeal nerves are vulnerable to damage in the neck and mediastinum, e.g. aortic aneurysm, malignant chest tumours, malignant glands and surgery in the neck (especially in the region of the thyroid gland). A unilateral vocal cord palsy due to a unilateral nerve lesion produces little disability other than slight hoarseness. Bilateral vocal cord paralysis is much more disabling, with marked hoarseness of the voice, a weak 'bovine' cough (because the cords cannot be strongly adducted) and respiratory stridor.

Myasthenia gravis

Bulbar muscle involvement in myasthenia gravis is quite common in this rare condition. The fatiguability of muscle function, which typifies myasthenia, is frequently very noticeable in the patient's speech and swallowing (Chapter 10, see pp. 164–6).

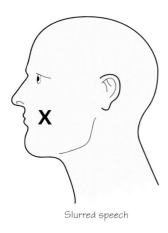

Slurred speech

Dysarthria

The speech disturbance in patients with dysarthria is a purely mechanical one caused by defective movement of the lips, tongue, palate, pharynx and larynx. Clear pronunciation of words is impaired due to the presence of a neuromuscular lesion.

Speaking is a complex motor function. Like complex movement of other parts of the body, normal speech requires the integrity of basic components of the nervous system, mentioned in Chapter 1, and illustrated again in Fig. 8.16. There are characteristic features of the speech when there is a lesion in each element of the nervous system identified in Fig. 8.16. These are the different types of dysarthria.

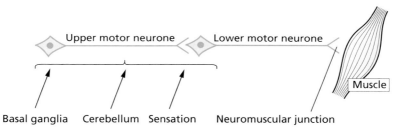

Fig. 8.16 Basic components of the nervous system required for normal movement.

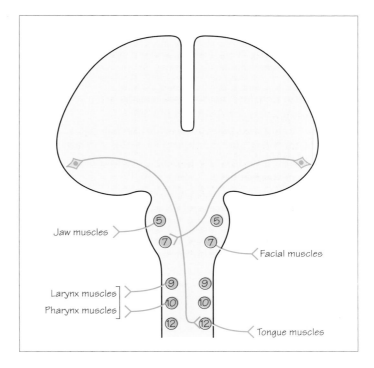

Fig. 8.17 The upper and lower motor neurones involved in speech.

It is important to remember the availability of communication aids for patients with severe dysarthria. These may be quite simple picture or symbol charts, alphabet cards or word charts. More 'high tech' portable communication aids that incorporate keyboards and speech synthesizers are also very valuable for some patients.

Upper motor neurone lesions

The upper motor neurones involved in speech have their cell bodies at the lower end of the precentral (motor) gyrus in each cerebral hemisphere. From the motor cortex, the axons of these cells descend via the internal capsule to the contralateral cranial nerve nuclei 5, 7, 9, 10 and 12, as shown in Fig. 8.17.

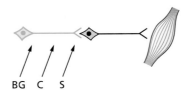

Speech is slow, indistinct, laboured and stiff in patients with pseudobulbar palsy

A unilateral lesion does not usually produce a major problem of speech pronunciation. There is some slurring of speech due to facial weakness in the presence of a hemiparesis.

Bilateral upper motor neurone lesions, on the other hand, nearly always produce a significant speech disturbance. Weakness of the muscles supplied by cranial nerves 5–12 is known as bulbar palsy if the lesion is lower motor neurone in type (see the next section in this chapter). It is known as pseudobulbar palsy if the weakness is upper motor neurone in type. Patients who have bilateral upper motor neurone weakness of their lips, jaw, tongue, palate, pharynx and larynx, i.e. patients with pseudobulbar palsy, have a characteristic speech disturbance, known as a spastic dysarthria. The speech is slow, indistinct, laboured and stiff. Muscle wasting is not present, the jaw-jerk is increased, and there may be associated emotional lability. The patient is likely to be suffering from bilateral cerebral hemisphere cerebrovascular disease, motor neurone disease or serious multiple sclerosis.

Lower motor neurone lesions, and lesions in the neuromuscular junction and muscles

The lower motor neurones involved in speech have their cell bodies in the pons and medulla (Fig. 8.17), and their axons travel out to the muscles of the jaw, lips, tongue, palate, pharynx and larynx in cranial nerves 5–12.

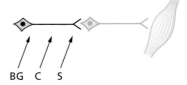

Speech is quiet, indistinct and nasal in patients with bulbar palsy

A single unilateral cranial nerve lesion does not usually produce a disturbance of speech, except in the case of cranial nerve 7. A severe unilateral facial palsy does cause some slurring of speech.

Multiple unilateral cranial nerve lesions are very rare.

Bilateral weakness of the bulbar muscles, whether produced by pathology in the lower motor neurones, neuromuscular junction or muscles, is known as bulbar palsy. One of the predominant features of bulbar palsy is the disturbance of speech. The other main features are difficulty in swallowing and incompetence of the larynx leading to aspiration pneumonia. The speech is quiet, indistinct, with a nasal quality if the palate is weak, poor gutterals if the pharynx is weak, and poor labials if the lips are weak. (Such a dysarthria may be rehearsed if one tries to talk without moving lips, palate, throat and tongue.)

Motor neurone disease, Guillain–Barré syndrome and myasthenia gravis all cause bulbar palsy due to lesions in the cranial nerve nuclei, cranial nerve axons and neuromuscular junctional regions of the bulbar muscles, respectively (see Chapter 10 and Fig. 8.15).

Basal ganglion lesions

The bradykinesia of Parkinson's disease causes the characteristic dysarthria of this condition. The speed and amplitude of movements are reduced. Speech is quiet and indistinct, and lacks up and down modulation. A monotonous voice from a fixed face, both voice and face lacking lively expression, is the typical state of affairs in Parkinson's disease.

Patients with chorea may have sudden interference of their speech if a sudden involuntary movement occurs in their respiratory, laryngeal, mouth or facial muscles.

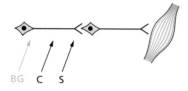

Parkinsonian patients have quiet, indistinct, monotonous speech

Cerebellar lesions

As already mentioned, the dysarthria of patients with cerebellar disease often embarrasses them because their speech sounds as if they are drunk. There is poor coordination of muscular action, of agonists, antagonists and synergists. There is ataxia of the speaking musculature, very similar to the limb ataxia seen in patients with cerebellar lesions. Speech is irregular, in both volume and timing. It is referred to as a scanning or staccato dysarthria.

Drugs that affect cerebellar function (alcohol, anticonvulsants), multiple sclerosis, cerebrovascular disease and posterior fossa tumours are some of the more common causes of cerebellar malfunction.

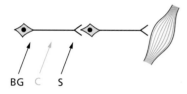

Speech is slurred, and irregular in volume and timing

CASE HISTORIES

Can you identify the most likely problem in each of these brief histories, and suggest a treatment?

a. 'I could see perfectly well last week. The right eye is still OK but the left one is getting worse every day. I can't see colours with it and I can't read small print. It hurts a bit when I look to the side.'

b. 'I see two of everything, side by side, but only when I look to the right. Apart from that, I'm fine.'

c. 'I'm getting terrible pains on the left of my face. I daren't touch it but it's just at the corner of my mouth, going down into my chin. It's so sharp, it makes me jump.'

d. 'I've had an ache behind my ear for a couple of days but this problem started yesterday. I'm embarrassed, I look so awful. I can't close my left eye, it keeps running. My mouth is all over to the right, I'm slurring my words, and making a real mess when I drink.'

e. 'I keep bumping into doorways and last week I drove into a parked car: I just didn't realize it was there. I think my eyesight is perfect but the optician said I needed to see a doctor straight away.'

f. 'I keep getting terribly dizzy. Rolling over in bed is the worst: everything spins and I feel sick. It's the same when I turn my head to cross the road. I am too frightened to go out.'

(For answers, see pp. 260–1.)

CHAPTER 9

Nerve root, nerve plexus and peripheral nerve lesions

Introduction

In this chapter, we are considering focal pathology in the peripheral nervous system. This means a study of the effect of lesions between the spinal cord and the distal connections of the peripheral nerves with skin, joints and muscles (as shown in Fig. 9.1). We shall become familiar with focal disease affecting nerve roots and spinal nerves, nerve plexuses and individual peripheral nerves. Focal disease infers a single localized lesion, affecting one nerve root or one peripheral nerve. Diffuse or generalized diseases affecting these parts of the nervous system, e.g. a peripheral neuropathy affecting all the peripheral nerves throughout the body, are the subject of Chapter 10.

Focal lesions of the lower cervical and lower lumbar nerve roots are common, as are certain individual peripheral nerve lesions in the limbs. Accurate recognition of these clinical syndromes depends on some basic neuro-anatomical knowledge. This is not formidably complicated but possession of a few hard anatomical facts is inescapable.

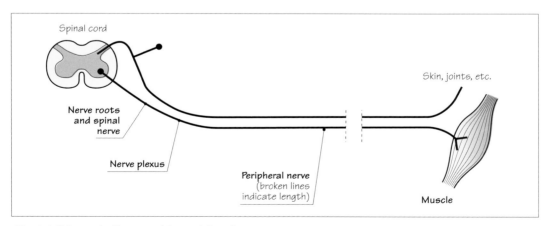

Fig. 9.1 Schematic diagram of the peripheral nervous system.

Nerve root lesions

Figure 9.2 is a representation of the position of the nerve roots and spinal nerve in relation to skeletal structures. The precise position of the union of the ventral and dorsal nerve roots, to form the spinal nerve, in the intervertebral foramen is a little variable. This is why a consideration of the clinical problems affecting nerve roots embraces those affecting the spinal nerve. A nerve root lesion, or *radiculopathy*, suggests a lesion involving the dorsal and ventral nerve roots and/or the spinal nerve.

The common syndromes associated with pathology of the nerve roots and spinal nerves are:
- *prolapsed intervertebral disc*;
- *herpes zoster*;
- *metastatic disease in the spine*.

Less common is the compression of these structures by a *neurofibroma*.

Prolapsed intervertebral disc

When the central, softer material, nucleus pulposus, of an intervertebral disc protrudes through a tear in the outer skin, annulus fibrosus, the situation is known as a prolapsed intervertebral disc. This is by far the most common pathology to affect nerve roots and spinal nerves. The susceptibility of these nerve elements to disc prolapses, which are most commonly posterolateral in or near the intervertebral foramen, is well shown in Fig. 9.2.

The typical clinical features of a prolapsed intervertebral disc, regardless of the level, are:

1. *Skeletal:*
   - pain, tenderness and limitation in the range of movement in the affected area of the spine;
   - reduced straight leg raising on the side of the lesion, in the case of lumbar disc prolapses.

2. *Neurological:*
   - pain, sensory symptoms and sensory loss in the dermatome of the affected nerve root;
   - lower motor neurone signs (weakness and wasting) in the myotome of the affected nerve root;
   - loss of tendon reflexes of the appropriate segmental value;
   - since most disc prolapses are posterolateral, these neurological features are almost always unilateral.

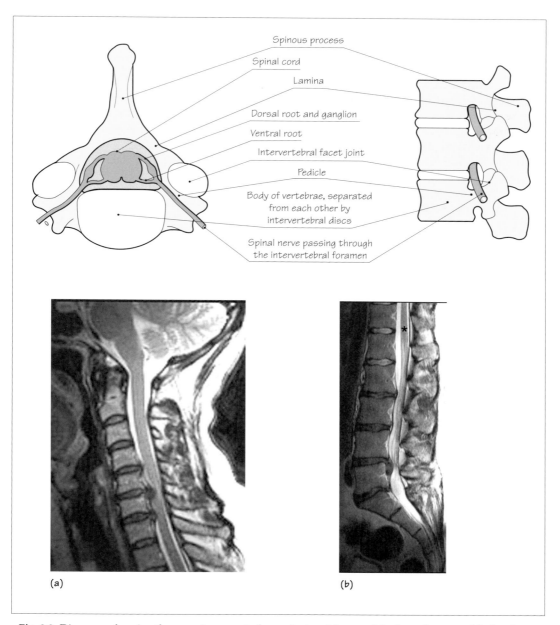

Fig. 9.2 Diagrams showing the superior aspect of a cervical vertebra, and the lateral aspect of the lumbar spine. Disc prolapse in the cervical region can cause cord and/or spinal nerve root compression (scan a). Disc prolapse in the lumbar region (scan b) can cause nerve root compression, but the spinal cord ends alongside L1 (asterisk) and is unaffected. In either region, additional degenerative changes in the facet joints may aggravate the problem.

Prolapsed intervertebral discs are most common between C4 and T1 in the cervical spine and between L3 and S1 in the lumbosacral spine. In the cervical region, there is not a great discrepancy between the level of the cervical spinal cord segment and the cervical vertebra of the same number, i.e. the C5 segment of spinal cord, the C5 nerve roots and the C4/5 intervertebral foramen, through which the C5 spinal nerve passes, are all at much the same level (see Fig. 6.1, p. 83). If the patient presents with a C5 neurological deficit, therefore, it is very likely that it will be a C4/5 intervertebral disc prolapse.

Figures 6.1 and 9.3 show that this is not the case in the lumbar region. The lower end of the spinal cord is at the level of the L1 vertebra. All the lumbar and sacral nerve roots have to descend

Common nerve roots to be compressed by prolapsed intervertebral discs:		
In the arm	C5	In the leg L4
	C6	L5
	C7	S1
	C8	

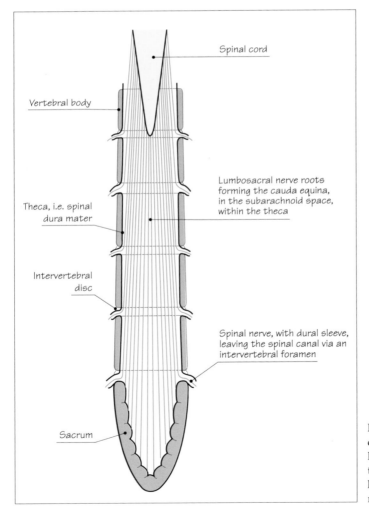

Fig. 9.3 Posterior view of the cauda equina. *NB* The pedicles, laminae and spinous processes of the vertebrae, and the posterior half of the theca, have been removed.

Labels on figure:
- Spinal cord
- Vertebral body
- Lumbosacral nerve roots forming the cauda equina, in the subarachnoid space, within the theca
- Theca, i.e. spinal dura mater
- Intervertebral disc
- Spinal nerve, with dural sleeve, leaving the spinal canal via an intervertebral foramen
- Sacrum

over a considerable length to reach the particular intervertebral foramen through which they exit the spinal canal. These nerve roots form the cauda equina, lying within the theca. Each nerve root passes laterally, within a sheath of dura, at the level at which it passes through the intervertebral foramen. Postero-lateral disc prolapses are likely to compress the emerging spinal nerve within the intervertebral foramen, e.g. an L4/5 disc prolapse will compress the emerging L4 root. More medially situated disc prolapses in the lumbar region may compress nerve roots of lower numerical value, which are going to exit the spinal canal lower down. This is more likely to happen if the patient has a constitutionally narrow spinal canal. (Some individuals have wide capacious spinal canals, others have short stubby pedicles and laminae to give a small cross-sectional area for the cauda equina.) It cannot be assumed therefore that an L5 root syndrome is the consequence of an L5/S1 disc prolapse; the trouble may be higher up. A more centrally prolapsed lumbar disc may produce bilateral leg symptoms and signs, involving more than one segment, often associated with sphincter malfunction due to lower sacral nerve root compression.

Figures 9.4 and 9.5 show the segmental value of the movements, reflexes and skin sensation most frequently involved in cervical and lumbar disc disease. From these diagrams, the area of pain and sensory malfunction, the location of weakness and wasting, and the impaired deep tendon reflexes can all be identified for any single nerve root syndrome. (Note that Figs 9.4 and 9.5 indicate weak movements, not the actual site of the weak and wasted muscles, which are of course proximal to the joints being moved.)

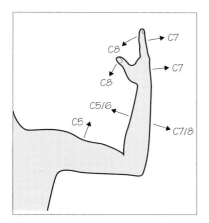
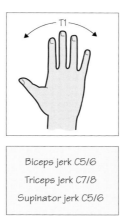
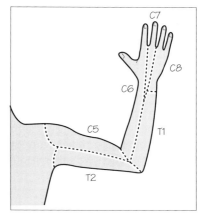

Fig. 9.4 Segmental nerve supply to the upper limb, in terms of movements, tendon reflexes and skin sensation.

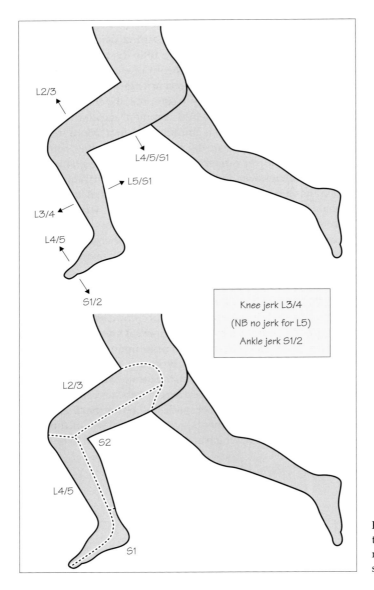

Knee jerk L3/4
(NB no jerk for L5)
Ankle jerk S1/2

Fig. 9.5 Segmental nerve supply to the lower limb, in terms of movements, tendon reflexes and skin sensation.

There are four main intervertebral disc disease syndromes.
1. The single, acute disc prolapse which is sudden, often related to unusually heavy lifting or exertion, painful and very incapacitating, often associated with symptoms and signs of nerve root compression, whether it affects the cervical or lumbar region.
2. More gradually evolving, multiple-level disc herniation in association with osteo-arthritis of the spine. Disc degeneration is associated with osteophyte formation, not just in the main intervertebral joint between body and body, but also in the

intervertebral facet joints. Figure 9.2 shows how osteo-arthritic changes in the intervertebral facet joint may further encroach upon the space available for the emerging spinal nerve in the intervertebral foramen. This is the nature of nerve root involvement in cervical and lumbar spondylosis.

3. Cervical myelopathy (Chapter 6, see p. 91) when **1**, or more commonly **2** above, causes spinal cord compression in the cervical region. This is more likely in patients with a constitutionally narrow spinal canal.

4. Cauda equina compression at several levels due to lumbar disc disease and spondylosis, often in association with a constitutionally narrow canal, may produce few or no neurological problems when the patient is at rest. The patient may develop sensory loss in the legs or weakness on exercise. This syndrome is not common, its mechanism is ill-understood, and it tends to be known as 'intermittent claudication of the cauda equina'.

Disc disease is best confirmed by MR scanning of the spine at the appropriate level.

Most acute prolapsed discs settle spontaneously with analgesics. Patients with marked signs of nerve root compression, with persistent symptoms or with recurrent symptoms, are probably best treated by microsurgical removal of the prolapsed material.

Cervical and lumbar spondylosis are difficult to treat satisfactorily, even when there are features of nerve root compression. Conservative treatment, analgesics, advice about bodyweight and exercise, and the use of collars and spinal supports are the more usual recommendations.

Symptomatic cauda equina compression is usually helped by surgery. The benefit of surgical treatment for spinal cord compression in the cervical region is less well proven.

Herpes zoster

Any sensory or dorsal root ganglion along the entire length of the neuraxis may be the site of active herpes zoster infection. The painful vesicular eruption of shingles of dermatome distribution is well known. Pain may precede the eruption by a few days, secondary infection of the vesicles easily occurs, and pain may occasionally follow the rash on a long-term basis (post-herpetic neuralgia). The dermatome distribution of the shingles rash is one of the most dramatic living neuro-anatomical lessons to witness.

The healing of shingles is probably not accelerated by the topical application of antiviral agents. In immunocompromised patients aciclovir should be given systemically. It is not clear that antiviral treatment prevents post-herpetic neuralgia.

Spinal tumours

Pain in the spine and nerve-root pain may indicate the presence of metastatic malignant disease in the spine. More occasionally, such pains may be due to a benign tumour such as a neuro-fibroma. The root pain may be either unilateral or bilateral. It is known as girdle pain when affecting the trunk, i.e. between T3 and L2. Segmental neurological signs in the form of lower motor neurone weakness, deep tendon reflex loss, and dermatome sensory abnormality may be evident, but the reason for early diagnosis and management is to prevent spinal cord com-pression, i.e. motor, sensory and sphincter loss below the level of the lesion (Chapter 6, see pp. 90–2).

Brachial and lumbosacral plexus lesions

Lesions of these two nerve plexuses are not common, so they will be dealt with briefly. Of the two, brachial plexus lesions are the more common. In both instances, pain is a common symp-tom, together with sensory, motor and deep tendon reflex loss in the affected limb.

Spinal nerves from C5 to T1 contribute to the brachial plexus, which runs from the lower cervical spine to the axilla, under the clavicle, and over the first rib and lung apex. Lesions of the brachial plexus are indicated in Fig. 9.6.

Spinal nerves from L2 to S2 form the lumbosacral plexus, which runs downwards in the region of the iliopsoas muscle, over the pelvic brim to the lateral wall of the pelvis. The com-mon pathology to affect this plexus is malignant disease, espe-cially gynaecological cancer in women.

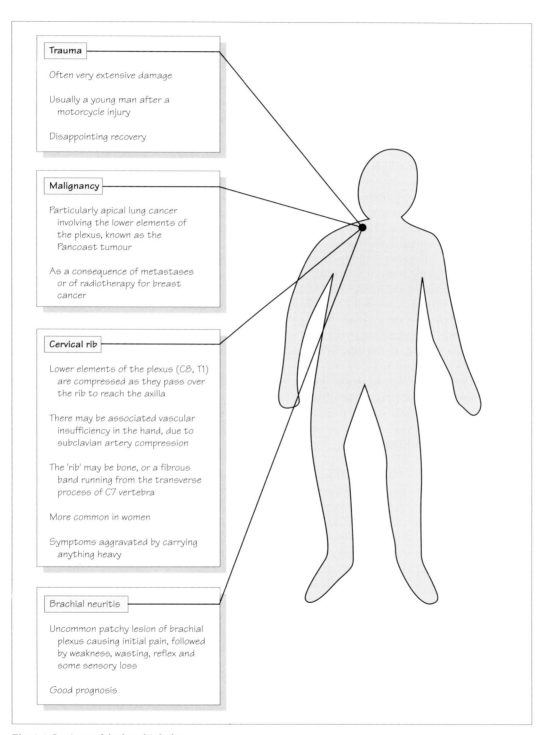

Trauma

Often very extensive damage

Usually a young man after a motorcycle injury

Disappointing recovery

Malignancy

Particularly apical lung cancer involving the lower elements of the plexus, known as the Pancoast tumour

As a consequence of metastases or of radiotherapy for breast cancer

Cervical rib

Lower elements of the plexus (C8, T1) are compressed as they pass over the rib to reach the axilla

There may be associated vascular insufficiency in the hand, due to subclavian artery compression

The 'rib' may be bone, or a fibrous band running from the transverse process of C7 vertebra

More common in women

Symptoms aggravated by carrying anything heavy

Brachial neuritis

Uncommon patchy lesion of brachial plexus causing initial pain, followed by weakness, wasting, reflex and some sensory loss

Good prognosis

Fig. 9.6 Lesions of the brachial plexus.

Peripheral nerve lesions

Individual peripheral nerves in the limbs may be damaged by any of five mechanisms.

1. *Trauma*: in wounds created by sharp objects such as knives or glass (e.g. median or ulnar nerve at the wrist), by inaccurate localization of intramuscular injections (e.g. sciatic nerve in the buttock), or by the trauma of bone fractures (e.g. radial nerve in association with a midshaft fracture of the humerus).

2. *Acute compression*: in which pressure from a hard object is exerted on a nerve. This may occur during sleep, anaesthesia or coma in which there is no change in the position of the body to relieve the compression (e.g. radial nerve compression against the posterior aspect of the humerus, common peroneal nerve against the lateral aspect of the neck of the fibula).

3. *Iatrogenically*: following prolonged tourniquet application (e.g. radial nerve in the arm), or as a result of an ill-fitting plaster cast (e.g. common peroneal nerve in the leg).

4. *Chronic compression*: so-called entrapment neuropathy, which occurs where nerves pass through confined spaces bounded by rigid anatomical structures, especially near to joints (e.g. ulnar nerve at the elbow or median nerve at the wrist).

5. As part of the clinical picture of *multifocal neuropathy*. There are some conditions that can produce discrete focal lesions in individual nerves, so that the patient presents with more than one nerve palsy either simultaneously or consecutively (e.g. leprosy, diabetes and vasculitis).

The speed and degree of recovery from injury or compression obviously depends on the state of the damaged nerve. No recovery will occur if the nerve is severed, unless it is painstakingly stitched together soon after injury by surgery. Damage which has injured the nerve sufficiently to cause axonal destruction will require regrowth of axons distally from the site of injury, a process which tends to be slow and incompletely efficient. Damage which has left the axons intact, and has only injured the myelin sheaths within the nerve, recovers well. Schwann cells reconstitute myelin quickly around intact axons.

Some peripheral nerve palsies are more common than others. Figures 9.7 and 9.8 show the common and uncommon nerve lesions in the upper and lower limbs, respectively. Brief notes about the uncommon nerve palsies are shown. The remainder of this chapter deals with the three common nerve palsies in the upper limbs and the two common ones in the legs.

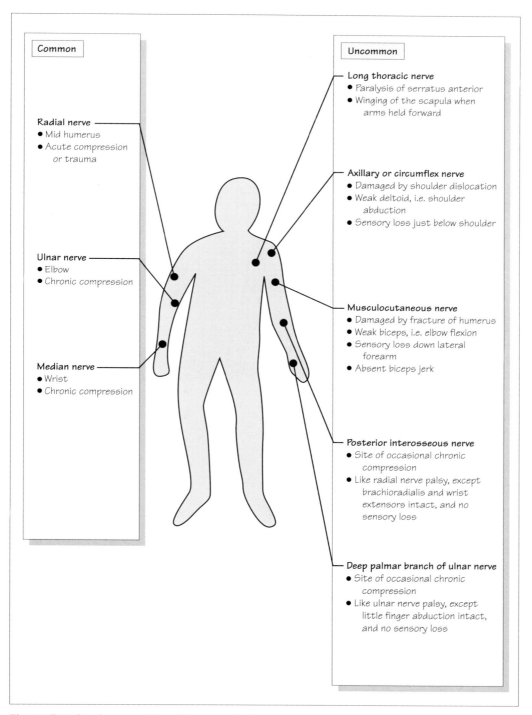

Common

Radial nerve
- Mid humerus
- Acute compression or trauma

Ulnar nerve
- Elbow
- Chronic compression

Median nerve
- Wrist
- Chronic compression

Uncommon

Long thoracic nerve
- Paralysis of serratus anterior
- Winging of the scapula when arms held forward

Axillary or circumflex nerve
- Damaged by shoulder dislocation
- Weak deltoid, i.e. shoulder abduction
- Sensory loss just below shoulder

Musculocutaneous nerve
- Damaged by fracture of humerus
- Weak biceps, i.e. elbow flexion
- Sensory loss down lateral forearm
- Absent biceps jerk

Posterior interosseous nerve
- Site of occasional chronic compression
- Like radial nerve palsy, except brachioradialis and wrist extensors intact, and no sensory loss

Deep palmar branch of ulnar nerve
- Site of occasional chronic compression
- Like ulnar nerve palsy, except little finger abduction intact, and no sensory loss

Fig. 9.7 Peripheral nerve palsies of the upper limb.

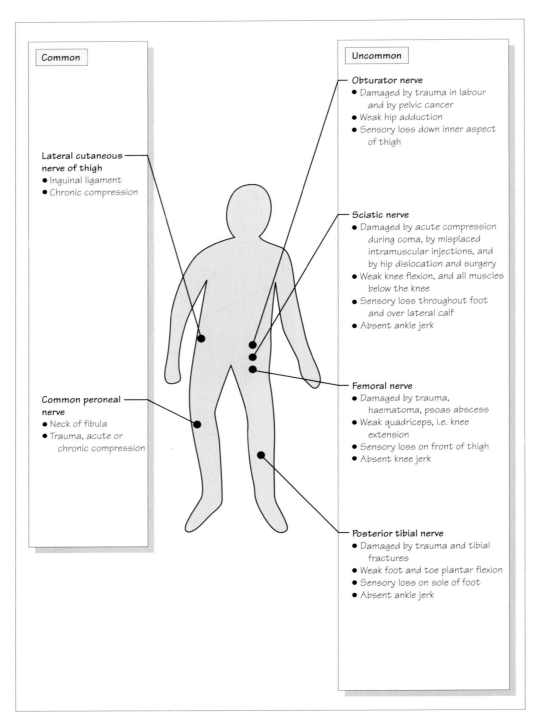

Fig. 9.8 Peripheral nerve palsies of the lower limb.

Radial nerve palsy (Fig. 9.9)

The nerve is most usually damaged where it runs down the posterior aspect of the humerus in the spiral groove. This may occur as a result of acute compression, classically when a patient has gone to sleep with his arm hanging over the side of an armchair (Saturday night palsy!). It may occur in association with fractures of the midshaft of the humerus.

The predominant complaint is of difficulty in using the hand, because of wrist drop. The finger flexors and small hand muscles are greatly mechanically disadvantaged by the presence of wrist, thumb and finger extensor paralysis. There are usually no sensory complaints.

The prognosis is good after acute compression, and more variable after damage in association with a fractured humerus. The function of the hand can be helped by the use of a special 'lively' splint which holds the wrist, thumb and fingers in partial extension.

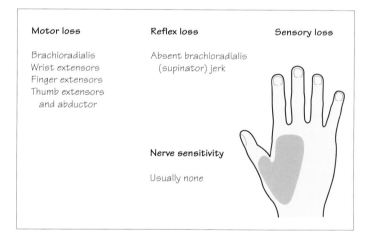

Motor loss

Brachioradialis
Wrist extensors
Finger extensors
Thumb extensors
and abductor

Reflex loss

Absent brachioradialis
(supinator) jerk

Sensory loss

Nerve sensitivity

Usually none

Fig. 9.9 Radial nerve palsy.

Ulnar nerve palsy (Fig. 9.10)

The commonest aetiology is chronic compression, either in the region of the medial epicondyle, or a little more distally where the nerve enters the forearm between the two heads of flexor carpi ulnaris. Sometimes the nerve is compressed acutely in this vicinity during anaesthesia or a period of enforced bedrest (during which the patient supports himself on the elbows whilst moving about in bed). The nerve may be damaged at the time of fracture involving the elbow, or subsequently if arthritic change or valgus deformity are the consequence of the fracture involving the elbow joint.

The patient complains of both motor and sensory symptoms, lack of grip in the hand, and painful paraesthesiae and numbness affecting the little finger and the ulnar border of the palm.

Persistent compression can be relieved by transposing the compressed nerve from behind to the front of the elbow joint. This produces good relief from the unpleasant sensory symptoms, and reasonable return of use of the hand even though there may be residual weakness and wasting of small hand muscles on examination.

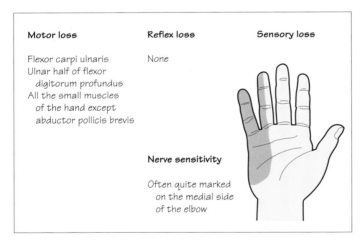

Motor loss	Reflex loss	Sensory loss

Flexor carpi ulnaris
Ulnar half of flexor
  digitorum profundus
All the small muscles
  of the hand except
  abductor pollicis brevis
	None	

	Nerve sensitivity	

	Often quite marked
	  on the medial side
	  of the elbow	

Fig. 9.10 Ulnar nerve palsy.

Median nerve palsy (Fig. 9.11)

Carpal tunnel syndrome is the commonest clinical expression of median nerve palsy, and is probably the commonest nerve entrapment syndrome. The median nerve becomes chronically compressed within the carpal tunnel, which consists of the bony carpus posteriorly and the flexor retinaculum anteriorly. The carpal tunnel has a narrower cross-sectional area in women than men, and patients with carpal tunnel syndrome have a significantly narrower cross-sectional area in their carpal tunnels than a control population.

Carpal tunnel syndrome is five times more common in women than men. It is more common in patients who have arthritis involving the carpus, and is more frequent in pregnancy, diabetes, myxoedema and acromegaly.

The patient complains of sensory symptoms. Painful paraesthesiae, swollen burning feelings, are felt in the affected hand and fingers, but often radiate above the wrist as high as the elbow. They frequently occur at night and interrupt sleep. They may occur after using the hands and arms. They are commonly relieved by shaking the arms. There are not usually any motor symptoms, except for possible impairment of manipulation of small objects between a slightly numb thumb, index and middle fingers.

Symptomatic control may be established by wearing a wrist-immobilizing splint or by the use of hydrocortisone injection into the carpal tunnel. Permanent relief often requires surgical division of the flexor retinaculum, a highly effective and gratifying minor operation.

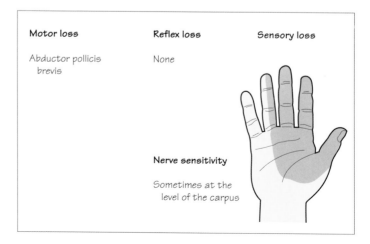

Motor loss	Reflex loss	Sensory loss
Abductor pollicis brevis	None	

Nerve sensitivity

Sometimes at the level of the carpus

Fig. 9.11 Median nerve palsy.

Common peroneal nerve palsy (Fig. 9.12)

The common peroneal (lateral popliteal) nerve runs a very superficial course around the neck of the fibula. It divides into the peroneal nerve to supply the lateral calf muscles which evert the foot, and into the anterior tibial nerve which innervates the anterior calf muscles which dorsiflex the foot and toes. The nerve is liable to damage from trauma, with or without fracture of the fibula. It is highly susceptible to acute compression during anaesthesia or coma, and from overtight or ill-fitting plaster casts applied for leg fractures.

The patient's predominant complaint is of foot drop, and the need to lift the leg up high when walking. He may complain of loss of normal feeling on the dorsal surface of the affected ankle and foot.

Treatment of common peroneal nerve palsy should be preventative wherever possible. A splint that keeps the ankle at a right angle may assist walking. The condition is not usually helped by any form of surgery.

Common peroneal nerve palsies due to acute compression have a good prognosis.

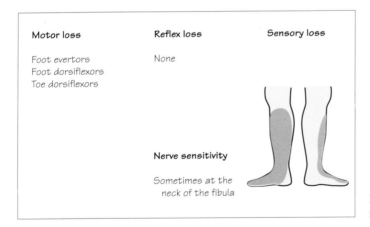

Motor loss	Reflex loss	Sensory loss
Foot evertors	None	
Foot dorsiflexors		
Toe dorsiflexors		
	Nerve sensitivity	
	Sometimes at the neck of the fibula	

Fig. 9.12 Common peroneal nerve palsy.

Meralgia paraesthetica (Fig. 9.13)

This irritating syndrome is the consequence of chronic entrapment of the lateral cutaneous nerve of the thigh as it penetrates the inguinal ligament, or deep fascia, in the vicinity of the anterior superior iliac spine.

As the nerve is sensory, there are no motor symptoms. The patient complains of annoying paraesthesiae and partial numbness in a patch of skin on the anterolateral aspect of the thigh. The contact of clothes is slightly unpleasant in the affected area.

No treatment of meralgia paraesthetica may be necessary if the symptoms are mild. Alternatively, nerve decompression or section at the site of compression both give excellent relief.

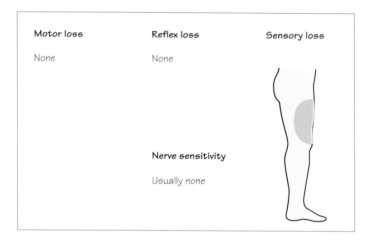

Fig. 9.13 Lateral cutaneous nerve of the thigh.

CASE HISTORIES

Which nerve or nerve root is the likely culprit in the following brief histories?

a. A middle-aged man who has difficulty walking because of weak dorsiflexion of the right foot.

b. A young man who cannot use his right hand properly and is unable to dorsiflex the right wrist.

c. A middle-aged lady who is regularly waking at night due to strong tingling and numbness of her hands and fingers.

d. An elderly lady with persistent tingling in her left little finger, and some weakness in the use of the same hand.

(For answers, see p. 261.)

10

Motor neurone disease, peripheral neuropathy, myasthenia gravis and muscle disease

Introduction

Fig. 10.1 The common peripheral neuromuscular disorders.

This chapter is about the common disorders that affect the peripheral nervous system and muscle (Fig. 10.1). They tend to produce a clinical picture of diffuse muscle weakness and wasting, and are sometimes difficult to distinguish from one another.

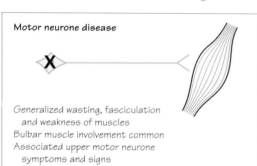

Motor neurone disease

Generalized wasting, fasciculation and weakness of muscles
Bulbar muscle involvement common
Associated upper motor neurone symptoms and signs
No sensory symptoms and signs
Steadily progressive and fatal

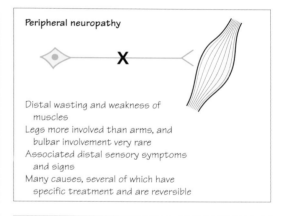

Peripheral neuropathy

Distal wasting and weakness of muscles
Legs more involved than arms, and bulbar involvement very rare
Associated distal sensory symptoms and signs
Many causes, several of which have specific treatment and are reversible

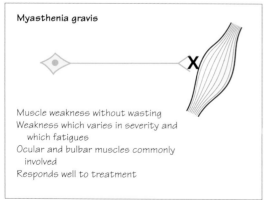

Myasthenia gravis

Muscle weakness without wasting
Weakness which varies in severity and which fatigues
Ocular and bulbar muscles commonly involved
Responds well to treatment

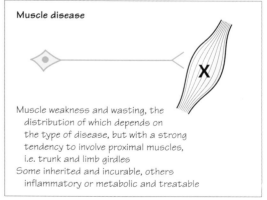

Muscle disease

Muscle weakness and wasting, the distribution of which depends on the type of disease, but with a strong tendency to involve proximal muscles, i.e. trunk and limb girdles
Some inherited and incurable, others inflammatory or metabolic and treatable

Motor neurone disease

This disease consists of a selective loss of lower motor neurones from the pons, medulla and spinal cord, together with loss of upper motor neurones from the motor cortex of the brain. The process is remarkably selective, leaving special senses, and cerebellar, sensory and autonomic functions intact. Progressive difficulty in doing things because of muscular weakness gradually overtakes the patient.

The cause of the neuronal loss in motor neurone disease (like the selective loss of neurones from other parts of the CNS, in diseases such as Alzheimer's and Parkinson's) is not understood.

There is variation in the clinical picture of motor neurone disease from one patient to another, which depends on:

- whether lower or upper motor neurones are predominantly involved;
- which muscles (bulbar, upper limb, trunk or lower limb) are bearing the brunt of the illness;
- the rate of cell loss. Most usually, this is steadily progressive over a few years, but in a minority of cases it may be much more gradual with long survival.

Motor neurone disease (MND) tends to start either as a problem in the bulbar muscles, or as a problem in the limbs, and initially the involvement tends to be either lower motor neurone or upper motor neurone in nature. This has led to four clinical syndromes at the outset of the illness, which are described in Fig. 10.2.

As the illness progresses and the loss of motor neurones becomes more generalized, there is a tendency for both upper and lower motor neurone signs to become evident in bulbar, trunk and limb muscles. Sometimes, the illness may remain confined to the lower motor neurones, or to the upper motor neurones, but the coexistence of both, in the absence of sensory signs, is the hallmark of motor neurone disease. A limb with weak, wasted, fasciculating muscles, in which the deep tendon reflexes are very brisk, and in which there is no sensory loss, strongly suggests motor neurone disease.

It is the involvement of bulbar and respiratory muscles that is responsible for the inanition and chest infections which account for most of the deaths in patients with motor neurone disease.

The glutamate antagonist riluzole slows progression and prolongs survival, but there is as yet no cure for motor neurone disease. This makes regular medical input more important, not less, and the neurologist should be part of an integrated team of professionals providing advice and support.

Key features of motor neurone disease

- Muscle weakness
- Muscle wasting
- Muscle fasciculation
- Exaggerated reflexes
- No loss of sensation

Bulbar weakness

The medulla oblongata used to be referred to as the 'bulb' of the brain. The cranial nerve nuclei 9, 10 and 12 reside in the medulla. This is why weakness of the muscles they supply (mouth, pharynx and larynx) is known as bulbar weakness or bulbar palsy. 'Bulbar palsy' and 'pseudobulbar palsy' imply that the cause is respectively in the lower and upper motor neurones supplying these muscles, and have specific physical signs (see pp. 131 and 134–5 and Fig. 10.2). MND characteristically causes a mixture of the two

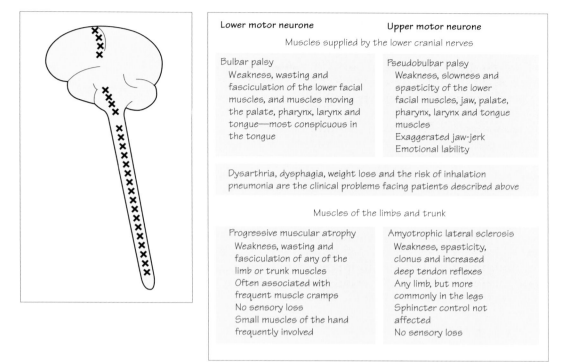

Lower motor neurone	Upper motor neurone
Muscles supplied by the lower cranial nerves	
Bulbar palsy Weakness, wasting and fasciculation of the lower facial muscles, and muscles moving the palate, pharynx, larynx and tongue—most conspicuous in the tongue	Pseudobulbar palsy Weakness, slowness and spasticity of the lower facial muscles, jaw, palate, pharynx, larynx and tongue muscles Exaggerated jaw-jerk Emotional lability
Dysarthria, dysphagia, weight loss and the risk of inhalation pneumonia are the clinical problems facing patients described above	
Muscles of the limbs and trunk	
Progressive muscular atrophy Weakness, wasting and fasciculation of any of the limb or trunk muscles Often associated with frequent muscle cramps No sensory loss Small muscles of the hand frequently involved	Amyotrophic lateral sclerosis Weakness, spasticity, clonus and increased deep tendon reflexes Any limb, but more commonly in the legs Sphincter control not affected No sensory loss

Fig. 10.2 The four clinical syndromes with which motor neurone disease may present.

The quality of life for patients can be helped by:
- humane explanation of the nature of the condition to the patient and his family, with the aid of self-help groups;
- sympathy and encouragement;
- drugs for cramp, drooling and depression;
- speech therapy, dietetic advice, and often percutaneous gastrostomy feeding for dysphagia;
- communication aids for dysarthria;
- non-invasive portable ventilators for respiratory muscle weakness;
- provision of aids and alterations in the house (wheelchairs, ramps, lifts, showers, hoists, etc.) as weakness progresses;
- nursing help and respite care;
- gentle and timely discussion and planning of terminal care, often involving hospice staff.

Peripheral neuropathy

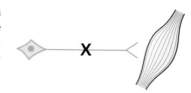

In this section, we are focusing on the axon of the anterior horn cell and the distal axon of the dorsal root ganglion cell. These myelinated nerve fibres constitute the peripheral nerves (Fig. 10.3). Each peripheral nerve, in reality, consists of very many myelinated nerve fibres.

In patients with peripheral neuropathy, there is malfunction in all the peripheral nerves of the body. Two types of pathology may occur. In some cases there may be distal axonal degeneration, explaining the distal distribution of symptoms and signs in the limbs. Alternatively segments of the nerve fibres become demyelinated (Fig. 10.4). The normal saltatory passage of the nerve impulse along the nerve fibre becomes impaired. The impulse either fails to be conducted across the demyelinated section, or travels very slowly in a non-saltatory way along the axon in the demyelinated section of the nerve. This means that a large volley of impulses, which should travel synchronously along the component nerve fibres of a peripheral nerve, become:

- diminished as individual component impulses fail to be conducted;
- delayed and dispersed as individual impulses become slowed by the non-saltatory transmission (Fig. 10.4). Neurotransmission is most impaired in long nerves under such circumstances simply because the nerve impulse is confronted by a greater number of demyelinated segments along the course of the nerve (Fig. 10.5). This is the main reason why the

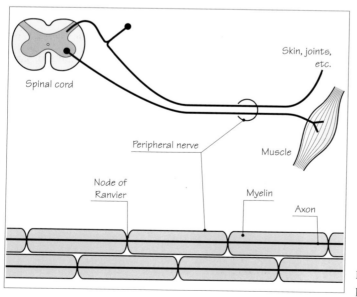

Fig. 10.3 Diagram to show the peripheral nerve components.

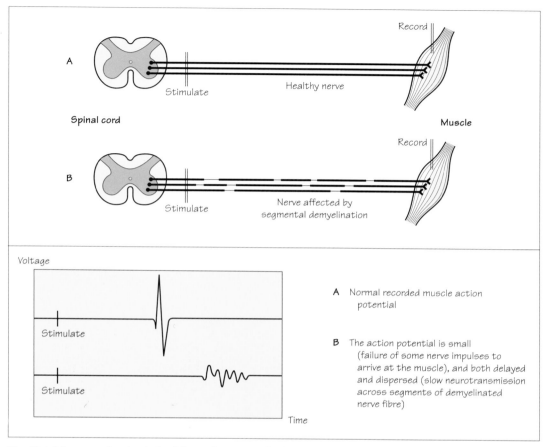

Fig. 10.4 Nerve conduction in healthy and segmentally demyelinated nerve fibres.

symptoms of neuropathy due to segmental demyelination are most evident distally in the limbs, why the legs and feet are more affected than the arms and hands, and why the distal deep tendon reflexes (which require synchronous neurotransmission from stretch receptors in the muscle to the spinal cord and back again to the muscle — the reflex arc) are frequently lost in patients with peripheral neuropathy.

The peripheral nerve pathology may predominantly affect sensory axons, motor axons, or all axons. Accordingly, the patient's symptoms and signs may be distal and sensory in the limbs, distal and motor in the limbs, or a combination of both. They are shown in greater detail in Fig. 10.6.

Fig. 10.5 Effect of nerve length upon neurotransmission in peripheral neuropathy.

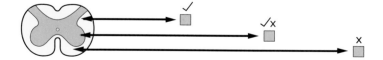

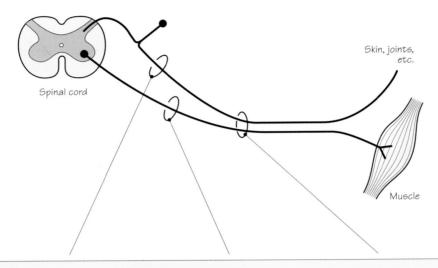

	Sensory	Motor	Reflex
Symptoms			
Upper limbs	Glove distribution of tingling, pins and needles and numbness	Weakness of grip and fingers	
	Difficulty in manipulating small objects in the fingers because of loss of sensation		
Lower limbs	Stocking distribution of tingling, pins and needles and numbness	Foot drop	
	Unsteadiness of stance and gait, especially in the dark or when eyes closed	Loss of spring at the ankles for running and climbing stairs	
Signs			
Upper limbs	Glove distribution of sensory loss, affecting any sensory modality	Distal lower motor neurone signs in hands	Loss of distal reflexes, e.g. supinator jerks
	Sensory ataxia in fingers and hands		
Lower limbs	Stocking distribution of sensory loss, affecting any sensory modality	Distal lower motor neurone signs in legs and feet	Loss of distal reflexes, especially ankle jerks
	Sensory ataxia in legs and gait		
	Rombergism (i.e. dependence on eyes for balance)		

Fig. 10.6 Symptoms and signs of peripheral neuropathy.

Common causes of peripheral neuropathy

In developed countries the commonest identifiable causes of peripheral neuropathy are alcohol and diabetes. In other parts of the world, vitamin deficiency and leprosy cause more disease, although this is gradually changing. In both settings, many cases of peripheral neuropathy remain unexplained. Figure 10.7 lists some of the most important causes of peripheral neuropathy.

Alcoholic neuropathy

Alcoholic neuropathy is common and usually more sensory than motor. How much it is caused by the direct toxic effect of alcohol on the peripheral nerves, and how much it is due to coexistent vitamin B_1 deficiency, is not completely known.

Vitamin B_{12} deficiency

Vitamin B_{12} deficiency is not a common cause of neuropathy, but is an important one to recognize because of its reversibility. Every effort should be made to reach the diagnosis before the irreversible changes of subacute combined degeneration of the spinal cord become established.

Deficiency	Vitamin B_1 in alcoholics Vitamin B_6 in patients taking isoniazid Vitamin B_{12} in patients with pernicious anaemia and bowel disease
Toxic	Alcohol Drugs, e.g. isoniazid, vincristine, aminodarone
Metabolic	Diabetes mellitus Chronic renal failure
Inflammatory	Guillain–Barré syndrome Chronic inflammatory demyelinating polyneuropathy
Paraneoplastic	Bronchial carcinoma and other malignancies
Connective tissue disease	Rheumatoid arthritis Systemic lupus erythematosus Polyarteritis nodosa
Hereditary	Hereditary motor and sensory neuropathy (HMSN) (also known as Charcot–Marie–Tooth disease)
Haematological	Paraproteinaemia
Idiopathic	Perhaps accounting for 50% of cases

Fig. 10.7 Common causes of peripheral neuropathy in the UK.

Diabetes mellitus

Diabetes mellitus is probably the commonest cause of peripheral neuropathy in the Western world. It occurs in both juvenile-onset insulin-requiring diabetes and maturity-onset diabetes. It may be the first clinical suggestion of the presence of diabetes. Excellent diabetic control has been shown to prevent neuropathy, but does not reverse it once it has developed.

The commonest form of neuropathy in diabetes is a predominantly sensory one. The combination of neuropathy and atherosclerosis affecting the nerves and arteries in the lower limbs very strongly predisposes the feet of diabetic patients to trophic lesions, which are slow to heal.

There are a few unusual forms of neuropathy that may occur in patients with diabetes:

- painful weakness and wasting of one proximal lower limb, so-called diabetic lumbosacral radiculo-plexopathy or diabetic amyotrophy;
- involvement of the autonomic nervous system giving rise to abnormal pupils, postural hypotension, impaired cardio-acceleration on changing from the supine to the standing position, impaired bladder, bowel and sexual function, and loss of normal sweating;
- a tendency for individual nerves to stop working quite abruptly, with subsequent gradual recovery. Common nerves to be involved are the 3rd and 6th cranial nerves and the common peroneal nerve in the leg. Involvement of several individual nerves in this way constitutes the clinical syndrome of multifocal neuropathy.

Hereditary motor and sensory neuropathy (HMSN, also known as Charcot–Marie–Tooth disease)

There are several forms of this, with a complex genetic classification. One of the more common, HMSN type I, is due to a duplication in the gene for peripheral myelin protein 22; this and some other forms can be diagnosed with a genetic test. The illness is usually evident in teenage life and very slowly worsens over many years. Motor involvement predominates, with lower motor neurone signs appearing in the feet and legs (especially in the anterolateral muscle compartments of the calves), and in the small muscles of the hands. Pes cavus and clawing of the toes are very common consequences. Sometimes, the pathology primarily involves the axons, but more often there is demyelination and remyelination to be found in the peripheral nerves.

> **Key features of HMSN**
>
> - Pes cavus
> - Distal wasting ('champagne bottle legs')
> - Distal weakness
> - Absent reflexes
> - Mild distal sensory loss

Causes of death

Guillain–Barré syndrome can be fatal, but most of the causes are avoidable:

- aspiration pneumonia
- DVT and pulmonary embolism
- cardiac arrhythmia

So monitor bulbar function, vital capacity and the heart, and anticoagulate

Guillain–Barré syndrome

Guillain–Barré syndrome is rather different from the other forms of peripheral neuropathy. This is because of its rapid evolution over several days, because it can produce a life-threatening degree of weakness, and because the underlying pathology clearly affects the nerve roots as well as the peripheral nerves.

The syndrome commonly occurs a week or two after an infection, such as *Campylobacter* enteritis, which is thought to trigger an autoimmune response.

The patient notices limb weakness and sensory symptoms which worsen day by day for 1–2 weeks (occasionally the progression may continue for as long as 4 weeks). Often, the illness stops advancing after a few days and does not produce a disability that is too major. Not uncommonly, however, it progresses to cause very serious paralysis in the limbs, trunk and chest muscles, and in the muscles supplied by the cranial nerves. Involvement of the autonomic nerves may cause erratic rises and falls in heart rate and blood pressure and profound constipation.

Patients with Guillain–Barré syndrome need to be hospitalized until it is certain that deterioration has come to an end, because chest and bulbar muscle weakness may make ventilation and nasogastric tube nutrition essential. Daily, or twice daily, estimations of the patient's vital capacity during the early phase of the disease can be a very valuable way of assessing the likelihood of the need for ventilatory support. Prompt administration of intravenous immunoglobulin or plasma exchange can prevent deterioration and the need for ventilation in many cases. Steroids have not been shown to be of proven benefit.

Patients with Guillain–Barré syndrome become very alarmed by the progressive loss of function at the start of their illness. They often need a good deal of psychological and physical support when the disability is severe and prolonged. The ultimate prognosis is usually very good, however. Incomplete recovery and recurrence are both well described, but by far the most frequent outcome of this condition is complete recovery over a few weeks or months, and no further similar trouble thereafter.

The pathology is predominantly in the myelin rather than in the axons of the peripheral nerves and nerve roots, i.e. a demyelinating polyneuropathy and polyradiculopathy. Recovery is due to the capability of Schwann cells to reconstitute the myelin sheaths after the initial demyelination. The involvement of the nerve roots gives rise to one of the diagnostic features of the condition, a raised CSF protein.

Myasthenia gravis

Myasthenia gravis is the rare clinical disease that results from impaired neuromuscular transmission at the synapse between the termination of the axon of the lower motor neurone and the muscle, at the motor end plate. Figure 10.8 is a diagram of a motor end plate. Neuromuscular transmission depends on normal synthesis and release of acetylcholine into the gap substance of the synapse, and its uptake by healthy receptors on the muscle membrane. The main pathological abnormality in myasthenia gravis at the neuromuscular junction is the presence of auto-antibody attached to receptor sites on the post-synaptic membrane. This auto-antibody both degrades and blocks acetylcholine receptor sites, thus impairing neuro-transmission across the synapse.

Myasthenia gravis is an autoimmune disease in which the auto-antibody appears clearly involved in the pathogenesis of the muscle weakness.

Myasthenia gravis is rather more common in women than men. In women, it tends to occur in young adult life, and in men it more commonly presents over the age of 50 years. Various subtypes of myasthenia gravis have been distinguished according to age and sex prevalence, HLA type associations, incidence of auto-antibodies, and other characteristics.

Muscle weakness, with abnormal fatiguability, and improve-ment after rest, characterize myasthenia gravis. Symptoms tend to be worse at the end of the day, and after repetitive use of mus-cles for a particular task, e.g. chewing and swallowing may be much more difficult towards the end of a meal than they were at the start. The distribution of muscle involvement is not uni-form, as shown in Fig. 10.9.

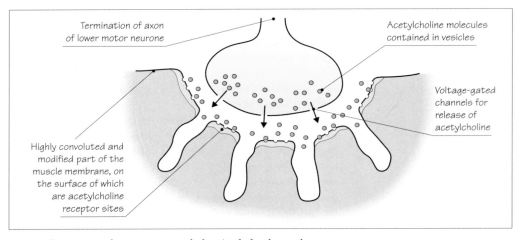

Fig. 10.8 Diagram to show a motor end plate in skeletal muscle.

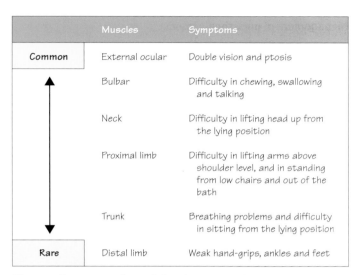

	Muscles	Symptoms
Common	External ocular	Double vision and ptosis
	Bulbar	Difficulty in chewing, swallowing and talking
	Neck	Difficulty in lifting head up from the lying position
	Proximal limb	Difficulty in lifting arms above shoulder level, and in standing from low chairs and out of the bath
	Trunk	Breathing problems and difficulty in sitting from the lying position
Rare	Distal limb	Weak hand-grips, ankles and feet

Fig. 10.9 Frequency of muscle involvement and symptoms in myasthenia gravis.

Confirmation of the diagnosis

Once suspected, the diagnosis of myasthenia gravis may be confirmed by:

1. The Tensilon test. Edrophonium chloride (Tensilon) is a short-acting anticholinesterase, which prolongs the action of acetylcholine at the neuromuscular junction for a few minutes after slow intravenous injection. This produces a transient and striking alleviation of weakness. There may also be an equally exciting bradycardia (reversed by atropine); the test should not be performed lightly in patients who are frail or have heart disease.

2. Detection of serum acetylcholine receptor antibodies. These antibodies are not found in the normal population, but are detected in about 50% of patients with purely ocular myasthenia, increasing up to about 90% of patients with more generalized myasthenia.

3. EMG studies. Sometimes it is helpful to show that the amplitude of the compound muscle action potential, recorded by surface electrodes over a muscle, decreases on repetitive stimulation of the nerve to the muscle.

4. Chest radiography and CT of the anterior mediastinum, to demonstrate an enlargement of the thymus gland. The association of myasthenia gravis with thymic enlargement is not yet fully understood. Of myasthenic patients, 10–15% have a thymoma, and 50–60% show thymic hyperplasia. Both sorts of pathology may enlarge the thymus, which can be clearly shown by suitable imaging procedures.

Management of myasthenia gravis

The management of myasthenia gravis includes:

1. The use of oral anticholinesterase drugs, pyridostigmine and prostigmine. These are prescribed at intervals during the day, and work quite effectively. Abdominal colic and diarrhoea, induced by the increased parasympathetic activity in the gut, can be controlled by simultaneous use of propantheline.

2. Immunosuppression by prednisolone or azathioprine. In patients with disabling symptoms inadequately controlled by oral anticholinesterase therapy, suppression of the autoantibody can radically improve muscle strength.

3. Thymectomy. Remission or improvement can be expected in 60–80% of patients after thymectomy, and must be considered in all patients. It may make the use of immunosuppressive drugs unnecessary, which is obviously desirable.

4. Plasma exchange to remove circulating auto-antibody to produce short-term improvement in seriously weak patients.

5. Great care of the myasthenic patient with severe weakness who is already on treatment. The muscle strength of such patients may change abruptly, and strength in the bulbar and respiratory muscles may become inadequate for breathing. The correct place for such patients is in hospital, with anaesthetic and neurological expertise closely to hand. There may be uncertainty as to whether such a patient is undertreated with anticholinesterase (myasthenic crisis), or overtreated so that the excessive acetylcholine at the neuromuscular junction is spontaneously depolarizing the postsynaptic membrane, i.e. depolarization block (cholinergic crisis). Fasciculation may be present when such spontaneous depolarization is occurring. Tensilon may be used to decide whether the patient is under- or overdosed, but *it is essential to perform the Tensilon test with an anaesthetist present in these circumstances*. If the weak state is due to cholinergic crisis, the additional intravenous dose of anticholinesterase may produce further critical paralysis of bulbar or respiratory muscles.

Management of myasthenia gravis

- Anticholinesterase
- Immunosuppression
- Thymectomy
- Plasma exchange
- Crisis management

Muscle disease

These are a group of rare diseases in which the primary pathology causing muscle weakness and wasting lies in the muscles themselves. They are classified in Fig. 10.10 and short notes about each condition are given in this section.

Inherited

1 Muscular dystrophies, whose genetic basis is increasingly understood in terms of gene and gene product identification.

Duchenne	X-linked recessive gene
Myotonic dystrophy	Autosomal dominant gene
Facio-scapulo-humeral	Autosomal dominant gene
Limb girdle	Not a single entity (variable inheritance)

2 Muscle diseases in which an inherited biochemical defect is present.

   Specific enzyme deficiencies occur which disrupt the pathways of carbohydrate or fat oxidation, often with accumulation of substrate within the muscle cell. The enzyme deficiency may be within the muscle cell cytoplasm, interfering with the utilization of glycogen or glucose, or it may be within the mitochondria of muscle cells (and cells of other organs) blocking the metabolism of pyruvate, fatty acids or individual elements of Krebs cycle.

   In other diseases of this sort, there is uncoupling of the electrical excitation of muscle fibres and their contraction. This is the case in McArdle's syndrome, and in malignant hyperpyrexia where sustained muscle contraction may occur in the absence of nerve stimulation.

Acquired

1 Immunologically mediated inflammatory disease, e.g.
      polymyositis
      dermatomyositis

2 Non-inflammatory myopathy, e.g.
      corticosteroids
      thyrotoxicosis

Fig. 10.10 Classification of muscle diseases.

Duchenne dystrophy

Duchenne dystrophy is the most serious inherited muscular dystrophy. The X-linked recessive inheritance gives rise to healthy female carriers and affected male children. The affected boys usually show evidence of muscular weakness before the age of 5 years, and die of profound muscle weakness (predisposing them to chest infections), or of associated cardiomyopathy, in late teenage life. In the early stages, the weakness of proximal muscles may show itself by a characteristic way in which these boys will 'climb up their own bodies with their hands' (Gower's sign) when rising from the floor to the standing position. They also show muscle wasting, together with pseudohypertrophy of the calf muscles (which is due to fat deposition in atrophied muscle tissue).

The affected boys have elevated levels of creatine kinase muscle enzyme in the blood, and the clinically unaffected carrier state in female relatives is often associated with some elevation of the muscle enzymes in the blood. The gene locus on the X chromosome responsible for Duchenne dystrophy, and its large gene product, dystrophin, have been identified. Molecular genetic diagnosis of affected patients and female carriers is possible, as is prenatal diagnosis.

This same region of the X chromosome is also implicated in the inheritance of a more benign variant of Duchenne dystrophy (later in onset and less rapidly progressive), known as Becker's musclar dystrophy.

The combination of family history, clinical examination, biochemical and genetic studies allows the detection of the carrier state, and the prenatal detection of the affected male fetus in the first trimester of pregnancy. Genetic counselling of such families has reached a high degree of accuracy. As a single gene disorder, Duchenne muscular dystrophy is one of the conditions in which gene therapy is being considered.

Key features of Duchenne muscular dystrophy

- Young
- Male
- Generalized weakness
- Muscle wasting
- Calf pseudohypertrophy
- Gower's sign

Key features of myotonic dystrophy

- Either sex
- Glum-looking from facial weakness and ptosis
- Frontal balding
- Glasses or previous cataract surgery
- Hand muscles show wasting and myotonia

Myotonic dystrophy

Myotonic dystrophy is characterized by 'dystrophy' of several organs and tissues of the body, and the dystrophic changes in muscle are associated with myotonic contraction.

The disease is due to an expanded trinucleotide repeat (see box on p. 75). This is inherited as an autosomal dominant, so men and women are equally affected, usually in early adult life. The mutation tends to expand with each generation, especially when transmitted from a woman to her child, causing a more severe phenotype which is described below. Genetic testing allows symptomatic, presymptomatic and prenatal diagnosis, where appropriate.

Some impairment of intellectual function, cataracts, premature loss of hair, cardiac arrhythmia and failure, gonadal atrophy and failure, all feature in patients with myotonic dystrophy, but the most affected tissue is muscle. The facial appearance may be characteristic, with frontal balding, wasting of the temporalis muscles, bilateral ptosis and bilateral facial weakness. Muscle weakness and wasting are generalized but the hands are often particularly affected.

The myotonia shows itself in two ways:

1. The patient has difficulty in rapid relaxation of tightly contracted muscle, contraction myotonia, and this is best seen by asking the patient to open the hand and fingers quickly after making a fist.

2. Percussion myotonia is the tendency for muscle tissue to contract when it is struck by a tendon hammer, and this is best seen by light percussion of the thenar eminence whilst the hand is held out flat. A sustained contraction of the thenar muscles lifts the thumb into a position of partial abduction and opposition.

From its appearance in early adult life, the illness runs a variable but slowly progressive course over several decades. The associated cardiomyopathy is responsible for some of the early mortality in myotonic dystrophy.

Some children of females with myotonic dystrophy may show the disease from the time of birth. Such babies may be very hypotonic, subject to respiratory problems (chest muscle involvement) and feeding problems (facial muscle involvement). Mental retardation is a feature of these children. Frequently, the birth of such a child is the first evidence of myotonic dystrophy in the family, since the mother's involvement is only mild.

Facio-scapulo-humeral dystrophy

Facio-scapulo-humeral dystrophy is generally a benign form of muscular dystrophy. It is due to an unusual dominantly inherited gene contraction near the telomere of chromosome 4, which can usually be detected for diagnostic purposes. It is often mild and asymptomatic. Wasting and weakness of the facial, scapular and humeral muscles may give rise to difficulties in whistling, and in using the arms above shoulder level and for heavy lifting. The thinness of the biceps and triceps, or the abnormal position of the scapula (due to weakness of the muscles which hold the scapula close to the thoracic cage), may be the features that bring the patient to seek medical advice. Involvement of other trunk muscles, and the muscles of the pelvic girdle, may appear with time.

Limb girdle syndrome

Weakness concentrated around the proximal limb muscles has a wide range of causes, including ones which are treatable. Limb girdle weakness should not be regarded as due to dystrophy (and therefore incurable) until thorough investigation has shown this to be the case. Even limb girdle dystrophy is heterogeneous, made up of a large number of pathologically and genetically distinct entities, for example involving many of the proteins which anchor the contractile apparatus of muscle to the muscle membrane. Other important causes of limb girdle syndrome are shown in the box.

> **Limb girdle weakness:**
>
> - polymyositis
> - myopathy associated with endocrine disease
> - metabolic myopathies
> - drug-induced myopathies, e.g. steroids
> - limb girdle dystrophy

Conditions caused by inherited biochemical defects

Muscle diseases in which an inherited biochemical defect is present are rare. Of these conditions, malignant hyperpyrexia is perhaps the most dramatic. Members of families in which this condition is present do not have any ongoing muscle weakness or wasting. Symptoms do not occur until an affected family member has a general anaesthetic, particularly if halothane or suxamethonium chloride is used. During or immediately after surgery, muscle spasm, shock and an alarming rise in body temperature occur, progressing to death in about 50% of cases.

The pathology of this condition involves a defect in calcium metabolism allowing such anaesthetic agents to incur a massive rise in calcium ions within the muscle cells. This is associated with sustained muscle contraction and muscle necrosis. The rise in body temperature is secondary to the generalized muscle contraction.

Polymyositis and dermatomyositis

The muscle problems in polymyositis and dermatomyositis are very similar. There is a mononuclear inflammatory cell infiltration and muscle fibre necrosis. In dermatomyositis, there is the additional involvement of skin, particularly in the face and hands. An erythematous rash over the nose and around the eyes, and over the knuckles of the hands, is most typical. Though all muscles may be involved, proximal limb, trunk and neck muscles are most frequently made weak by polymyositis with occasional involvement of swallowing.

The condition most usually develops subacutely or chronically and is unassociated with muscle tenderness. Problems when trying to use the arms above shoulder level, and difficulty when standing up out of low chairs and the bath, are the most frequent complaints.

Both conditions are autoimmune diseases involving skeletal and not cardiac muscle. Dermatomyositis, especially in older men, can be triggered by underlying malignancy.

Both dermatomyositis and polymyositis respond to immunosuppressive therapy. High-dose steroids, with or without other immunosuppressants, gradually reduced to reasonable long-term maintenance levels, constitute the treatment of choice. Effective control of the disease can be established in the majority of cases.

Acquired non-inflammatory myopathy

Acquired non-inflammatory myopathy can occur in many circumstances (alcoholism, drug-induced states, disturbances of vitamin D and calcium metabolism, Addison's disease, etc.), but the two common conditions to be associated with myopathy are *hyperthyroidism* and *high-dose steroid treatment*.

Many patients with hyperthyroidism show weakness of shoulder girdle muscles. This is usually asymptomatic. Occasionally, more serious weakness of proximal limb muscles and trunk muscles may occur. The myopathy completely recovers with treatment of the primary condition.

Patients on high-dose steroids, especially fluorinated triamcinolone, betamethasone and dexamethasone, may develop significant trunk and proximal limb muscle weakness and wasting. The myopathy is reversible on withdrawal of the steroids, on reduction in dose, or on change to a non-fluorinated steroid.

Investigation of patients with generalized muscle weakness and wasting

The last section of this chapter discusses the common investigations that are carried out in patients with generalized muscle weakness and wasting. Of the four conditions discussed in this chapter, myasthenia gravis does not produce muscle wasting, and is usually distinguishable by virtue of the ocular and bulbar muscle involvement, the abnormal degree of fatiguability, and the response to anticholinesterase. The other three conditions may be quite distinct on clinical grounds too, but investigation is frequently very helpful in confirmation of diagnosis.

Figure 10.11 shows the investigations that are carried out on patients of this sort.

Test	Motor neurone disease	Peripheral neuropathy	Muscle disease
Biochemistry Creatine kinase	Normal	Normal	Elevated
Electrical studies Electromyography	Denervation	Denervation	Muscle disease
Motor and sensory nerve conduction studies	Normal	Delayed conduction velocities and reduced nerve action potentials	Normal
Histology Histochemistry Immunofluorescence Electron microscopy			
Muscle biopsy	Denervation	Denervation	Specific commentary on the nature of the muscle disease, i.e. dystrophy, polymyositis or acquired myopathy
Nerve biopsy		Sometimes helpful in establishing the precise cause of peripheral neuropathy	
Molecular genetics	No help in conventional MND	Helpful in hereditary motor and sensory neuropathy	Helpful in the inherited muscle diseases

Fig. 10.11 The investigations performed in patients with generalized muscle weakness and wasting.

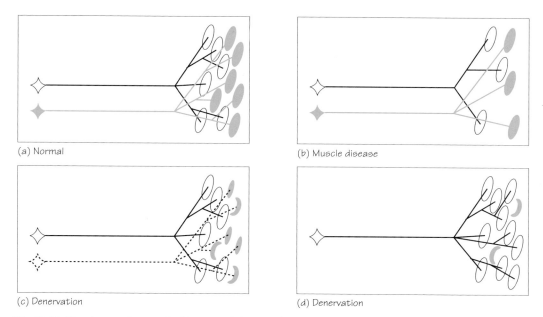

Fig. 10.12 The changes in muscle disease and denervation.
(a) Two normal motor units. Each lower motor neurone supplies several muscle fibres.
(b) In muscle disease (dystrophy, polymyositis or acquired myopathy), there is loss or damage directly affecting muscle fibres. The number of functional muscle fibres decreases. Therefore, in muscle disease, there is *a normal number of abnormally small motor units*.
(c) Damage to one lower motor neurone, either in the cell body (as in motor neurone disease), or in the axon (as in peripheral neuropathy), results in denervated muscle fibres within the motor unit.
(d) The surviving lower motor neurone produces terminal axonal sprouts which innervate some of the muscle fibres of the damaged motor unit. Therefore, in muscles affected by a denervating disease, there is *a reduced number of abnormally large motor units*.

It is important that the consequences of denervation and muscle disease on the motor unit are understood, and these are shown in Fig. 10.12. Both electromyography (the recording of muscle at rest and during contraction) and muscle biopsy are able to detect the changes of chronic partial denervation and of primary muscle disease.

CASE HISTORIES

Case 1

A 55-year-old bank manager reports a 12-month history of numbness and burning in his feet. He takes ranitidine for dyspepsia but has no other medical history. He is married with grown-up children. He has no family history of neurological disease. His GP has checked his full blood count (MCV mildly raised at 101, otherwise normal), electrolytes and glucose (normal).

On examination he is generally thin but has no muscle wasting, fasciculation or weakness. His ankle reflexes are absent. Both plantar responses are flexor. He has impaired appreciation of pain and temperature sensation below mid-shin on both sides. He can feel light touch and joint position normally. Romberg's test is negative (i.e. he can stand to attention with his eyes shut, without falling over).

a. What type of neurological problem does he have?
b. What is the most likely cause?

Case 2

A previously healthy 26-year-old junior doctor asks your advice. She has been choking on drinks for 2 weeks and last night a patient complained about her slurred speech. She is extremely anxious because her uncle died of motor neurone disease. She lives on her own in a hospital flat; she has not registered with a GP.

On examination she is anxious and breathless. Her speech is nasal and becomes softer as she talks. Her palatal movements are reduced. Her tongue looks normal. Her jaw-jerk is normal. Examination of the other cranial nerves is normal. She has no limb wasting, fasciculation or weakness. Her reflexes are brisk. There is no sensory loss.

a. What is the most likely diagnosis?
b. How would you manage her case?

(For answers, see pp. 261–3.)

CHAPTER 11

Unconsciousness

Introduction and definitions

Patients who become unconscious make their relatives and their doctors anxious. A structured way of approaching the unconscious patient is useful to the doctor so that he behaves rationally and competently when those around him are becoming alarmed.

Unconsciousness is difficult to define. Most people know what is meant by the word. One way of defining unconsciousness is by asking the reader how he would recognize that a person he had just found was unconscious. Answers to this question would probably include statements like this, 'in a deep sleep, eyes closed, not talking, not responding to his name or instructions, not moving his limbs even when slapped or shaken'.

In terms of neurophysiology and neuro-anatomy, it is not completely clear on what consciousness depends. Consciousness involves the normally functioning cerebrum responding to the arrival of visual, auditory and somatic afferent stimulation as shown in Fig. 11.1.

The ideal circumstances for normal loss of consciousness, in sleep, are entirely compatible with this concept—eyes closed in a darkened room, where it is quiet, in a bed where the body is comfortable, warm and still.

Abnormal states of unconsciousness occur firstly if there is some generalized impairment of cerebral hemisphere function preventing the brain from responding to normal afferent stimulation, or secondly, if the cerebral hemispheres are deprived of normal afferent stimulation due to pathological lesions in the brainstem, blocking incoming visual, auditory and somatic sensory stimuli. The concept of unconsciousness being the consequence of either a diffuse cerebral problem, or a major brainstem lesion, or both, is useful from the clinical point of view.

A patient may present to the doctor with attacks of unconsciousness between which he feels well, i.e. blackouts, or he may be in a state of ongoing unconsciousness which persists and demands urgent management, i.e. persistent coma. We will consider these two situations separately.

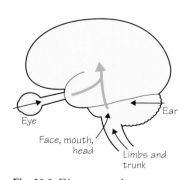

Fig. 11.1 Diagram to show important factors maintaining consciousness.

Eye

Face, mouth, head

Limbs and trunk

Ear

Attacks of unconsciousness or blackouts

Here it is most likely that the patient, feeling perfectly well, will consult the doctor about some blackouts which have been occurring. Very often a relative will be with him, since the attack has caused as much anxiety in the witnessing relative as in the patient. It is not common for doctors to witness transient blackouts in patients, for obvious reasons. *The value of a competent witness's account is enormous in forming a diagnosis. Arriving at a firm diagnosis in a patient who has suffered unwitnessed attacks is often much more difficult.*

The common causes of blackouts are illustrated in Fig. 11.2.

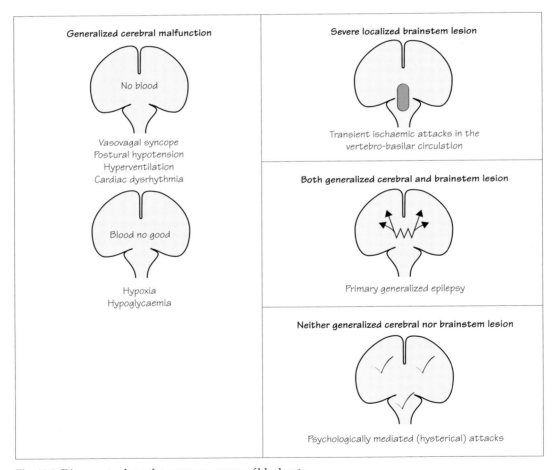

Generalized cerebral malfunction

No blood

Vasovagal syncope
Postural hypotension
Hyperventilation
Cardiac dysrhythmia

Blood no good

Hypoxia
Hypoglycaemia

Severe localized brainstem lesion

Transient ischaemic attacks in the
vertebro-basilar circulation

Both generalized cerebral and brainstem lesion

Primary generalized epilepsy

Neither generalized cerebral nor brainstem lesion

Psychologically mediated (hysterical) attacks

Fig. 11.2 Diagram to show the common causes of blackouts.

Causes of blackouts

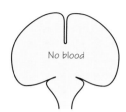

Vasovagal syncope

As a consequence of increased vagal and decreased sympathetic activity, the heart slows and blood pools peripherally. Cardiac output decreases and there is inadequate perfusion of the brain when the patient is in the upright position. He loses consciousness, falls, becomes horizontal, venous return improves, cardiac output improves and consciousness is restored. The attack is worse if the patient is held upright and it is relieved or prevented by lowering the patient's head below the level of the heart.

Common features of vasovagal syncope are as follows:
- they are more common in teenage and young adult life;
- they may be triggered by standing for a long time, and by emotionally upsetting circumstances (hearing bad news, hearing or seeing explicit medical details, experiencing minor medical procedures, e.g. venipuncture, sutures);
- the patient has a warning of dizziness, visual blurring, feeling hot or cold, sweating, pallor;
- the patient is unconscious for a short period (30–120 seconds) only, during which time there may be a brief flurry of myoclonic jerks but then the patient is flaccid and motionless;
- the patient feels nauseated and sweaty on recovery, but is back to normal within 15 minutes or so.

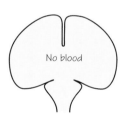

Postural hypotension

In circumstances of decreased sympathetic activity affecting the heart and peripheral circulation, the normal cardio-acceleration and peripheral vasoconstriction that occurs when changing from the supine to the erect position does not occur, and cardiac output and cerebral perfusion are inadequate in the standing position, resulting in loss of consciousness. The situation rectifies itself as described above in vasovagal syncope. The cause of the decreased sympathetic activity is usually pharmacological (overaction of antihypertensive agents or as a side-effect of very many drugs given for other purposes), though it is occasionally due to a physical lesion of the sympathetic pathways in the central or peripheral nervous system.

Postural hypotension should be suspected if the patient:
- is middle-aged or elderly, and is on medication of some sort;
- complains of dizziness or lightheadedness when standing;
- only experiences attacks in the standing position and can abort them by sitting or lying down;
- has a systolic blood pressure which is lower by 30 mmHg or more when in the standing position than when supine.

Hyperventilation

Patients who overbreathe, wash out carbon dioxide from their blood. Arterial hypocapnia is a very strong cerebral vasoconstrictive stimulus. The patient starts to feel lightheaded, unreal and increasingly dissociated from her surroundings.

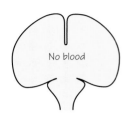

The clues to hyperventilation being the cause of blackouts are:

- the patient is young and female;
- the patient is in a state of anxiety;
- the patient mentions that she has difficulty in 'getting her breath' as the attack develops;
- distal limb paraesthesiae and/or tetany are mentioned (due to the increased nerve excitability which occurs when the concentration of ionized calcium in the plasma is reduced during respiratory alkalosis);
- the attacks can be culminated by reassurance and rebreathing into a paper bag;
- the symptoms may be reproducible by voluntary hyperventilation.

Cardiac arrhythmia

When left ventricular output is inadequate because of either cardiac tachyarrhythmia or bradyarrhythmia, cardiac output and cerebral perfusion may be inadequate to maintain consciousness. The cardiac arrhythmia is most usually (but not exclusively) caused by ischaemic heart disease. The most classical form of this condition, known as the Stokes–Adams attack, occurs when there is impaired atrioventricular conduction leading to periods of very slow ventricular rate and/or asystole.

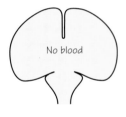

Cardiac arrhythmia should be suspected if:

- the patient is middle-aged or elderly;
- the attacks are unrelated to posture;
- there is a history of ischaemic heart disease;
- the patient has noticed palpitations;
- episodes of dizziness and presyncope occur as well as episodes in which consciousness is lost;
- marked colour change and/or loss of pulse have been observed by witnesses during the attacks;
- the patient has a rhythm abnormality at the time of examination;
- ischaemic, rhythm or conduction abnormalities are present in the ECG.

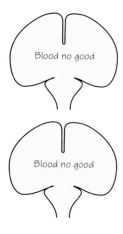

Hypoxia

Hypoxia is a very uncommon cause of attacks of unconsciousness. Even in patients with severe respiratory embarassment, e.g. major asthmatic attack, consciousness is usually retained.

Hypoglycaemia

Except in diabetic patients who are taking oral hypoglycaemic agents or insulin, hypoglycaemia is another very uncommon cause of blackouts. This is because alternative causes of hypoglycaemia (e.g. insulinoma of the pancreas) are rare.

Amongst diabetics, hypoglycaemia should be high on the list of possible causes of blackouts.

Hypoglycaemic attacks:
- may be heralded by feelings of hunger and emptiness;
- are associated with the release of adrenaline (one of the body's homeostatic mechanisms to release glucose from liver glycogen stores in the face of hypoglycaemia). This explains the palpitations, tremor and sweating that characterize hypoglycaemic attacks;
- may not proceed to full loss of consciousness; they may simply cause episodes of abnormal speech, confusion or unusual behaviour;
- may proceed quite rapidly through faintness and drowsiness to coma, especially in children;
- are most conclusively proved by recording a low blood glucose level during an attack, but clearly this is not always possible.

Vertebro-basilar transient ischaemic attacks

Vertebro-basilar transient ischaemic attacks rarely cause loss of consciousness without additional symptoms of brainstem dysfunction. Thrombo-embolic material, derived from the heart or proximal large arteries in the chest and neck, may lodge in the small arteries which supply the brainstem. They may cause ischaemia of the brainstem tissue until lysis or fragmentation of the thrombo-embolic material occurs.

Vertebro-basilar ischaemia is suggested:
- if the patient is middle-aged or elderly;
- if the patient is known to be arteriopathic (i.e. history of myocardial infarction, angina, intermittent claudication or stroke), or has a definite source of emboli;
- if the patient is having transient ischaemic attacks that do not involve loss of consciousness, e.g. episodes of monocular blindness, speech disturbance, hemiplegia, hemianaesthesia, diplopia, ataxia, etc.

Epilepsy

Chapter 12 deals with epilepsy in detail. Epilepsy may be generalized or focal. In generalized epilepsy the abnormal electrical
activity starts in deep midline brain structures and spreads to all
parts of the cerebral cortex simultaneously. This gives rise to
tonic–clonic and absence seizures in which consciousness is
invariably lost.

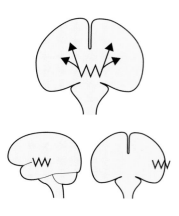

In focal epilepsy, the abnormal electrical activity is localized
to one area of the cerebral cortex. In focal seizures, there is
grossly deranged function in that part of the brain where
the epileptic activity is occurring, whilst the rest of the brain
remains relatively normal. So long as the seizure remains
localized, consciousness is maintained. It is only when focal
epileptic activity occurs in the temporal lobe, when regions
subserving memory are disrupted during the attack, that
patients seek help for blackouts which they cannot properly
remember. Memory, rather than consciousness, is lost in such
attacks.

'Psychogenic non-epileptic' attacks

Some patients attract attention to themselves, at a conscious or
subconscious level, by having blackouts. The attacks may consist of apparent loss of consciousness and falling, sometimes
with convulsive movement of the limbs and face. The patient
may report no memory or awareness during the attack, or he
may acknowledge awareness at a very distant level without any
ability to respond to his environment or control his body during
the attack.

Such psychologically mediated non-epileptic attacks:
- are more common in teenage and young adult life;
- are associated with self-reported previous physical or sexual
  abuse;
- may be suggested by the coordinated purposeful kinds of
  movements which are witnessed in the attacks (shouting,
  grasping, pelvic thrusting, turning the head from side to
  side);
- may occur in association with epilepsy. It is easy to understand why a young person with epilepsy might respond to
  adversity by having non-epileptic attacks rather than developing some other psychosomatic disorder;
- are disabling, very difficult to manage, and potentially
  dangerous if treated inappropriately with anticonvulsant
  drugs such as intravenous benzodiazepines.

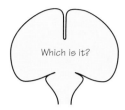

Which is it?

Making the diagnosis in a patient with blackouts

Making the diagnosis is best achieved by giving oneself enough time to talk to the patient so that he can describe all that happens before, during and after the attacks, and similarly by talking to a witness so that he can describe all the observable phenomena of the patient's attack. Physical examination of the patient with blackouts is very frequently normal, so it cannot be relied upon to yield very much information of use. Occasionally, it may be necessary to admit the patient to hospital so that the attacks may be observed by medical and nursing staff.

The investigations that may prove valuable in patients with blackouts are:

- EEG and ECG, with prolonged monitoring of the brain and heart by these techniques, if the standard procedures are not diagnostic;
- blood glucose and blood gas estimations (ideally at the time of the attacks) may help to prove either hypoglycaemia or hyperventilation as the basis of the attacks.

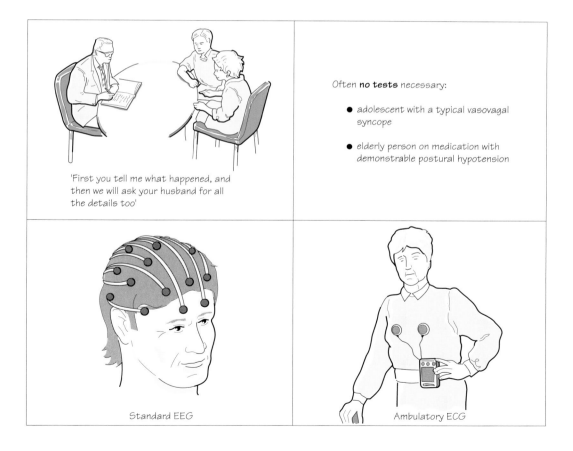

'First you tell me what happened, and then we will ask your husband for all the details too'

Often **no tests** necessary:

- adolescent with a typical vasovagal syncope

- elderly person on medication with demonstrable postural hypotension

Standard EEG

Ambulatory ECG

Treatment of the common causes of blackouts

Apart from a general explanation of the nature of the attacks to the patient and his family, there are two other aspects of management.

Specific treatment suggestions

Vasovagal syncope: lower head at onset.

Postural hypotension: remove offending drug, consider physical and pharmacological methods of maintaining the standing blood pressure (sleep with bed tilted slightly head up, fludrocortisone).

Hyperventilation: reassurance, and exercises to control breathing.

Cardiac arrhythmia: pharmacological or implanted pacemaker control of cardiac rhythm.

Hypoglycaemia: attention to drug regime in diabetics, removal of insulinoma in the rare instances of their occurrence.

Vertebro-basilar TIAs: treat source for emboli, aspirin.

Epilepsy: anticonvulsant drugs.

'Psychogenic non-epileptic' attacks: try to establish the reason for this behaviour, and careful explanation to the patient.

Care of personal safety

People who are subject to sudden episodes of loss of consciousness:

- should not *drive motor vehicles*;
- should consider showering rather than *taking a bath*;
- may not be safe in some *working environments* which involve working at heights, using power tools, working amongst heavy unguarded machinery, working with electricity wires;
- may have to curtail some *recreational activities* involving swimming or heights.

A firm but sympathetic manner is necessary in pointing out these aspects of the patient's management.

Sensible, but often unpopular restrictions

Before leaving the causes of blackouts, there are two rare neurological conditions to mention briefly. One condition predisposes the patient to frequent short episodes of sleep, *narcolepsy*, and the other gives rise to infrequent episodes of selective loss of memory, *transient global amnesia*.

Narcolepsy

- Sudden irresistible need to sleep, for short periods
- Legs give way, when highly amused or angry

In this condition, which is familial and very strongly associated with the possession of a particular HLA tissue type, the patient has a tendency to sleep for short periods, e.g. 10–15 minutes. The sleep is just like ordinary sleep to the observer, but is unnatural in its duration and in the strength with which it overtakes the patient. Such episodes of sleep may occur in circumstances where ordinary people feel sleepy, but narcoleptic patients also go to sleep at very inappropriate times, e.g. whilst talking, eating or driving.

The condition is associated with some other unusual phenomena:

- *cataplexy*: transient loss of tone and strength in the legs at times of emotional excitement, particularly laughter and annoyance, leading to falls without any impairment of consciousness;
- *sleep paralysis*: the frightening occurrence of awakening at night unable to move any part of the body for a few moments;
- *hypnogogic hallucinations*: visual hallucinations of faces occurring just before falling asleep in bed at night.

Narcolepsy, and its associated symptoms, are helped by dexamphetamine, clomipramine and modafinil.

Transient global amnesia

A short period, lasting hours, of very selective memory loss, other cerebral functions remaining intact

This syndrome, which tends to occur in patients over the age of 50, involves loss of memory for a few hours. During the period of amnesia, the patient cannot remember recent events, and does not retain any new information at all. All other neurological functions are normal. The patient can talk, write and carry out complicated motor functions (e.g. driving) normally. Throughout the episode, the patient repeatedly asks the same questions of orientation. Afterwards, the person is able to recall all events up to the start of the period of amnesia, remembers nothing of the period itself, and has a somewhat patchy memory of the first few hours following the episode.

Transient global amnesia may occur a few times in a patient's life. Its pathological mechanism remains poorly understood, but may be related to that of migraine aura.

Persistent coma

Assessment of conscious level

The observations that might be made by someone who finds an unconscious body were mentioned at the beginning of this chapter: 'in a deep sleep, eyes closed, not talking, not responding to instructions, not moving even when slapped or shaken'. These natural comments have been brought together and elaborated in the Glasgow Coma Scale. This is used very effectively to indicate and monitor a patient's level of unconsciousness. The Glasgow Coma Scale records the level of stimulus required to make the patient open his eyes and also records the patient's best verbal and motor responses, as shown in Fig. 11.3. It may be helpful to amplify the scores with a written description of the patient's precise responses to command or pain, in case subsequent staff are less familiar with the numerical scale.

The responses of the Glasgow Coma Scale depend upon the cerebrum's response to afferent stimulation. This may be impaired either because of impaired cerebral hemisphere function or because of a major brainstem lesion interfering with access of such stimuli to the cerebral hemispheres. Direct evidence that there is a major brainstem lesion may be evident in an unconscious patient (Fig. 11.4). Dilatation of the pupils and lack of pupillary constriction to light indicate problems in the midbrain, i.e. 3rd cranial nerve dysfunction. Impaired regulation of

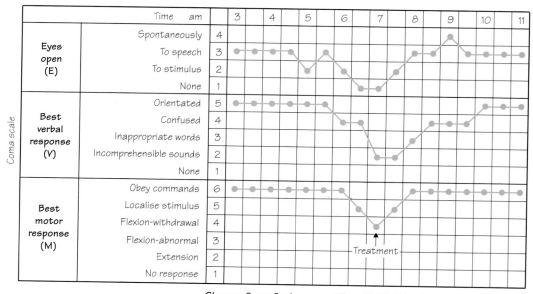

Glasgow Coma Scale score at 7am: E1, V2, M4 = 7

Fig. 11.3 Scheme to show the Glasgow Coma Scale. (After Teasdale G. & Jennett B. (1974) *Lancet* **ii**, 81–3.)

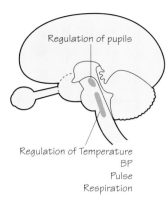

Regulation of pupils

Regulation of Temperature
BP
Pulse
Respiration

Fig. 11.4 Diagram to show important functions of the brainstem.

body temperature, blood pressure, pulse and respiration may all indicate trouble in the pons/medulla, where the centres controlling these vital functions exist.

When confronted with a patient in coma, a well-trained doctor will assess:

- vital functions of respiration, temperature control, pulse and blood pressure;
- pupil size and reactivity;
- the patient's eyes, speech and motor responses according to the Glasgow Coma Scale.

This approach to the assessment of conscious level holds good regardless of the particular cause of coma.

Causes of coma

There is a simple mnemonic to help one to remember the causes of coma (Fig. 11.5). In considering the causes of coma it is helpful to think again in terms of disease processes which impair cerebral hemisphere function generally on the one hand, and in terms of lesions in the brainstem blocking afferent stimulation of the cerebrum on the other. The common causes of coma are illustrated in this way in Fig. 11.6 overleaf.

	A E I O U	
A = Apoplexy	Brainstem infarction Intracranial haemorrhage	
E = Epilepsy	Post-ictal or inter-ictal coma Status epilepticus	
I = Injury	Concussion—major head injury	
I = Infection	Meningo-encephalitis Cerebral abscess	
O = Opiates	Standing for all CNS depressant drugs, including alcohol	
U = Uraemia	Standing for all metabolic causes for coma. Quite a useful way of remembering all possibilities here is to think of coma resulting from extreme deviation of normal blood constituents	
	Oxygen	Anoxia
	Carbon dioxide	Carbon dioxide narcosis
	Hydrogen ions	Diabetic keto-acidosis
	Glucose	Hypoglycaemia
	Urea	Renal failure
	Ammonia	Liver failure
	Thyroxine	Hypothyroidism

Fig. 11.5 A simple mnemonic for the recall of the causes of coma.

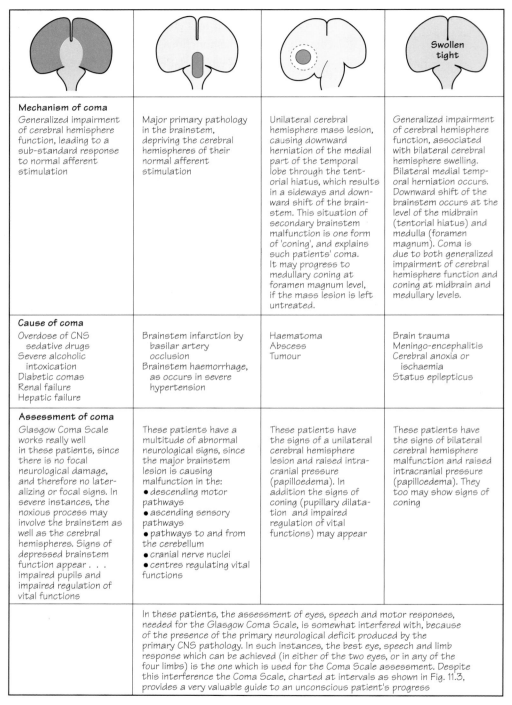

			Swollen tight
Mechanism of coma			
Generalized impairment of cerebral hemisphere function, leading to a sub-standard response to normal afferent stimulation	Major primary pathology in the brainstem, depriving the cerebral hemispheres of their normal afferent stimulation	Unilateral cerebral hemisphere mass lesion, causing downward herniation of the medial part of the temporal lobe through the tentorial hiatus, which results in a sideways and downward shift of the brainstem. This situation of secondary brainstem malfunction is one form of 'coning', and explains such patients' coma. It may progress to medullary coning at foramen magnum level, if the mass lesion is left untreated.	Generalized impairment of cerebral hemisphere function, associated with bilateral cerebral hemisphere swelling. Bilateral medial temporal herniation occurs. Downward shift of the brainstem occurs at the level of the midbrain (tentorial hiatus) and medulla (foramen magnum). Coma is due to both generalized impairment of cerebral hemisphere function and coning at midbrain and medullary levels.
Cause of coma			
Overdose of CNS sedative drugs Severe alcoholic intoxication Diabetic comas Renal failure Hepatic failure	Brainstem infarction by basilar artery occlusion Brainstem haemorrhage, as occurs in severe hypertension	Haematoma Abscess Tumour	Brain trauma Meningo-encephalitis Cerebral anoxia or ischaemia Status epilepticus
Assessment of coma			
Glasgow Coma Scale works really well in these patients, since there is no focal neurological damage, and therefore no lateralizing or focal signs. In severe instances, the noxious process may involve the brainstem as well as the cerebral hemispheres. Signs of depressed brainstem function appear . . . impaired pupils and impaired regulation of vital functions	These patients have a multitude of abnormal neurological signs, since the major brainstem lesion is causing malfunction in the: • descending motor pathways • ascending sensory pathways • pathways to and from the cerebellum • cranial nerve nuclei • centres regulating vital functions	These patients have the signs of a unilateral cerebral hemisphere lesion and raised intracranial pressure (papilloedema). In addition the signs of coning (pupillary dilatation and impaired regulation of vital functions) may appear	These patients have the signs of bilateral cerebral hemisphere malfunction and raised intracranial pressure (papilloedema). They too may show signs of coning
	In these patients, the assessment of eyes, speech and motor responses, needed for the Glasgow Coma Scale, is somewhat interfered with, because of the presence of the primary neurological deficit produced by the primary CNS pathology. In such instances, the best eye, speech and limb response which can be achieved (in either of the two eyes, or in any of the four limbs) is the one which is used for the Coma Scale assessment. Despite this interference the Coma Scale, charted at intervals as shown in Fig. 11.3, provides a very valuable guide to an unconscious patient's progress		

Fig. 11.6 Scheme to show the common causes of coma.

- Airway
- Level of coma
- Cause of coma
- Caution over lumbar puncture
- Treat cause
- Routine care of unconscious patient

Investigation and management of a patient in coma

1. Check that the patient's airway is clear, that breathing is satisfactory, and that the patient's colour is good.

2. Assess the level of coma, looking at vital functions, pupils and items of the Glasgow Coma Scale as mentioned above.

3. Try to establish the cause of the coma by taking a history from relatives or witnesses, physical examination and appropriate tests. It is obviously important to have the common causes of coma (A, E, I, O, U) clearly in one's mind whilst questioning, examining and ordering investigations.

4. Remember the danger of lumbar puncture in patients in whom coning is imminent or present (see p. 44). Reduction of the CSF pressure below the foramen magnum may encourage further downward herniation at the tentorial or foramen magnum level, so *no lumbar puncture if papilloedema is present, or until a head scan has excluded a mass lesion or any brain swelling*.

5. Treat the specific cause of the coma as soon as this is established, e.g. anticonvulsants for epilepsy, antibiotics for meningitis, intravenous glucose for hypoglycaemia, specific antagonists for specific CNS depressant drug poisonings.

6. Establish the routine care of an unconscious patient regardless of the cause (Fig. 11.7).

(a) Observations: assessment every 15–30 minutes of vital functions, pupils and Glasgow Coma Scale, to monitor improvement or deterioration in the patient's condition.

(b) Airway, ventilation, blood gases.

(c) Blood pressure, to maintain adequate perfusion of the body, particularly of the brain and kidneys.

(d) Fluid and electrolyte balance.

(e) Nutrition and hydration.

(f) Avoidance of sedative or strong analgesic drugs.

(g) General nursing care of eyes, mouth, bladder, bowels, skin and pressure areas, passive limb mobilization to prevent venous stagnation and contractures, chest physiotherapy.

Fig. 11.7 Diagram to show the routine care of the unconscious patient.

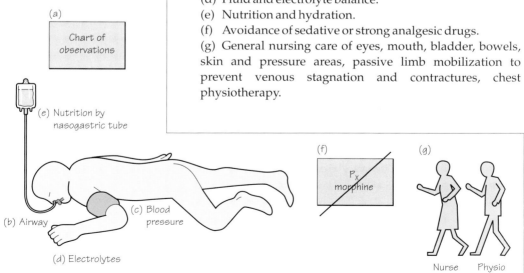

Prognosis for coma

Patients whose coma has been caused by drug overdose may remain deeply unconscious for prolonged periods and yet have a satisfactory outcome. They may need respiratory support during their coma if brainstem function is depressed, but proceed to make a full recovery.

Prolonged coma from other causes has a much less satisfactory outcome. As an example of this, if one takes a group of unconscious patients, whose coma is not due to drug overdose, who:

- show no eye opening (spontaneous or to voice),
- express no comprehensible words,
- fail to localize painful stimuli,
- remain like this for more than 6 hours,

more than 50% of them will die, and recovery to independent existence will occur in a minority of the rest. This background knowledge must remain in the doctor's mind when counselling relatives of patients in coma, and when planning the care of patients in prolonged coma.

Some patients who fail to recover from coma enter a state of unawareness of self and environment, in which they can breathe spontaneously and show cycles of eye closure and opening which may simulate sleep and waking. This is known as the vegetative state, which can become permanent. It is difficult, and takes a long time, to determine the precise state of awareness in such unfortunate patients.

Brainstem death

Deeply unconscious patients whose respiration has to be maintained on a ventilator, whose coma is not caused by drug overdose, clearly have a worsening prognosis as each day goes by. Amongst this group of patients, there will be some who have a zero prognosis, whose brainstems have been damaged to such an extent that they will never breathe spontaneously again.

Guidelines exist to help doctors identify patients who have undergone brainstem death whilst in coma which has been supported by intensive care and mechanical ventilation (Fig. 11.8). Testing for brainstem death must be done by two independent, senior and appropriately trained specialists if treatment is to be withdrawn.

Preconditions

In coma on ventilator | The patient is deeply comatose, and maintained on a ventilator on account of failure of spontaneous respiration

Diagnosis certain | The coma is due to irreversible structural brain damage. The diagnosis is certain, and is a disorder which can lead to brainstem death

No drugs
No hypothermia
No metabolic abnormality | Any of which might be having a reversible effect on the brainstem

No paralytic drugs | The patient's unresponsiveness is not due to neuromuscular paralytic agents

Tests

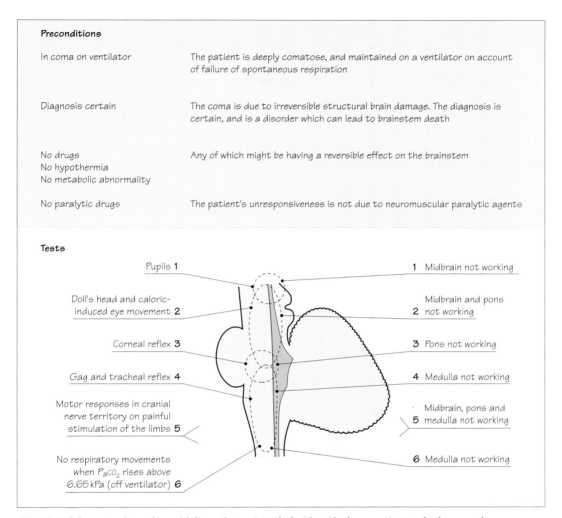

Pupils **1** — **1** Midbrain not working

Doll's head and caloric-induced eye movement **2** — Midbrain and pons **2** not working

Corneal reflex **3** — **3** Pons not working

Gag and tracheal reflex **4** — **4** Medulla not working

Motor responses in cranial nerve territory on painful stimulation of the limbs **5** — Midbrain, pons and **5** medulla not working

No respiratory movements when P_aCO_2 rises above 6.65 kPa (off ventilator) **6** — **6** Medulla not working

Fig. 11.8 Scheme to show the guidelines that exist to help identify those patients who have undergone brainstem death whilst in coma.

CASE HISTORIES

Case 1

A 78-year-old man is referred after three blackouts. He feels momentarily 'dizzy' and then loses consciousness. He comes round on the floor. On the first occasion he sustained a nasty facial laceration, called an ambulance and was taken to the emergency department, where his examination, full blood count, glucose and ECG were all normal. The second happened as he was finishing his lunch and he slumped out of his chair. He recovered rapidly and did not call an ambulance. The third happened when he was walking his dog but he was able to get home unaided. He has not bitten his tongue on any occasion.

He lives alone and none of the attacks has been witnessed. He smokes 10 cigarettes per day. He takes bendrofluazide for hypertension. He is otherwise well.

You find no abnormalities on examination.

a. What is the differential diagnosis?
b. What further questions would you ask?
c. What tests would you request?

Case 2

A young man is brought to the emergency department by ambulance. He has been found unconscious on waste ground. The ambulance staff cannot provide any other history, but he has a recent prescription for the antibiotic oxytetracycline and the anticonvulsant sodium valproate in his wallet.

He is breathing normally and maintaining normal oxygen saturation. His temperature, pulse and blood pressure are normal. There are no external signs of injury. He does not have neck stiffness. There is no spontaneous eye opening, speech or movement. He makes no response to verbal command but briefly opens his eyes, groans and tries to push your hand away in response to painful stimulation. There is no asymmetry in his motor responses. When you open his eyelids, his eyes are roving slowly from side to side. Limb tone and reflexes are normal with flexor plantar responses. General examination is normal apart from acne. His finger-prick glucose is normal.

a. What is your differential diagnosis?
b. How would you manage his case?

(For answers, see pp. 263–4.)

CHAPTER 12

Epilepsy

12

Introduction and definitions

The word epilepsy conjures up something rather frightening and undesirable in most people's minds, because of the apprehension created in all of us when somebody temporarily loses control of his body, especially if unconsciousness, violent movement and impaired communication are involved. Epilepsy is the word used to describe a tendency to episodes, in which a variety of clinical phenomena may occur, caused by abnormal electrical discharge in the brain, between which the patient is his normal self. What actually happens to the patient in an epileptic attack depends upon the nature of the electrical discharge, in particular upon its location and duration.

The most major form of epilepsy is the generalized tonic–clonic seizure, which involves sudden unconsciousness and violent movement, often followed by coma. This form of seizure has traditionally been called grand mal. Unless otherwise stated, mention of an epileptic attack would generally infer the occurrence of a tonic–clonic seizure.

Amongst patients and doctors a single epileptic attack may be called an epileptic fit, a fit, an epileptic seizure, an epileptic convulsion or a convulsion. The words tend to be used synonymously. This is a somewhat inaccurate use of words since a convulsion (violent irregular movement) is one component of some forms of epilepsy. There is also a confusing tendency for older patients and doctors to use the traditional term petit mal for any form of epilepsy which is not too massive or prolonged. Petit mal originally had a rather restricted and specific meaning which has been lost over time; we describe the modern terminology in the following sections. Patients and their families very ·ften use softer words other than epilepsy, fits, seizures or convulsions, which is quite natural. Within families, words like blackout, episode, funny do, attack, blank spell, dizzy turn, fainting spell, trance, daze and petit mal abound when describing epileptic attacks.

Epilepsy causes attacks which are:
- brief
- stereotyped
- unpredictable

We can see that the use of words is often imprecise here. 'A minor fit' may mean one thing to one person and another thing to somebody else, and it may certainly be used by a patient or relative to describe any form of epileptic or non-epileptic attack. We must be tolerant of this amongst patients, but there is always a need to clarify exactly what has happened in an individual attack in an individual patient. Errors in management rapidly appear when the doctor does not know the precise features of each of the patient's attacks.

The word epilepsy is generally used to indicate a tendency to suffer from epileptic attacks, i.e. more than one attack and perhaps an ongoing tendency. Some medical and non-medical people are upset by the use of the word epilepsy when applied to someone who has only ever had one epileptic attack.

Common forms of epilepsy

There are two main types of epilepsy: *primary generalized* and *focal.* In primary generalized epilepsy, electrical discharges arise within deep midline structures of the brain and spread rapidly and simultaneously to all parts of the cerebral cortex (Fig. 12.1). In focal epilepsy, the electrical discharges start in one part of the cerebral cortex and spread to a greater or lesser extent to other regions (see Figs 12.5 and 12.8).

The distinction between these two main forms of epilepsy is important, because they have different causes and respond to different drugs. Confusion arises because focal seizures can start in one area and eventually spread to all of the cerebral cortex, resulting in a tonic–clonic seizure. This kind of attack is called a secondarily generalized tonic–clonic seizure.

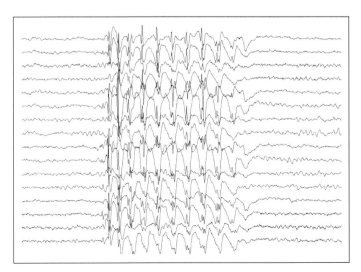

Fig. 12.1 EEG recording typical of primary generalized epilepsy.

Primary generalized epilepsy

There are three common manifestations of primary generalized epilepsy:
- primary generalized tonic–clonic seizures;
- absence seizures;
- myoclonic seizures.

Individual patients often have a mixture of these seizure types.

Primary generalized tonic–clonic seizures (Fig 12.2)

- There is no warning or aura.
- *Tonic phase.* The patient loses consciousness and suddenly stiffens, as all the muscles in his body enter a state of sustained (tonic) contraction. The limbs and neck usually extend. The patient falls stiffly with no attempt to break his fall. He makes a loud groan as air is forced out of the chest through tightened vocal cords. He does not breathe and becomes cyanosed. The tonic phase is brief, usually a matter of seconds, so that observers notice a cry, a fall and stiffening of the body before the clonic phase commences.
- *Clonic phase.* The sustained muscle contraction subsides into a series of random, disorganized jerks and jitters involving any and all muscles. These convulsive movements are in no way purposeful, coordinated or predictable. The tongue may protrude as the jaw closes, causing tongue biting. Urinary incontinence is frequent. Breathing recommences in the same disorganized way. It is noisy and inefficient and cyanosis usually persists. Saliva accumulates in the mouth which, together with the disorganized respiration, results in froth spilling from the mouth. The patient remains unconscious. The clonic phase typically lasts a minute or two, but can be briefer and can occasionally be very much longer.
- *Phase of coma.* After the convulsive movements stop, the patient is in coma. Breathing becomes regular and coordinated. The patient's colour returns to normal so long as the upper airway is clear. The period of time that the patient remains in coma relates to the duration of the previous tonic and clonic phases.
- There follows a state of confusion, headache, restlessness and drowsiness before final recovery. This may last for hours. For a day or two, the patient may feel mentally slow and notice aching pains in the limbs subsequent to the convulsive movement, together with a sore tongue.

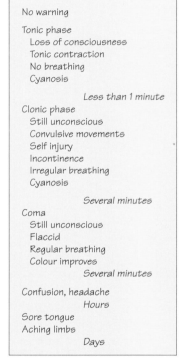

No warning

Tonic phase
  Loss of consciousness
  Tonic contraction
  No breathing
  Cyanosis
                    Less than 1 minute
Clonic phase
  Still unconscious
  Convulsive movements
  Self injury
  Incontinence
  Irregular breathing
  Cyanosis
                    Several minutes
Coma
  Still unconscious
  Flaccid
  Regular breathing
  Colour improves
                    Several minutes
Confusion, headache
                    Hours
Sore tongue
Aching limbs
                    Days

Fig. 12.2 Scheme to show typical severe tonic–clonic epilepsy.

Photosensitivity

Occasional patients with all the types of primary generalized epilepsy may have seizures triggered by flashing light, for example from the television, computer games or flickering sunshine when driving past a row of trees, and have to avoid such stimuli. Almost all such patients also get spontaneous seizures unrelated to visual stimulation

The description given above is of a severe attack. They may not be as devastating or prolonged. The tonic and clonic phases may be over in a minute and the patient may regain consciousness within a further minute or two. He may feel like his normal self within an hour or so.

During a tonic–clonic epileptic attack, cerebral metabolic rate and oxygen consumption are increased, yet respiration is absent or inefficient with reduced oxygenation of the blood. The brain is unable to metabolize glucose anaerobically, so there is a tendency for accumulation of lactic and pyruvic acid in the brain during prolonged seizure. This hypoxic insult to the brain with acidosis is the probable cause of post-epileptic (post-ictal) coma and confusion.

Absence seizures (Fig. 12.3)

Whole attack lasts less than 10 seconds

Young person

Sudden onset, sudden end . . . switch-like

Unaware, still, staring

May occur several times a day

Fig. 12.3 Scheme to show typical absence epilepsy.

Absence seizures are much less dramatic and may indeed pass unnoticed. The attack is sudden in onset, does not usually last longer than 10 seconds, and is sudden in its ending. The patient is usually able to tell that an episode has occurred only because he realizes that a few moments have gone by of which he has been quite unaware. Conversation and events around him have moved on, and he has no recall of the few seconds of missing time.

Observers will note that the patient suddenly stops what he is doing, and that his eyes remain open, distant and staring, possibly with a little rhythmic movement of the eyelids. Otherwise the face and limbs are usually still. The patient remains standing or sitting, but will stand still if the attack occurs while walking. There is no response to calling the patient by name or any other verbal or physical stimulus. The attack ends as suddenly as it commences, sometimes with a word of apology by the patient if the circumstances have been such as to make him realize an attack has occurred.

Absence seizures usually commence in childhood, so at the time of diagnosis the patient is usually a child or young teenager. It is quite common for absence seizures to occur several times a day, sometimes very frequently so that a few attacks may be witnessed during the initial consultation.

Myoclonic seizures (Fig. 12.4)

Myoclonic seizures take the form of abrupt muscle jerks, typically causing the upper limbs to flex and the patient to drop anything that they are holding. The jerks may occur singly or in a brief run. Consciousness is not usually affected. They often happen in the first hour of the day, especially if the patient has consumed alcohol the night before. Myoclonic seizures almost always occur in association with the other generalized seizure types, and their significance in this setting is that they help to confirm a diagnosis of primary generalized epilepsy (most often a specific syndrome called juvenile myoclonic epilepsy). Isolated myoclonic jerks can occur in a wide range of conditions with no relation to epilepsy, including waking and falling asleep in normal people (see Chapter 5, p. 77).

> One or more brief jerks
>
> Duration up to a few seconds
>
> Consciousness preserved
>
> Coexists with tonic-clonic and absence seizures

Fig. 12.4 Scheme to show typical myoclonic epilepsy.

Focal epilepsy

If the primary site of abnormal electrical discharge is situated in one area of the cortex in one cerebral hemisphere, the patient will be prone to attacks of *focal epilepsy* (Fig. 12.5).

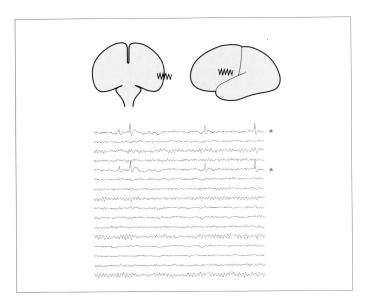

Fig. 12.5 EEG recording typical of focal epilepsy. In this figure, the focal EEG abnormality might generate focal motor twitching of the right side of the face. The recordings marked by an asterisk are from adjacent locations of the brain, and show spike discharges.

The phenomena that occur in focal epileptic attacks entirely depend on the location of the epileptogenic lesion. The most obvious form of focal epileptic attack is when the localized epileptic discharge is in part of the motor cortex (precentral gyrus) of one cerebral hemisphere. During the attack, disorganized

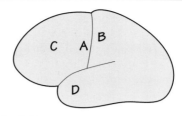

A *Focal motor seizures*
Strong convulsive movements of one part of the contralateral face, body or limbs

B *Focal sensory seizures*
Strong, unpleasant, slightly painful, warm, tingling, or electrical sensations in one part of the contralateral face, body or limbs

C *Frontal lobe epilepsy*
Strong, convulsive turning of the eyes, head and neck towards the contralateral side ('adversive seizure', epileptic activity in the frontal eye fields) or complex posturing with one arm flexed and one arm extended like a fencer (epileptic activity in the supplementary motor area)

D *Temporal lobe epilepsy*
Strong, disorganized aberration of temporal lobe function (see text and Fig. 12.7)

Fig. 12.6 Scheme to show the common forms of focal epilepsy.

Subjective
Déjà vu
Memories rushing through the brain
Loss of memory during the attack
Hallucination of smell/taste
Sensation rising up the body

Objective
Diminished contact with the environment
Slow, confused
Repetitive utterances
Repetitive movements (automatisms)
Lip-smacking and sniffing movements

Fig. 12.7 Scheme to show the subjective experiences and objective observations in a patient with temporal lobe epilepsy.

strong convulsive movement will occur in the corresponding part of the other side of the body. These are focal motor seizures (Fig. 12.6).

Figure 12.6 illustrates the common forms of focal epilepsy. *Focal motor seizures, focal sensory seizures* and *frontal lobe seizures* are quite straightforward. *Temporal lobe epilepsy* deserves a special mention, not least because it is probably the commonest form of focal epilepsy. It is necessary to remember what functions reside in the temporal lobe in order to understand what might happen when epileptic derangement occurs in this part of the brain. Apart from speech comprehension in the dominant temporal lobe, the medial parts of both temporal lobes are significantly involved in smell and taste function, and in memory (Fig. 12.7).

NB Any indication that a patient's epilepsy is focal should lead to a search for an explanation of localized cortical pathology, i.e. Why is this area of cerebral cortex behaving in this way? What is wrong with it? In other words, these patients need a brain scan, preferably using MRI.

Focal epileptic discharges may remain focal, but sometimes the abnormal electrical discharge spreads over the surface of the cerebral hemisphere and then triggers generalized epileptic discharges involving all parts of both cerebral hemispheres (Fig. 12.8).

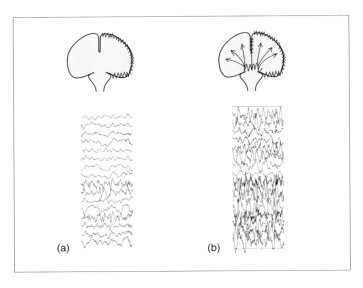

Fig. 12.8 (a) EEG showing seizure discharges that have spread across all of the left hemisphere (lower eight tracings). (b) A few seconds later the seizure discharges have become generalized and more intense.

If the focal discharge begins in one part of the motor cortex, the first symptom might be convulsive twitching of the right side of the face, spreading rapidly into the right arm and then the right leg before affecting the whole body in a secondarily generalized tonic–clonic seizure. This particular kind of attack is known as *Jacksonian epilepsy* (after the nineteenth-century neurologist Hughlings Jackson).

Any warning or 'aura' in the moments before a tonic–clonic seizure indicates that it is a manifestation of focal epilepsy rather than primary generalized epilepsy, with the implication that there is a problem with a localized area of the cerebral cortex which must be investigated. The nature of the aura depends on the location of this area, and it can take any of the forms listed in Figs 12.6 and 12.7. Sometimes the patient himself may not be aware of the warning, if for example it simply consists of turning the eyes and head to the side or extending one limb. This highlights the importance of talking to someone who has seen the patient right through an attack.

The main indication that a tonic–clonic seizure has a focal cause and that the patient does not suffer from primary generalized epilepsy sometimes occurs *after* the fit rather than before it. A tonic–clonic seizure which is followed by a focal neurological deficit (e.g. weakness of the right side of the body), lasting for an hour or two, strongly indicates a localized cortical cause for the fit (in or near the left motor cortex in this example). The tell-tale post-epileptic unilateral weakness is known as *Todd's paresis*. It may be apparent to the patient, but is commonly recognized only by a doctor examining the patient shortly after the tonic–clonic seizure has ceased.

Febrile convulsions

The young, immature brain of children is less electrically stable than that of adults. It appears that a child's EEG is made more unstable by fever.

Tonic–clonic attacks occurring at times of febrile illnesses are not uncommon in children under the age of 5 years. Such attacks are usually transient, lasting a few minutes only. In the majority of cases, the child has only one febrile convulsion, further convulsions in subsequent febrile illnesses being unusual rather than the rule.

A febrile convulsion generates anxiety in the parents. The attack itself is frightening, especially if prolonged, and its occurrence makes the parents wonder if their child is going to have a lifelong problem with epilepsy.

The very small percentage of children with febrile convulsions who are destined to suffer from epileptic attacks unassociated with fever later in life are identifiable to a certain extent by the presence of the following risk factors:

- a family history of non-febrile convulsions in a parent or sibling;
- abnormal neurological signs or delayed development identified before the febrile convulsion;
- a prolonged febrile convulsion, lasting longer than 15 minutes;
- focal features in the febrile convulsion before, during or after the attack.

Those who do go on to have epilepsy in later life usually have a pathology called mesial temporal sclerosis affecting one hippocampus, giving rise to focal epilepsy with temporal lobe seizures. They may be cured by having the abnormal hippocampus surgically resected.

Epilepsy syndromes

There are a large number of recognizable epilepsy syndromes, which are mainly rare, but two require special mention.

Juvenile myoclonic epilepsy

This is the commonest cause of tonic–clonic seizures starting in teenagers. It is a form of primary generalized epilepsy, so the tonic–clonic seizures come on without warning. They often follow a late night with too much alcohol. The patient may not volunteer the characteristic history of myoclonic seizures unless asked, having thought that their messy breakfasts were due to clumsiness rather than epilepsy. Similarly their absence seizures may have been attributed to day-dreaming. Crucially, juvenile myoclonic epilepsy is not usually fully controlled by carbamazepine or phenytoin, but it is by sodium valproate or lamotrigine. It is upsetting for all concerned when patients receive the wrong treatment for many years, with all the disability that attends poorly controlled epilepsy.

Lennox–Gastaut syndrome

Lennox (no relation) and Gastaut described one of the most severe forms of so-called epileptic encephalopathy, where a range of metabolic and genetic disorders of brain development give rise to severe learning disability and epilepsy. In addition to all the seizures types described above, patients with Lennox–Gastaut syndrome (LGS) may have seizures characterized by isolated tonic or clonic phases. They also experience a very distressing type of seizure called *atonic seizures*, in which there is abrupt loss of consciousness, muscle power and tone. The patient falls abruptly, often injuring his head or face. The prognosis in LGS is very poor, although some of the newer anticonvulsants have a partial effect in reducing seizure frequency.

Non-epileptic attacks

The differential diagnosis of epilepsy, including non-epileptic attacks of psychogenic origin, has been discussed in Chapter 11 (see p. 180). It is worth repeating here that non-epileptic seizures generally resemble tonic–clonic seizures but tend to be more prolonged, to involve more coordinated and purposeful movements (arching the back repetitively, turning the head from side to side, grasping attendants) and to preserve reflexes which are lost in tonic–clonic seizures (pupil, lash and tendon stretch reflexes and flexor plantar responses). Cyanosis does not occur unless the diagnosis has been missed and the patient has been given sufficient intravenous lorazepam or diazepam to suppress respiration. Because of the risk of iatrogenic respiratory arrest, it is important, but sometimes difficult, to distinguish lengthy non-epileptic attacks from status epilepticus.

Status epilepticus

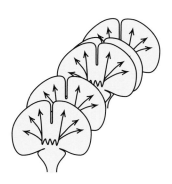

Unless otherwise stated the term status epilepticus indicates the occurrence of one tonic–clonic seizure after another without recovery of consciousness between attacks. During tonic–clonic seizures, there exists a state of increased cerebral metabolism and oxygen requirement and decreased respiratory efficiency and cyanosis. If further tonic–clonic seizures occur at short intervals, it is easy to understand that increasing metabolic acidosis and oedema will occur in the brain, and progressively increasing coma will overtake the patient. There is evidence that, even if hypoxia and metabolic acidosis are prevented, seizures themselves can cause permanent brain damage if they last more than 1 hour (as a toxic consequence of excessive release of excitatory neurotransmitters). Hence, urgent control of seizures and attention to respiration are required in patients with tonic–clonic status, usually needing admission to an intensive care unit. The treatment is discussed in more detail on p. 208. Even with careful management, status epilepticus has a significant mortality rate and it is common for survivors to have new cognitive or physical difficulties or more refractory epilepsy.

Diagnosis

Clinical history and a good witness's account

Epilepsy is a difficult condition to diagnose, and mistakes (both underdiagnosis and overdiagnosis) are not infrequent. Certainty of diagnosis in patients with epilepsy depends mainly on the establishment of a clear picture of the features of the attack both from the patient and from a witness. This applies to the diagnosis of any sort of blackout, as emphasized in Chapter 11. One has to go through the precise details of how the patient felt before, during (if conscious) and after the attack, and also obtain a clear description of how the patient behaved during each stage from a witness. One cannot overstate the importance of the clinical history in evaluating attacks. Investigations, such as EEG, should be used to support a diagnostic hypothesis based on the clinical information. Diagnostic certainty is always much more difficult in unwitnessed episodes of loss of consciousness.

The following comments can be made about the differential diagnosis of the different forms of epilepsy.

- *Tonic–clonic seizures* have to be differentiated from the other causes of attacks of loss of consciousness mentioned in Chapter 11 (see Fig. 11.2, p. 176). Cardiovascular disorders are the main consideration (simple faints and vasovagal syncope in young patients, arrhythmias and postural hypotension in older patients). Confusion often arises because of the brief flurry of myoclonic jerks that sometimes accompany syncope of any cause. Non-epileptic attacks of a psychogenic kind are a common source of diagnostic difficulty in specialist clinics. Diabetics on treatment of any sort should prompt one to think of hypoglycaemia. In general, tongue biting, irregular noisy breathing, strong convulsive movement, incontinence, post-ictal confusion and limb pains all suggest tonic–clonic epilepsy.
- *Absence seizures* may be confused with absent-minded daydreaming, or with wilful inattention of a young person to his environment. The sudden nature of the start and finish of the trance, switch-like, typifies absence epilepsy.
- *Focal motor seizures* do not really have a differential diagnosis.
- *Focal sensory seizures* may be difficult to differentiate from episodes of transient cerebral ischaemia, but are usually shorter and more frequent, and cause tingling rather than numbness.
- *Frontal lobe seizures* can be confused with dystonia (see Chapter 5, p. 75) and can appear so bizarre that they are thought to have a behavioural basis.

Listen to the patient

Listen to a witness
- in detail
- in person
- on the phone
- via letter

- *Temporal lobe seizures* mainly have to be distinguished from anxiety and panic attacks. Attacks which are provoked in any way, or which last more than a few minutes, are unlikely to be due to temporal lobe epilepsy. Attacks which involve unusual behaviour requiring alert, clear thought and/or well-coordinated physical behaviour (fighting, shoplifting) are most unlikely to be due to epilepsy.

Establishing the cause of epilepsy

> **Think about the cause**
>
> - Family history
> - Past history
> - System review
> - Alcohol history
> - Drug history
> - Focal neurological symptoms or signs

Apart from accurate information regarding the attacks, there is further information to be elucidated at the interview and examination. If the attacks are thought to be epileptic, an enquiry should be mounted as to the cause of the epilepsy. Primary generalized epilepsy (primary generalized tonic–clonic, absence or myoclonic seizures, with or without photosensitivity) is familial, so questioning may reveal other members of the family who suffer from epileptic attacks. Any form of focal epilepsy (and some cases with no apparent focal features) reflects the presence of intracranial pathology. Most commonly, this pathology is an area of scarring subsequent to some previous active pathology, though sometimes epileptic attacks may occur when the pathological process is in the active phase:

- following birth trauma to the brain;
- following trauma to the skull and brain later in life;
- during or following meningitis, encephalitis or cerebral abscess;
- at the time of, or as a sequel to, cerebral infarction, cerebral haemorrhage or subarachnoid haemorrhage;
- as a result of the inevitable trauma of neurosurgery.

Sometimes, the epileptic attacks are caused by biochemical insults to the brain, rather than by localized physical disease, such as:

- during alcohol or drug withdrawal;
- during hepatic, uraemic, hypoglycaemic comas;
- whilst on major tranquillizing or antidepressant drugs.

At the front of one's mind must be the possibility that the patient's epilepsy is an early symptom of a brain tumour. Brain tumours are not a common cause of epilepsy, but they are not to be missed. Epilepsy of adult onset, especially if focal and/or associated with evolving abnormal neurological signs, should initiate strong thoughts about the possibility of a tumour.

Physical examination

Physical examination is clearly important since it may reveal abnormal neurological signs which indicate evidence of:
- previous intracranial pathology;
- current intracranial pathology;
- evolving intracranial pathology as indicated above.

EEG and other investigations

The EEG is not a test for epilepsy. In the appropriate clinical setting (i.e. a patient with a history suggestive of epilepsy) it may provide additional support for the diagnosis and help in distinguishing between the generalized and focal types of epilepsy. But remember:
- 10% of the normal population show mild, non-specific EEG abnormalities, such as slow waves in one or both temporal regions;
- 30% of patients with epilepsy will have a normal EEG between their attacks (falling to 20% if the EEG includes a period of sleep).

In other words, the EEG can mislead through both false positives and false negatives, and must be requested and interpreted with care. Prolonged ambulatory EEG recording (an immensely laborious activity) can be useful in very difficult cases with frequent attacks, allowing the EEG to be sampled during the attack itself. But even here there is a false-negative problem, with 10% of focal seizures arising deep in a fold of the cerebral cortex and failing to give rise to abnormal discharges on the EEG.

Imaging of the brain, preferably with MR rather than CT scanning, is an important part of the assessment of focal epilepsy, and in cases where the type of epilepsy is uncertain. It is probably unnecessary in patients with primary generalized epilepsy confirmed by EEG.

The other routine tests (glucose, calcium, ECG) are very rarely informative.

Summary of the stages in diagnosis in a patient with epilepsy

1. Listen to the patient.
2. Listen to witnesses.
3. Wonder why the patient has epilepsy.
4. Try to establish a cause:
   - from the history;
   - from the examination.

5. Investigate by EEG, often by MR brain scan, sometimes by other tests.
6. Assess patient reaction and the consequences of the diagnosis of epilepsy in his or her life.

Management

'On the spot'

If somebody suddenly has a tonic–clonic fit, people close at hand should:

1. look after the patient's airway (by putting the patient into the recovery position when you can and pulling the jaw forward);

2. prevent self-injury during strong convulsive movements (by keeping the patient away from hard, sharp or hot objects).

Relatives of newly diagnosed epileptic patients certainly appreciate advice of this sort. In an adult, one would generally wait for the convulsions to cease and for the patient to regain consciousness. If one can establish that the patient is subject to epileptic fits, no further medical action is required. If the patient has never had a fit before, and especially if there are focal features to the fits or post-ictal stage, further medical advice will be required either immediately or in the next few days. In children with febrile convulsions, diazepam may be administered *per rectum* if it is available, and further medical attention should be sought if the convulsion has not stopped (with or without diazepam) within 5 minutes.

Explanation

Generally supportive comments and explanation about epilepsy, appropriate to the level of intelligence of the patient and his relatives, constitute the first steps in the management of newly diagnosed epilepsy. The actual word epilepsy greatly upsets some families. It is a good idea to ask the patient and relatives what epilepsy means to them as a starting point for explanation and reassurance. Not uncommonly, it is the relatives, rather than the patient, who are more anxious about attacks involving unconsciousness. They need to be reassured that although the epileptic attack may have looked profoundly life-threatening, death during epileptic convulsions is actually extremely rare. Associations of epilepsy with mental subnormality, madness, brain tumours, epileptic 'homes', incurability, transmission to the next generation, etc. are all likely to be introduced during this phase of explanation, and it is important that the doctor has a chance of correcting preconceived ideas in the patient or his family at the outset.

The facts that young people tend to grow out of their tendency to epilepsy, and that epilepsy can be controlled by drugs in the majority of cases, need to be clearly stated.

Drug therapy

Positive motivation towards taking anticonvulsant drugs, which have side-effects, and which may need to be taken regularly for several years, is not automatic in patients with epilepsy. It will be optimized by careful explanation about the drugs, and allowing time for the patient to express his feelings about the prospect of taking the pills regularly.

You need to help the patient to decide which drug has the best chance of controlling the seizures with the least risk of side-effects that would be unacceptable from their point of view. Patients will prioritize possible side-effects differently depending on their circumstances: sedation may be a major concern to an academic; teratogenic hazard may be the greatest worry to a woman who is planning a family. Once you have chosen a drug, this should be introduced gradually with the aim of finding the smallest dose that completely suppresses the seizures. If the patient builds the dose up to a level that is causing side-effects and is still having seizures, then you need to move on to another drug. Serum anticonvulsant levels are not an important part of this titration process, but can be a way of making sure the patient is actually taking the pills.

Primary generalized epilepsy usually responds to drug treatment. The first-line drugs are sodium valproate and lamotrigine. Myoclonus often responds to the addition of clonazepam, and absences may respond specifically to ethosuximide. There are several second-line options, including phenobarbitone, topiramate and levetiracetam.

The choice of drugs for focal epilepsy is even wider, but only 80% of patients achieve complete control. The first-line drugs are carbamazepine, sodium valproate and lamotrigine. If none of these drugs work on their own, then the possibility of surgical treatment should be considered (see p. 210) before moving on to a combination of a first-line and a second-line drug (phenytoin, topiramate, levetiracetam, gabapentin, phenobarbitone, etc.). If the patient responds to the combination, think about withdrawing the first-line drug to see if control is maintained on the second-line drug alone. In general, most patients prefer to take a single drug because this reduces the risk of side-effects; from the doctor's point of view, it also reduces the risk of interactions between the two drugs and, in the case of those anticonvulsants metabolized by the liver, interactions with other drugs such as the oral contraceptive and warfarin.

Most anticonvulsants have both idiosyncratic (occasional and unpredictable) side-effects and dose-dependent ones. The most important side-effects of the first-line drugs are shown in the table on the next page. Teratogenicity (for example neural tube defects) is a serious concern when treating young women.

	Idiosyncratic side-effects	Dose-dependent side-effects	Approximate teratogenic risk
Valproate	Weight gain, transient hair loss, liver dysfuction	Tremor, sedation	>10%
Carbamazepine	Rash, hyponatraemia	Ataxia, sedation	5%
Lamotrigine	Rash, influenza-like symptoms	Sedation	2–3%

They should be counselled about this before starting treatment and again before any planned pregnancy. Folate supplements may reduce some of this risk.

It is generally possible to treat most patients with a twice-daily regimen (phenobarbitone, phenytoin and slow-release preparations of sodium valproate can be given once daily). This helps patients to remember their pills. Sticking to a thrice-daily schedule is very difficult.

Once anticonvulsant treatment is started, it is usual to maintain the treatment for a minimum of 2 or 3 years. If the seizures have been fully controlled, treatment can be withdrawn gradually but there is a high risk (about 40% overall) of seizures returning. The risk is much higher in some forms of epilepsy such as juvenile myoclonic epilepsy, in patients where it has taken several different drugs to achieve control, and where the epilepsy was caused by a structural brain lesion that is still present. Even patients with lower risk may prefer to stay on treatment rather than take a chance of losing their driving licence by having another attack.

Febrile convulsions

- Cool the child
- Rectal diazepam
- Consider meningitis

The main things to remember here are the early use of rectal diazepam, steps to cool the child (including paracetamol), correct management of any underlying infection (with particular consideration to the possibility of meningitis) and reassurance of parents about the benign nature of febrile convulsions.

Status epilepticus

Any form of status epilepticus is an indication for hospitalization to establish control of the seizures, but in the case of tonic–clonic status the problem is a medical emergency requiring admission to an intensive care unit. There are three main directions of treatment of grand mal status:

1. Routine care of the unconscious patient (see Chapter 11, p. 187).

2. Control of seizure activity in the brain. This means the maintenance of the patient's normal anticonvulsant regime, supplemented by the use of intravenous anticonvulsants; diazepam or lorazepam early; phenytoin or phenobarbitone if seizures persist; thiopentone to produce general anaesthesia if seizures have failed to come under control within 60 minutes.

3. Maintenance of optimal oxygenation of the blood. This may mean the use of oxygen and an airway, but may be the main indication for anaesthesia, paralysis and ventilation. It is important to remember the control of seizure activity in the brain of the paralyzed. Vigorous anticonvulsant therapy must be continued.

- Emergency admission
- Care of the unconscious patient
- Continue and intensify anticonvulsant therapy
  - i.v. benzodiazepine
  - i.v. phenytoin
  - i.v. barbiturates
- Maintain oxygenation

Sensible restrictions

Until satisfactory control of epileptic attacks has been established, and for a little while longer, it is important for patients with most forms of epilepsy to be aware of the dangers of bathing, driving, riding a bicycle, heights, open heavy machinery, swimming and water sports. Advice to each patient has to be individualized, bearing in mind the type and frequency of his epileptic attacks. In the UK, the driving licensing authorities have definite guidelines for patients and doctors to follow, and it is the doctor's role to make sure that the patient understands where he stands in relation to these. A patient who has had one or more attacks of epilepsy has to refrain from driving until 1 year has elapsed, regardless of whether the patient is on medication or not. This is the general rule in the UK, which has exceptions for nocturnal attacks and 'provoked' attacks. Very gentle but firm explanation is often required when pointing out the need for these restrictions.

- Driving
- Other potentially dangerous pursuits
- Understand frustration

Most patients with photosensitive epilepsy can attend discos where lights flash at rates too slow to stimulate epilepsy. Such patients should avoid video games and sit well back from the TV screen.

Occupation

The financial benefits and personal prestige of working are important in the life of a patient with epilepsy, just as for everybody else. Nevertheless, it is more difficult for people with epilepsy to become employed. Some occupations are completely closed to patients with epilepsy, e.g. jobs requiring an HGV or PSV driving licence, and jobs in the armed forces, police or fire services. Some occupations may be very difficult for patients with incompletely controlled epilepsy, e.g. teaching, working with young children, nursing, and working near fire or water, at heights, or around unguarded machinery. Individual employers may need education and encouragement to accept that their employee with epilepsy can continue to work normally. In many countries disability discrimination legislation is helping to strengthen their resolve.

Special considerations in women with epilepsy

1. As already mentioned, the metabolism and transport systems of anticonvulsant drugs interact with those of oral contraceptive drugs, so special advice and monitoring are necessary if the two sorts of medication are to be taken concurrently.

2. All anticonvulsant drugs seem to be teratogenic to some extent. Stopping all medication and experiencing uncontrolled epilepsy during pregnancy may pose a greater risk to mother and fetus, although scientific data are extremely scanty. The aim should probably be to control all but the mildest forms of epilepsy using a single drug of low teratogenicity, in the lowest effective dose. The metabolism of most anticonvulsant drugs is increased during pregnancy, so drug level monitoring may show the need for slightly increased anticonvulsant dosage during pregnancy.

3. Most anticonvulsants appear in the mother's milk during lactation, but not in quantities that affect the neonate. Mothers on anticonvulsants should breast feed if this is their wish.

4. Focal epilepsy, due to an epileptogenic cortical scar, is not an hereditary condition. Idiopathic, primary generalized, epilepsy is a familial condition so a little genetic counselling may be necessary in such cases. The risk of epilepsy in a child born to a couple, one of whom suffers from idiopathic epilepsy, is small. If both parents suffer from epilepsy, the risk becomes much greater (up to 1 in 4).

5. Care of infants and toddlers may be difficult for a parent who is unlucky enough to suffer from epileptic attacks which remain frequent despite drug therapy.

> - Interaction of anticonvulsants and oral contraceptives
> - Teratogenicity of anticonvulsants
> - Genetics
> - Breast feeding
> - Childcare

Psychological factors

1. Unpredictable attacks of one sort or another, the word 'epilepsy', the need to take tablets, restrictions on driving and some recreational activities, exclusion from some occupations and difficulty in obtaining employment may all make patients with epilepsy feel second class, depressed, victimized or aggressive. The size of this psychological reaction is a measure of the patient's personality on the one hand, and of the support he receives from his family and doctor on the other.

2. Patients and relatives have particular problems accommodating seizures which are themselves prolonged, or from which it takes the patient a long time to recover. Self-injury in the seizures, and severe automatisms (shouting, undressing, running, hitting) are also very upsetting.

3. Stress is probably not a major factor in causing individual attacks in a person prone to epileptic fits. It is perfectly natural for patients to look round for causes explaining the occurrence of attacks, but the main difficulty of most patients' epilepsy is its complete unpredictability.

4. Emotional thought and behaviour are aspects of normal temporal lobe function. In patients with abnormal temporal lobes, for whatever reason, there may be some abnormalities of such functions in addition to temporal lobe epilepsy. This is not an inevitable association but it is one to bear in mind when managing patients with this form of epilepsy.

5. If an epileptic patient has difficulty coping with life and develops psychosomatic symptoms, it is possible that he will start to have blackouts that are not epileptic but emotional in origin. This need for careful differentiation applies to individual attacks, and also to status epilepticus versus prolonged non-epileptic attacks. It emphasizes the need to establish the precise features of a patient's attacks for correct management.

> The patient's reaction, and that of his family, are important to understand, and to modify if inappropriate

Surgical treatment

Occasionally, in a patient with a highly localized epileptogenic focus, which is producing intractable epileptic attacks, the focal area of the brain may be removed with benefit. Identification of the small percentage of patients with epilepsy who are likely to benefit from such surgery has improved very significantly in the last decade. It is more common in patients with focal pathology which has been clearly demonstrated on the medial side of the temporal lobe by sophisticated EEG and imaging techniques (MR scan). Outcomes are best in children and young adults; older patients may have difficulty in picking up the threads of a life disrupted by epilepsy even if the seizures themselves are abolished.

> Surgical treatment should be considered if:
> - drugs are failing
> - a focus can be confidently identified, with concordance between:
>   clinical features
>   EEG
>   MR scan
> - the focus is resectable
> - the patient wishes to proceed

CASE HISTORIES

Case 1

A psychiatric colleague asks you to see a patient who has been referred to him because of possible psychosis. The 34-year-old business woman gives a 6-month history of experiences which she believes have religious meaning. She finds it hard to put the experiences into words but describes a warm sensation in her stomach which rises rapidly to her head and is accompanied by a pleasant feeling of tranquillity and a feeling that she understands all the mysteries of the world. This lasts less than a minute. The experiences happen unpredictably several times each week. Between these times she feels entirely normal and has no psychiatric symptoms apart from anxiety about the cause of her symptoms.

Neurological examination is normal.

a. What is the most likely diagnosis?
b. How would you manage her case?

Case 2

A previously healthy 25-year-old security guard is admitted to the emergency department in status epilepticus. His generalized tonic–clonic seizures started 25 minutes ago. He is cyanosed despite supplementary oxygen, with a tachycardia and fever of 39.0°C.

a. Outline your emergency management.

Ten minutes later the seizures have stopped but he remains deeply unconscious and he is transferred to ITU, intubated and ventilated. Over the next hour his fever increases to 39.8°C.

b. What would you advise now?

(For answers, see pp. 264–5.)

13

CHAPTER 13

Headache and facial pain

Introduction

Any pain in the head or face must reflect activity in some pain-sensitive structure, and attempts have been made to classify headache and face pains on this basis. The idea seems intellectually attractive but has little else to commend it. In practice it is more useful to think of four broad categories of head and face pain (see the table below), and to become familiar with the common disorders in each category. By far the most common are the longstanding headaches which affect the patient most of the time, namely tension headaches and analgesic-dependent headaches, and the longstanding but intermittent headaches of migraine. Contrary to public belief, it is extremely rare for brain tumours to present with chronic headache without additional symptoms.

	Head pain	Face pain
Chronic, continual	Tension headache Analgesic-dependent headache	Atypical facial pain
Chronic, episodic	Migraine Cluster headache Icepick headache	Trigeminal neuralgia
Subacute, evolving	Raised intracranial pressure Meningo-encephalitis Giant cell arteritis	
Acute, severe	Subarachnoid haemorrhage Benign sex headache	

Tension headache

Tension headache is very common. It is frequently described as a tight band around the head, often radiating into the neck. Most of us have experienced headaches of this kind from time to time, when tired or stressed. Patients who seek medical advice about tension headaches tend to get them most of the time and with considerable severity. The source of the pain is believed to be chronic contraction of the neck and facial muscles.

'You've got to do something Doctor.'

There is usually a background of stress and worry, sometimes with clinically significant anxiety or depression. The patient is often concerned about the possibility of a brain tumour, creating a vicious circle where headaches cause anxiety and anxiety causes more headaches.

Treatment therefore starts with trying to help the patient to understand the nature of the headache, with reassurance (based upon a careful neurological examination) that there is no serious physical cause. Some patients cannot be reassured without a brain scan but this is not a good use of resources from a medical point of view. Modification of lifestyle may be desirable but cannot always be achieved. Relaxing therapies and small night-time doses of amitriptyline may be beneficial. Underlying depression should be treated if present. Regular analgesic use is generally counterproductive (see p. 216). It is often difficult to satisfy patients complaining of tension headaches.

Migraine

Migraine affects about 15% of women and 8% of men. It is familial. Most patients experience their first attack before the age of 40 years. It characteristically causes episodes of headache, lasting between a few hours and a few days; the patient feels normal between these attacks.

'I'm OK in between, but when it comes I'm awful, I'm sick and I can't see properly.'

Attacks may be precipitated by a wide range of triggers, and commonly by a combination of these. Most patients have a prodrome, for example yawning or passing urine frequently. Some then have an aura, which characteristically evolves over a period of about 20 minutes. The commonest is visual, with an area of blurred vision or an arc of scintillating zigzags slowly spreading across the visual field. Less commonly there may be tingling, for example in one hand spreading slowly to the ipsilateral tongue, or dysphasia, or unilateral weakness, or a succession of all three. It used to be thought that these aura symptoms reflected cerebral ischaemia, but recent research has shown that the phenomena have a neuronal rather than a vascular basis.

The next phase of the attack is the headache itself, although older patients may find they gradually stop experiencing this.

The headache is typically throbbing, severe, felt at the front of the head and worse on one side, and lasts for several hours. It is often accompanied by pallor, nausea or vomiting, and an intense desire to lie still in a quiet darkened room. A period of sleep will often terminate an attack. A few unfortunate patients have attacks that last for a couple of days.

Patients with migraine have no abnormal physical signs on examination. So long as this is the case, brain scanning is not required.

It is not always possible to persuade the patient to pursue the life of sustained tranquillity and regularity that seems to suit migraine best. They should, nonetheless, be encouraged to avoid their triggers where possible. Individual attacks may respond to simple analgesia taken promptly, if necessary together with a dopamine antagonist, e.g. aspirin and metoclopramide. Failing that, serotonin agonists such as ergotamine and the triptan family of drugs can be of great benefit. If vomiting is pronounced, such agents can be given sublingually, by nasal spray, by suppository or by injection. Some patients respond well, only to get a rebound attack the following day. This is a particular problem with ergotamine but can also occur with the triptans and can lead to overuse of medication and a chronic headache (see overleaf).

Preventive treatment should be considered if migraine attacks are frequent or when there are rebound attacks. Regular administration of beta-adrenergic blockers such as atenolol, the tricyclic amitriptyline and the anticonvulsant sodium valproate all have significant benefits. Current research suggests that some of the newer anticonvulsants may be even more effective, supporting the view that migraine may be a disorder of ion channels.

Some triggers for migraine

- Stress and fatigue
- Relaxation after stress ('Saturday morning migraine')
- Skipping meals
- Binge eating
- Specific foods (cheese, citrus fruits, etc.)
- Specific drinks:
    caffeine (too much or
        sudden withdrawal)
    red wine (too much)
- Menstruation or ovulation
- Oral contraceptive
- Early post-partum period
- Menopause
- Bright sunshine, flicker or patterns
- Strong smells
- Hypertension
- Head injury

Cluster headache

Cluster headache gets its name from its tendency to occur repetitively, once or twice each day, for several weeks, with long intervals of a year or more until it recurs in the same way. During the cluster, the attacks themselves are brief, lasting between 30 and 120 minutes. They often occur at the same time in each 24-hour cycle, with a predilection for the early hours of the morning. Functional brain imaging studies have shown activation of the brain's clock and central pain-sensitive areas at the onset of the attack.

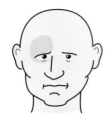

'Mainly at night, I could set the clock by it. Really severe.'

Cluster headache is much less common than migraine, and mainly affects men. The pain is excruciatingly severe, located around one eye, and accompanied by ipsilateral signs of autonomic dysfunction including redness and swelling, nasal congestion, or Horner's syndrome. The pain can sometimes be controlled by inhaling high-flow oxygen or injecting sumatriptan.

Prophylactic treatment can be enormously helpful, starting with steroids and verapamil and moving on to methysergide or anticonvulsants (such as topiramate) if necessary.

Icepick headaches

Icepick headaches are momentary jabbing pains in the head. They often occur in people who also have migraine, or tension headaches, or both. They are alarming but entirely benign. Reassurance is usually all that is required but regular administration of non-steroidal anti-inflammatory drugs can suppress them.

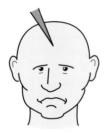

'I'm scared of them.'

Analgesic-dependent headache

Patients with either tension headaches or migraine can develop headaches due to overuse of analgesia, especially the milder opiates such as co-proxamol and codeine, ergotamine and the triptans. They develop a daily headache, often with a throbbing quality, that is transiently relieved by the offending drug. Treatment consists of explanation, gradual introduction of headache prophylaxis (such as amitriptyline) and planned, abrupt discontinuation of the analgesic. The daily headaches usually settle after a short but unpleasant period of withdrawal headache.

'I daren't stop the pills.'

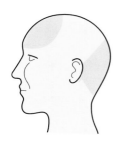

'It's not too bad really. Mainly in the mornings when I wake.'

Raised intracranial pressure

Patients with raised intracranial pressure often have little or no headache, and when they do have headache, it often lacks specific features. The diagnosis of raised intracranial pressure therefore largely relies upon the detection of the focal symptoms and signs of the causative intracranial space-occupying lesion (tumour, haematoma, abscess, etc.) or the other features of raised intracranial pressure (impairment of conscious level, vomiting, papilloedema). Such features tend to arise in the context of a subacute and clearly deteriorating illness, and require prompt investigation with brain scanning. Lumbar puncture should not be performed unless a focal cause has been confidently excluded.

The headaches of raised intracranial pressure tend to be worse when the patient is lying flat, and may therefore wake the patient from sleep or be present on waking. Migraine is, however, a much more common cause of headaches with these features. As a general rule, raised-pressure headaches are more likely to be occipital and mild.

Low intracranial pressure

'I'm OK lying down, but the headache's awful when I'm upright.'

Low-pressure headaches have the opposite characteristic: they are relieved by lying flat but rapidly return when the patient resumes an upright posture. They may follow a lumbar puncture (diagnostic or accidental during epidural anaesthesia), due to a persistent leak of CSF through the hole in the theca. They can also occur spontaneously, because of a leak arising in a thoracic nerve root sheath following coughing or air travel. They often settle with bedrest and caffeine supplements.

Benign sex headache

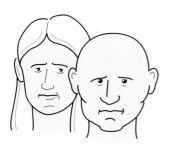

'Right at the moment when I'm most excited.'

Benign sex headache causes a sudden, severe headache which occurs at the moment of orgasm in men or women. The first attack may be difficult to distinguish from subarachnoid haemorrhage (which can, of course, occur at times of exertion). It is very reassuring if one discovers a history of previous attacks under similar circumstances. Happily, and unlike subarachnoid haemorrhage, benign sex headaches are not associated with loss of consciousness or vomiting. The attacks tend to disappear spontaneously but beta-adrenergic blockers can be a very effective preventive treatment.

Giant cell arteritis

In elderly people, the extracranial and the intra-orbital arteries may become affected with an arteritis which is painful and dangerous. The danger lies in the fact that the lumen of these arteries may become obliterated because of the thickening of their walls and associated thrombosis.

Patients with giant cell arteritis generally feel unwell, short of energy and apathetic. The condition overlaps with polymyalgia rheumatica, in which similar symptoms are associated with marked stiffness of muscles.

The arteritis causes headache and tenderness of the scalp (when resting the head on the pillow, and when brushing the hair), because of the inflamed arteries. The superficial temporal arteries may be tender, red, swollen and non-pulsatile. The condition is sometimes known as temporal arteritis because of the very frequent involvement of the superficial temporal arteries, but the facial arteries are often involved, as are other arteries in the scalp.

The arterial occlusive aspects of the disease chiefly concern the small branches of the ophthalmic artery in the orbit. Sudden and irreversible blindness due to infarction of the distal part of the optic nerve is the main danger.

Giant cell arteritis is an emergency requiring urgent estimation of the ESR (usually elevated above 60 mm/hour, with an accompanying elevation in C-reactive protein) and immediate high-dose steroid treatment. In all but the most clear-cut cases, the diagnosis should be rapidly confirmed with a temporal artery biopsy. Most patients will continue to need steroids in much diminished doses for a couple of years, and sometimes for much longer.

'I don't feel at all well, Doctor. I can't put my head on the pillow.'

Subdural haematoma

Elderly people, alcoholics and people on anticoagulants who bang their heads may subsequently develop a collection of blood in the subdural space. This condition is described in more detail elsewhere (see pp. 64 and 232). The usual presentation is with cognitive decline. Occasional cases present with a subacute headache and raised intracranial pressure.

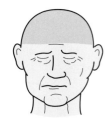

'He's sleepy, slow and unsteady. He wet the bed last night.'

Subarachnoid haemorrhage and meningitis

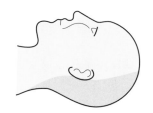

'Never had a headache like this before. My neck feels stiff.'

When the meninges are irritated and inflamed, pain is felt throughout the head and neck, especially in the occipital region. Forward flexion of the neck moves the inflamed meninges, and is involuntarily resisted by the patient. This gives rise to the classical sign of meningeal irritation (meningism) known as 'neck stiffness'.

The headache and neck stiffness are severe and sudden in onset when the meningeal irritation is due to blood in the subarachnoid space (subarachnoid haemorrhage) (see pp. 32–7). The symptoms and signs evolve a little more gradually in the case of meningitis caused by pyogenic bacteria and acute viral infection (see pp. 242–4). Evidence of raised intracranial pressure (depression of conscious level, papilloedema) and abnormal neurological signs are not uncommon in patients with subarachnoid haemorrhage or meningitis. Urgent admission to hospital (for CT brain scanning, lumbar puncture, antibiotics, etc.) is the ideal early management of patients with headaches associated with neck stiffness.

Trigeminal neuralgia

'Sudden cruel severe stabs of pain which make me jump.'

Trigeminal neuralgia causes sudden, momentary pains like electric shocks (lancinating pain) in the distribution of one trigeminal nerve. The pain is unilateral, usually in the maxillary or mandibular territory, close to the mouth or nose. Each stab of pain is severe and sudden enough to make the patient jump (hence the French term *tic douloureux*). There may be a background ache between the stabs. The pain may recur many times a day and tends to be triggered by contact with the skin of the affected area. Cold wind on the face, washing, shaving, teeth-cleaning, talking, eating and drinking may all trigger the pain, and the patient may reduce or stop these activities.

Trigeminal neuralgia tends to occur in patients over the age of 55 years, often with a history of hypertension, and may be due to irritation of the proximal part of the trigeminal nerve by an adjacent blood vessel. Younger patients and those with abnormal physical signs should be investigated to exclude other rare causes such as multiple sclerosis and compression of the trigeminal nerve by a neuroma or meningioma.

Trigeminal neuralgia tends to wax and wane spontaneously but is usually controlled by anticonvulsants like carbamazepine, lamotrigine or gabapentin. Failing this, the pain can be controlled by selectively damaging the nerve with, for example, a radiofrequency lesion (with a risk of troublesome facial numbness and subsequent recurrence of pain) or by surgical decompression of the trigeminal nerve (with all the risks of neurosurgery, including brainstem stroke).

Atypical facial pain

Atypical facial pain causes a dull, persistent ache around one cheek with a great deal of accompanying misery. The pain is constant, not jabbing. Most patients are women aged between 30 and 50 years. Physical examination and investigations are normal. Like tension headaches, atypical facial pain is hard to relieve. Tricyclic antidepressants can, however, be curative.

'I'm beginning to think I'm neurotic.'

Post-herpetic neuralgia

In the face and head, herpes zoster infection most commonly affects the ophthalmic division of the trigeminal nerve. The condition is painful during the acute vesicular phase and, in a small percentage of patients, the pain persists after the rash has healed. The occurrence of persistent pain, post-herpetic neuralgia, does not relate to the age of the patient or the severity of the acute episode, nor is it definitely reduced by the early use of antiviral agents.

'It's been there every day since I had the shingles.'

Post-herpetic neuralgia can produce a tragic clinical picture. The patient is often elderly (since shingles is more common in the elderly) with a constant burning pain in the thinned and de-pigmented area that was affected by the vesicles. Not infrequently, the patient cannot sleep properly, loses weight and becomes very depressed.

The pain rarely settles of its own accord but can be ameliorated by tricyclic antidepressants, gabapentin and topical capsaicin ointment. Capsaicin is a derivative of chilli pepper that suppresses activity in substance P-containing sensory neurones; care must be taken to keep it out of the eye.

Post-concussion syndrome

Patients of any age who have an injury to their head resulting in concussion may suffer a group of symptoms during the months or years afterwards, even though physical examination and investigation are normal.

The head injury is usually definite but mild, with little or no post-traumatic amnesia. Subsequently, the patient may complain of headaches (which are frequent or constant and made worse by exertion), poor concentration and memory, difficulty in taking decisions, irritability, depression, dizziness, intolerance of alcohol and exercise.

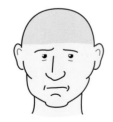

'I've not been myself ever since that accident.'

The extent to which these symptoms are physical (and the mechanism of this) or psychological, and the extent to which they are maintained by the worry of medico-legal activity in relation to compensation, is not clear and probably varies a good deal from case to case.

Other causes of headache and facial pain

It is important to remember that pains in the head and face may be non-neurological in nature, and more the province of the general practitioner or other medical or surgical specialists. Some of these conditions are very common. They are shown below.

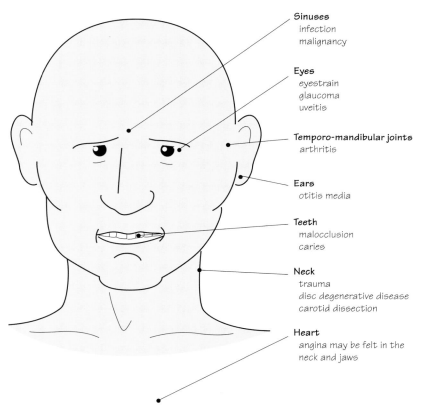

Sinuses
infection
malignancy

Eyes
eyestrain
glaucoma
uveitis

Temporo-mandibular joints
arthritis

Ears
otitis media

Teeth
malocclusion
caries

Neck
trauma
disc degenerative disease
carotid dissection

Heart
angina may be felt in the
neck and jaws

Fig. 13.1 Non-neurological causes of headache and facial pain.

CASE HISTORIES

The diagnosis of headache and facial pains concentrates very much on the history. Abnormal examination findings are important but rare, except in the acute and evolving headaches. Patients often use key phrases which start to point you towards the correct diagnosis. In reality you would want to hear a great deal more before committing yourself to a diagnosis, but see if you can identify the likely causes in these cases.

a. 'It was like being hit on the back of the head with a baseball bat.'

b. 'It's a tight band around my head, holding it in a vice, like something's expanding inside.'

c. 'Every night at 2 o'clock, like someone is squeezing my eyeball very hard.'

d. 'Mainly in the mornings and when I bend over.'

e. 'All over my head, it feels so tender, I've never felt so bad in all my years.'

f. 'Maybe once or twice a month, at the front on this side.'

g. 'Cruel, sudden, I can't brush my teeth.'

h. 'Awful when I sit up, fine lying flat.'

i. 'Endless, nagging ache in this cheek: I'm desperate.'

j. 'It's very embarrassing, doctor, it always happens just as I'm, you know. . . .'

(For answers, see pp. 265–6.)

CHAPTER 14

Dementia

Introduction

Dementia is a progressive loss of intellectual function. It is common in the developed world and is becoming more common as the age of the population gradually increases, putting more people at risk of neurodegenerative disease. In the developing world there are other serious causes, including the effects of HIV–AIDS and untreated hypertension. Patients with dementia place a major burden on their families and on medical and social services. Reversible causes of dementia are rare. Treatment is generally supportive or directed at relieving symptoms, and is usually far from perfect. But dementia is now an area of intense scientific study, bringing the prospect of more effective therapies in the future.

Recognizing dementia is easy when it is severe. It is much harder to distinguish early dementia from the forgetfulness due to anxiety, and from the mild cognitive impairment that often accompanies ageing (usually affecting memory for names and recent events), which does not necessarily progress to more severe disability. It is also important to distinguish dementia from four related but clinically distinct entities: delirium (or acute confusion), learning disability, pseudodementia and dysphasia.

Dementia

- Progressive
- Involvement of more than one area of intellectual function (such as memory, language, judgement or visuospatial ability)
- Sufficiently severe to disrupt daily life

Delirium

Delirium is a state of confusion in which patients are not fully in touch with their environment. They are drowsy, perplexed and uncooperative. They often appear to hallucinate, for example misinterpreting the pattern on the curtains as insects. There are many possible causes, including almost any systemic or CNS infection, hypoxia, drug toxicity, alcohol withdrawal, stroke, encephalitis and epilepsy. Patients with a pre-existing brain disease, including dementia, are particularly susceptible to delirium.

Learning disability

Learning disability is the currently accepted term for a condition that has in the past been referred to as mental retardation, mental handicap or educational subnormality. The difference between dementia and learning disability is that patients with dementia have had normal intelligence in their adult life and then start to lose it, whereas patients with learning disability have suffered some insult to their brains early in life (Fig. 14.1) which has prevented the development of normal intelligence. While dementia is progressive, learning disability is static unless a further insult to the brain occurs. The person with learning disability learns and develops, slowly and to a limited extent.

Early disruption of brain function results in any of:

1. Impaired thinking, reasoning, memory, language, etc.

2. Behaviour problems because of difficulty in learning social customs, controlling emotions or appreciating the emotional needs of others.

3. Abnormal movement of the body, because of damage to the parts of the brain involved in movement (motor cortex, basal ganglia, cerebellum, thalamus, sensory cortex) giving rise to:

- delayed milestones for sitting, crawling, walking;
- spastic forms of cerebral palsy including congenital hemiplegia and spastic diplegia (or tetraplegia);
- dystonic ('athetoid') form of cerebral palsy (where the intellect is often normal);
- clumsy, poorly coordinated movement;
- repetitive or ritualistic stereotyped movements.

4. Epilepsy, which may be severe and resistant to treatment.

It is now clear that in developed countries anoxic birth injury, once thought to account for most cases of learning disability and cerebral palsy, is actually an unusual cause; genetic disorders are the major culprit. Parents may appreciate early diagnosis, genetic counselling and in a few cases prenatal diagnosis.

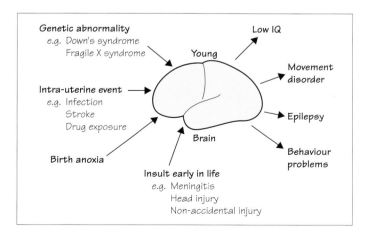

Fig. 14.1 Diagram to show the common insults that can occur to the developing brain, and their consequences.

Pseudodementia

A few patients may deliberately affect loss of memory and impaired intellectual function, usually in response to a major life crisis. Anxiety commonly interferes with the ability to take in new information. In the main, however, pseudodementia refers to the impaired thinking that occurs in some patients with depression. Severely depressed patients may be mentally and physically retarded to a major degree. There may be long intervals between question and answer when interviewing such patients. The patient's feelings of unworthiness and lack of confidence may be such that he is quite uncertain whether his thoughts and answers are accurate or of any value. Patients like this often state quite categorically that they cannot think or remember properly, and defer to their spouse when asked questions. Their overall functional performance, at work or in the house, may become grossly impaired because of mental slowness, indecisiveness, lack of enthusiasm and impaired energy.

'. . . I can't remember . . I think you'd better ask my wife . .'

Dysphasia

The next clear discrimination is between dementia and dysphasia. It is very likely that talking to the patient, in an attempt to obtain details of the history, will have defined whether the problem is one of impaired intellectual function, or a problem of language comprehension and production, or both. The discrimination is important, not least because of the difficulty in assessing intellectual function in a patient with significant dysphasia. Moreover, dysphasia can be mistaken for delirium, leading to the neglect of a treatable focal brain problem such as encephalitis.

Patients with dysphasia have a language problem. This is not dissimilar to being in a foreign country and finding oneself unable to understand (receptive dysphasia), or make oneself understood (expressive dysphasia).

Figure 14.2 sets out the two main types of dysphasia (as seen in the majority of people, in whom speech is represented in the left cerebral hemisphere). Not infrequently, a patient has a lesion in the left cerebral hemisphere which is large enough to produce a global or mixed dysphasia. Broca's and Wernicke's areas are both involved; verbal expression and comprehension are both impaired.

Involvement of nearby areas of the brain by the lesion causing the dysphasia may result in other clinical features. These are shown in Fig. 14.3. Stroke, ischaemic or haemorrhagic, and cerebral tumour are the common sorts of focal pathology to behave in this way.

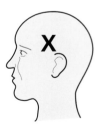

Language problem

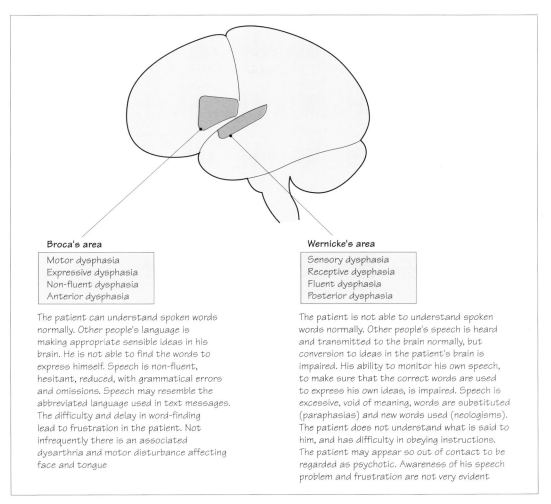

Broca's area

> Motor dysphasia
> Expressive dysphasia
> Non-fluent dysphasia
> Anterior dysphasia

The patient can understand spoken words normally. Other people's language is making appropriate sensible ideas in his brain. He is not able to find the words to express himself. Speech is non-fluent, hesitant, reduced, with grammatical errors and omissions. Speech may resemble the abbreviated language used in text messages. The difficulty and delay in word-finding lead to frustration in the patient. Not infrequently there is an associated dysarthria and motor disturbance affecting face and tongue

Wernicke's area

> Sensory dysphasia
> Receptive dysphasia
> Fluent dysphasia
> Posterior dysphasia

The patient is not able to understand spoken words normally. Other people's speech is heard and transmitted to the brain normally, but conversion to ideas in the patient's brain is impaired. His ability to monitor his own speech, to make sure that the correct words are used to express his own ideas, is impaired. Speech is excessive, void of meaning, words are substituted (paraphasias) and new words used (neologisms). The patient does not understand what is said to him, and has difficulty in obeying instructions. The patient may appear so out of contact to be regarded as psychotic. Awareness of his speech problem and frustration are not very evident

Fig. 14.2 The two broad groups of dysphasia.

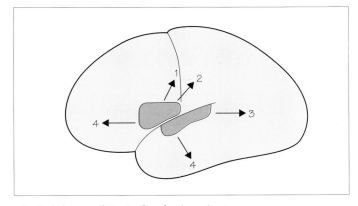

1 Weakness of the right face, hand and arm

2 Sensory impairment in the right face, hand and arm

3 Difficulties with:
   written words . . . dyslexia and dysgraphia
   numbers . . . dyscalculia
   visual field . . . right homonymous hemianopia

4 Impairment of memory, alteration of behaviour

Fig. 14.3 The common associated neurological abnormalities in dysphasic patients.

Features of dementia

The commonly encountered defects in intellectual function that occur in patients with dementia, together with the effects that such defects have, are shown below. Because the dementing process usually develops slowly, the features of dementia evolve insidiously, and are often 'absorbed' by the patient's family. This is why dementia is often advanced at the time of presentation.

> . . . a forgetful person, in no real distress, who can no longer do their job, can no longer be independent, and who cannot really sustain any ordinary sensible conversation

Defect in:	Effects
Memory	• Disorientation, especially in time • Impaired knowledge of recent events • Forgets messages, repeats himself, loses things about the house • Increasing dependence on familiar surroundings and daily routine
Thinking, understanding, reasoning and initiating	• Poor organization • Ordinary jobs muddled and poorly executed • Slow, inaccurate, circumstantial conversation • Poor comprehension of argument, conversation and TV programmes • Difficulty in making decisions and judgements • Fewer new ideas, less initiative • Increasing dependence on relatives
Dominant hemisphere function	• Reduced vocabulary, overuse of simple phrases • Difficulty in naming things and word-finding • Occasional misuse of words • Reading, writing and spelling problems • Difficulties in calculation, inability to handle money
Non-dominant hemisphere function	• Easily lost, wandering and difficulty dressing (spatial disorientation)
Insight and emotion	• Usually lacking in insight, facile • Occasionally insight is intact, causing anxiety and depression • Emotional lability may be present • Socially or sexually inappropriate behaviour

Testing intellectual function (with some reference to anatomical localization)

Talking to the patient, in an attempt to obtain details of the history, will have indicated the presence of impairment of intellectual function in most instances. The next tasks are to find out how severely affected intellectual function is, and whether all aspects of the intellect are involved, i.e. global dementia, or whether the problem is localized.

Dysphasia

Establish first whether there is significant expressive or receptive dysphasia, because these make it hard to use most of the other bedside tests of intellectual function. The features of dysphasia are described in Fig. 14.2
- Listen for expressive dysphasia: hesitant speech, struggling to find the correct word and using laborious ways round missing words (circumlocution)
- Test for receptive dysphasia by asking the patient to follow increasingly complex commands, e.g. 'close your eyes,' 'put one hand on your chest and the other on your head,' 'touch your nose, put on your spectacles, and stand up'
- In both situations the patient may use the wrong words

Bilateral frontal and temporal regions

- Look for and ask about behavioural changes of frontotemporal disorder:
  - self-neglect, apathy and social withdrawal
  - socially or sexually inappropriate behaviour
  - excessive and uncharacteristic consumption of alcohol or sweet foods
  - lack of insight into these changes
- Test orientation in time and place, and recall of current affairs (if the patient does not follow the news, try sport or their favourite soap opera)
- Test attention and recall, asking the patient to repeat a name and address immediately and after 5 minutes
- Test frontal lobe function. Ask the patient to give the meaning of proverbs (looking for literal or 'concrete' interpretations rather than the abstract meaning), or to generate a list of words beginning with a particular letter (usually very slow and repetitive)

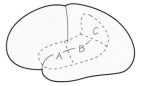

Dominant hemisphere

Spoken language (A)
- Test vocabulary, naming of objects, misuse of words and ability to follow multicomponent commands

Written language (B)
- Test reading, writing and calculation

Parietal dysfunction (C)
- Test for contralateral limb sensory inattention or visual field inattention

Non-dominant hemisphere

- Test for contralateral limb sensory inattention or visual field inattention
- Ask about loss of spatial awareness, where the patient becomes lost in familiar surroundings, or struggles with the correct arrangement of clothes on his body (dressing dyspraxia)
- Test ability to draw a clock and copy a diagram of intersecting pentagons

Causes of dementia

The commoner causes of dementia are listed below, followed by brief notes about each of the individual causes.

1. Alzheimer's disease.
2. Dementia with Lewy bodies.
3. Vascular dementia.
4. Other progressive intracranial pathology:
   - brain tumour;
   - chronic subdural haematoma;
   - chronic hydrocephalus;
   - multiple sclerosis;
   - Huntington's disease;
   - Pick's disease;
   - motor neurone disease;
   - Creutzfeldt–Jakob disease.
5. Alcohol and drugs.
6. Rare infections, deficiencies, etc.:
   - HIV–AIDS;
   - syphilis;
   - B vitamin deficiency;
   - hypothyroidism.

Alzheimer's disease

This is very common, especially with increasing age, and accounts for about 65% of dementia in the UK. Onset and progression are insidious. Memory is usually affected first, followed by language and spatial abilities. Insight and judgement are preserved to begin with. After a few years all aspects of intellectual function are affected and the patient may become frail and unsteady. Epilepsy is uncommon.

The main pathology is in the cerebral cortex, initially in the temporal lobe, with loss of synapses and cells, neurofibrillary tangles and senile plaques. These changes also affect subcortical nuclei, including the ones that provide acetylcholine to the cerebral cortex. This may contribute to the cognitive decline; cholinesterase inhibitors such as rivastigmine and donepezil sometimes provide symptomatic improvement.

People with the apolipoprotein E e4 genotype are at increased risk of developing Alzheimer's disease, and mutations in the amyloid precursor protein gene and the presenilin genes can cause familial Alzheimer's disease. Environmental factors are probably also important.

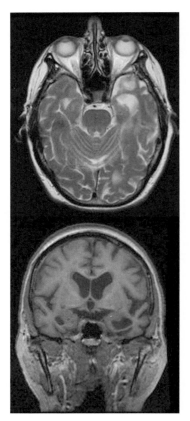

Atrophy of both temporal lobes due to Alzheimer's disease.

Dementia with Lewy bodies

Dementia with Lewy bodies accounts for about 15% of dementia in the UK. The intellectual symptoms are similar to those of Alzheimer's disease but patients are much more likely to develop parkinsonism, visual hallucinations and episodes of confusion.

The distribution of pathology is also similar, but affected neurones form Lewy bodies rather than tangles. The cholinergic deficit is more profound, and the response to cholinesterase therapies usually more marked. Neuroleptic drugs can exacerbate the parkinsonism to a severe, or even fatal, degree.

Vascular dementia (see also p. 31)

This accounts for about 10% of UK dementia. Most cases are caused by widespread small vessel disease within the brain itself, due to hypertension or diabetes, giving rise to extensive and diffuse damage to the subcortical white matter. These patients present with failing judgement and reasoning, followed by impaired memory and language, together with a complex gait disturbance, consisting of small shuffling steps (*marche à petits pas*). Emotional lability and pseudobulbar palsy are often present, with a brisk jaw-jerk and spastic dysarthria.

A few cases are due to carotid atheroma giving rise to multiple discrete cerebral infarcts, i.e. multi-infarct dementia. These patients have a stepwise evolution with events that can be recognized as distinct strokes and which give rise to focal neurological deficits (such as hemiparesis, dysphasia or visual field defect). Intellectual impairment accrues as these deficits start to summate.

Treatment of vascular risk factors, especially hypertension and hyperlipidaemia, can have a useful preventive effect in both forms of vascular dementia.

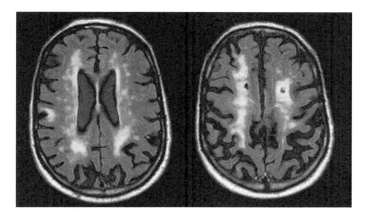

Extensive signal change in the white matter due to small vessel disease.

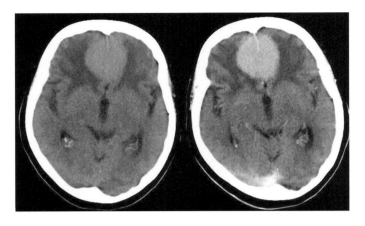

CT scan demonstrating a frontal meningioma with surrounding cerebral oedema. The tumour enhances after contrast administration (right-side image).

Other progressive intracranial pathology

Frontal and temporal tumours occasionally become large enough to cause significant intellectual impairment before producing tell-tale features like epilepsy, focal deficit or raised intracranial pressure.

Patients with chronic subdural haematoma are usually elderly, alcoholic or anticoagulated. They may not recall the causative head injury, but become drowsy, unsteady and intellectually impaired over a few weeks. Because the collection of blood is outside the brain, focal neurological signs appear late.

Any process which causes hydrocephalus slowly may declare itself by failing intellectual ability, slowness, inappropriate behaviour and drowsiness, often with gait disturbance, incontinence of urine and headache.

Neurosurgery may help all these patients.

Severe multiple sclerosis can cause dementia, often with emotional lability.

Dementia that particularly affects frontal lobe functions, with disinhibited and illogical behaviour, is characteristic of Huntington's disease, the dementia that sometimes accompanies motor neurone disease, and Pick's disease. This pattern of dementia, where language and spatial abilities are affected late, if at all, is particularly challenging to manage. The patient has no insight into the nature of his problems, often neglects himself and refuses help.

Creutzfeldt–Jakob disease (CJD) classically causes a very rapidly progressive and devastating dementia with ataxia and myoclonic jerks. The patient gets worse day by day and is helpless and bed-bound within weeks or months, dying within a year. It is mercifully very rare.

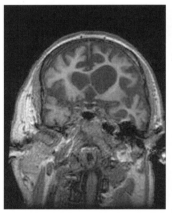

Severe atrophy of the frontal and temporal lobes due to Pick's disease.

Transmission and CJD

There are two aspects to mention:

1. Whereas most cases of classic CJD are caused by spontaneous deposition of an abnormal form of prion protein within the patient's brain, a few cases have been caused by iatrogenic, person to person, transmission of this abnormal protein through pituitary extracts, corneal grafts and neurosurgical procedures.

2. The variant form of CJD, which occurs mainly in the UK, takes a slightly slower course and affects younger people. It is thought to be due to transmission of the closely related prion disease in cattle, bovine spongiform encephalopathy, to people by human consumption of contaminated beef.

Alcohol and drugs

In addition to the rather flamboyant syndromes seen in alcoholics who become deficient in vitamin B_1, namely Wernicke's encephalopathy and Korsakoff's psychosis, it is being increasingly recognized that chronic alcoholism is associated with cerebral atrophy and generalized dementia.

Patients, especially those who are elderly, may become confused and forgetful whilst on medication, especially antidepressants, tranquillizers, hypnotics, analgesics and anticonvulsants.

It is most important to bear in mind alcohol and drugs before embarking upon a detailed investigation of dementia.

Rare infections, deficiencies and metabolic disorders

HIV–AIDS

HIV–AIDS can cause dementia, either through a primary HIV encephalitis or through the CNS complications of immunodeficiency such as opportunistic infection (toxoplasmosis, cryptococcal meningitis) and lymphoma. The risk of all of these is greatly reduced by current highly active retroviral therapy regiments, but tragically these are least available in the countries with the greatest prevalence and need.

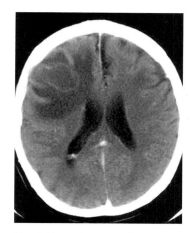

Frontal toxoplasmosis abscess due to HIV–AIDS.

Tertiary syphilis

Tertiary syphilis was the AIDS of the nineteenth century but is now rare because of improvements in public health and the widespread use of penicillin, which is lethal to the spirochaete *Treponema pallidum*. It gives rise to general paralysis of the insane (a dementia with prominent frontal lobe features), tabes dorsalis (with loss of proprioception and reflexes in the lower limbs), taboparesis (a mixture of the two) and meningovascular syphilis (with small vessel strokes, especially of the brainstem) (see p. 248 for further details). Blood tests for syphilis should be a routine part of the investigation of dementia.

B vitamin deficiency

Vitamin B_1 deficiency in Western society occurs in alcoholics whose diet is inadequate, and in people who voluntarily modify their diet to an extreme degree, e.g. patients with anorexia nervosa or extreme vegetarians.

Impairment of short-term memory, confusion, abnormalities of eye movement and pupils, together with ataxia, constitute the features of Wernicke's encephalopathy. Though associated with demonstrable pathology in the midbrain, this syndrome is often rapidly reversible by urgent intravenous thiamine replacement.

Less reversible is the chronic state of short-term memory impairment and confabulation which characterize Korsakoff's psychosis, mainly seen in advanced alcoholism.

Whether *vitamin B_{12} deficiency* causes dementia remains uncertain. Certainly, peripheral neuropathy and subacute combined degeneration of the spinal cord are more definite neurological consequences of deficiency in this vitamin.

Hypothyroidism

Hypothyroidism is usually rather evident clinically by the time significant impairment of intellectual function is present. It is a cause worth remembering in view of its obvious reversibility.

Investigation of dementia

Usually an accurate history, with collateral information from family and friends, together with a full physical examination, will highlight the most likely cause for an individual patient's dementia.

It is worth thinking whether the problem has begun in the temporal and parietal lobes (with poor memory, then language and spatial problems, usually indicating Alzheimer's disease or dementia with Lewy bodies) or in the frontal lobes (with changes in behaviour, raising the possibility of surgically treatable pathology like tumour or hydrocephalus). It is important to ask about the patient's past medical history (vascular risk factors) and family history (vascular risk factors again, and genetic dementias such as Huntington's disease, familial Alzheimer's disease and Pick's disease). It is particularly important to ask about the patient's social circumstances, because of the need to provide support and care during an illness that is usually arduous and prolonged.

The examination must include tests of memory, language, spatial ability and reasoning as already outlined. It must include a search for neurological clues to the cause of the dementia (see table on opposite page), and a careful examination of the

---

Clinical clues to the cause of dementia

Myoclonus	Neurodegenerative disease: usually Alzheimer's or dementia with Lewy bodies but think of CJD if the myoclonus is severe
Parkinsonism	Dementia with Lewy bodies
Focal deficit	Tumour or vascular dementia
Drowsiness	Delirium not dementia; hydrocephalus; subdural haematoma
Chaotic gait	Vascular dementia; hydrocephalus; Huntington's disease; syphilis; CJD

---

mental state, looking for symptoms and signs of anxiety and depression that may be contributing to the clinical problem.

Bedside testing of intellectual function can be usefully supplemented by standardized neuropsychological testing; this is especially helpful in distinguishing between early dementia and the worried well.

Blood tests rarely detect treatable pathology, but should routinely include:

- full blood count and ESR;
- electrolytes, glucose, calcium and liver function tests;
- thyroid function tests;
- syphilis serology;
- vitamin B_{12};
- antinuclear antibody.

In selected cases these should be supplemented with more specific tests, after appropriate counselling, such as HIV serology, genetic tests for Huntington's disease and so on.

Brain imaging, with a CT scan to rule out tumour, hydrocephalus and vascular disease, is now routine in developed countries. MR brain scanning may be useful in delineating the rarer focal brain atrophies such as Pick's disease and has a research role in monitoring disease progression. Other tests, such as CSF examination or pressure monitoring, are sometimes required.

Management of dementia

Careful explanation is important. Patients vary greatly in the amount of information that they want and can absorb, and establishing this in an individual person requires patience and sensitivity. Family members tend to want more information, especially if there may be genetic implications. The family must be helped to realize that the demented patient will continue to be dependent on them, will thrive better on a familiar routine each day, and may need care to prevent injury from hazards around the home. Additional help and support may be available from disease-specific self-help groups like the Alzheimer Society; voluntary care organizations that provide someone to sit with the patient while the carer pursues activities out of the house; social services facilities like day centres; or old age psychiatry services including community nurses and day hospitals. Ultimately many patients require full-time nursing care.

It may be necessary to encourage the healthy spouse to seek power of attorney, and to obtain advice regarding pensions, investments and wills from a solicitor.

Clearly any treatable underlying condition will be treated. In Alzheimer's disease, and especially in dementia with Lewy bodies, a careful trial of a cholinesterase inhibitor (such as rivastigmine, donepezil or galantamine) may produce transient symptomatic benefit. Unfortunately many patients do not improve or experience adverse effects, and should not continue the treatment unnecessarily. Coexisting conditions such as anxiety and depression can often be usefully treated.

Most of the drugs that are prescribed for people with dementia are, however, sedatives or neuroleptics directed at modifying undesirable or dangerous behaviours, such as irritability or wandering. There is surprisingly little evidence that such treatments are effective, and increasing evidence that they may be hazardous. In an ideal world they would be used very sparingly, with greater emphasis on non-pharmacological ways of modifying behaviour and supporting carers.

- Explanation
- Practical support
- Careful trials of symptomatic therapy
- Power of attorney

CASE HISTORIES

Case 1

A man of 76, who has suffered from atrial fibrillation for 15 years and takes regular warfarin therapy, starts to cause concern in his wife. He is usually very alert for his age, keeping well abreast of current affairs, and a source of inspiration to his children and grandchildren. She is unable to date the precise onset of his symptoms, but it is all very recent. She has been surprised by her husband forgetting items when shopping, his mistakes over the grandchildren's names, his lack of concern, and his tendency to sleep more in the daytime. The GP is consulted but cannot really confirm any definite impairment of neurological function, and examination is normal except for his controlled atrial fibrillation. Thyroid function tests are checked and are normal.

Over the next 3 weeks the situation does not improve. All the family can see the change in the patient, who is now mentioning generalized headaches.

a. What are your thoughts about diagnosis?
b. And your management?

Case 2

A 69-year-old woman is brought to the emergency department by her distressed husband. Over the last 2 days she has become increasingly agitated. She has repeatedly seen people around their home, and thinks that he is involved in a conspiracy to house illegal immigrants. She has become aggressive when he tries to persuade her that there is in fact no-one else in the house and no conspiracy. He feels that she has been more forgetful over recent months, and has developed difficulty in navigating around the familiar streets of their town centre. He also describes a recent episode of confusion which settled after 2 days of treatment for a presumed urinary tract infection.

She is highly aroused, shouting angrily for help. She cannot cooperate with a detailed neurological examination but uses all four limbs effectively and has normal eye and facial movements. Her chest is clear and she is afebrile.

a. What are the diagnostic possibilities here, and how would you manage her?

(For answers, see pp. 266–7.)

CHAPTER 15

Infections of the nervous system

Introduction

In this chapter, we will try to simplify our understanding of such a large area of neurological disease, identifying the features that many of these infections have in common. We will pay most attention to those that are already common in the UK, or which are becoming more common in the early twenty-first century.

Having said this, the human nervous system can be infected by a wide range of organisms:

- parasites (hydatid cysts and cysticercosis);
- protozoa (*Toxoplasma*);
- *Rickettsia* (Rocky Mountain spotted fever);
- mycoplasma (*M. pneumoniae*);
- spirochaetes (syphilis, leptospirosis, Lyme disease);
- fungi (*Cryptococcus, Candida*);
- chronic mycobacteria (tuberculosis and leprosy);
- pyogenic bacteria (*Haemophilus influenzae*, meningococcus);
- chronic viruses (AIDS, SSPE (subacute sclerosing panencephalitis), etc.);
- acute viruses (herpes simplex and herpes zoster, poliovirus).

Common localized infections

Viral infections

Some viruses have a predilection for particular elements of the nervous system.

Acute poliomyelitis

Poliomyelitis

Acute poliomyelitis is very uncommon in the UK nowadays, because of the effective immunization programme. Rare cases are usually the consequence of inadequate primary or 'booster' immunization. It remains a serious problem in some other parts of the world.

After a gastro-enterological infection, the virus takes up residence in the lower motor neurones (in the spinal cord and brainstem). Paralysis ensues, which is often patchy and asymmetrical in the body. Where the infection has been very severe in the neuraxis, lower motor neurones do not recover and the paralysis is permanent. Some of the damage to motor neurones is less complete, and frequently there is recovery of some muscle function after a few weeks. Permanently affected muscles remain wasted and areflexic.

Herpes zoster infections

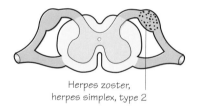

Herpes zoster, herpes simplex, type 2

Herpes zoster infections, or *shingles*, have been described in Chapters 8 (pp. 123 and 125), 9 (p. 143) and 13 (p. 220). The virus probably enters the dorsal root ganglion cells in childhood at the time of chickenpox infection, and remains there in some sort of dormant condition. Later in life, as a result of some impairment in immunological surveillance (e.g. age, immunosuppressive treatment, lymphoma, leukaemia), the virus becomes activated and causes shingles.

Herpes simplex infections

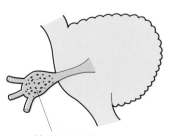

Herpes simplex, type 1

Cold sores around the mouth and nose are the commonest clinical expressions of herpes simplex virus *type 1* infection. A similar dormant state to that in herpes zoster infections occurs here, with the herpes simplex virus resident in the trigeminal nerve ganglion. The altered immunological status that accompanies another viral infection (usually a 'cold') allows the herpes simplex virus to become activated in the ganglion, and cause the skin rash in trigeminal territory.

In the case of herpes simplex virus *type 2* infections, the site of latent infection is the dorsal root ganglion in the sacral region, and reactivation leads to *genital herpes*, in which the vesicular ulcerative lesions occur in the urogenital tract and perineal region.

Pyogenic bacterial infections

Cerebral abscess and *spinal extradural abscess* are the consequences of localized pyogenic bacterial infection. Cerebral abscess is the more common of the two. Figure 15.1 shows the common clinical features of these two conditions.

Cerebral abscess

In the case of cerebral abscess, the continuing mortality from this condition is due to delay in diagnosis. The presence of a cerebral abscess must be anticipated whenever some of the features depicted in the left part of Fig. 15.1 occur. In particular, the presence of one of the local infective conditions which can give rise to cerebral abscess must put one 'on guard'.

The non-specific features of an infection, i.e. fever, elevated white cell count and ESR, may not be very marked in patients with cerebral abscess. Epilepsy, often with focal features, is common in patients with a brain abscess. The diagnosis should be established before the focal neurological deficit (the nature of which will depend upon the site of the abscess) and evidence of raised intracranial pressure are too severe.

Urgent CT brain scan and referral to the local neurosurgical centre are the correct lines of management of patients with suspected cerebral abscess. Lumbar puncture is contra-indicated and potentially dangerous. Neurosurgical drainage, bacteriological diagnosis and intensive antibiotic treatment are required for a successful outcome.

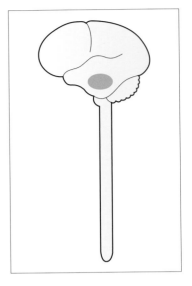

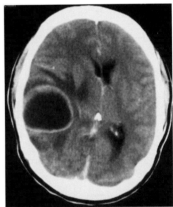

CT brain scan showing a large cerebral abscess, with surrounding cerebral oedema and shift of midline structures to the opposite side.

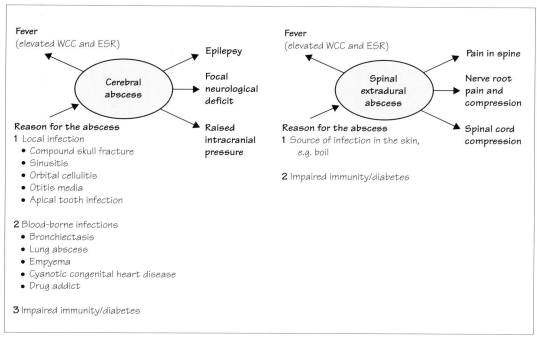

Fever
(elevated WCC and ESR)

Cerebral abscess

Epilepsy

Focal neurological deficit

Raised intracranial pressure

Reason for the abscess
1 Local infection
  • Compound skull fracture
  • Sinusitis
  • Orbital cellulitis
  • Otitis media
  • Apical tooth infection

2 Blood-borne infections
  • Bronchiectasis
  • Lung abscess
  • Empyema
  • Cyanotic congenital heart disease
  • Drug addict

3 Impaired immunity/diabetes

Fever
(elevated WCC and ESR)

Spinal extradural abscess

Pain in spine

Nerve root pain and compression

Spinal cord compression

Reason for the abscess
1 Source of infection in the skin, e.g. boil

2 Impaired immunity/diabetes

Fig. 15.1 Common localized pyogenic bacterial infections.

Spinal extradural abscess

Patients with a spinal extradural abscess present like any patient with a localized spinal cord lesion, except that pain and tenderness in the spine are often very conspicuous. The clinical picture is one that worsens very quickly. There may be clinical evidence of infection, and possibly some predisposition to infection.

Urgent MR scanning of the relevant part of the spine leading to decompressive surgery, organism identification (usually *Staphylococcus aureus*), and antibiotic therapy constitute the correct management.

Other localized infections

Localized *tuberculous* infection may occur in the brain, known as a tuberculoma, or in the spine.

Localized *Toxoplasma* or *fungal brain abscesses* may occur in immunodeficient or immunosuppressed patients, especially those with AIDS (see p. 233).

Common acute generalized CNS infections

Acute meningo-encephalitis is probably the best term to describe acute generalized viral or bacterial infections of the nervous system. Clinically and pathologically, there is almost always some degree of encephalitis in *acute meningitis*, and some degree of meningitis in *acute encephalitis*. Frequently, both aspects are apparent clinically. The close apposition of the meninges to the highly convoluted surface of the brain makes it very unlikely that meninges and brain tissue could escape sharing the same acute inflammatory illness.

Figure 15.2 shows the features of acute meningo-encephalitis. The emphasis on meningitic and encephalitic features varies from one patient to another, and according to the particular infecting agent. The drowsiness and coma may be due to raised intracranial pressure, or to direct involvement of the brainstem in the encephalitic process. The raised intracranial pressure may be due to brain swelling (encephalitis), failure of CSF absorption over the surface of the brain (meningitis), or thrombosis of the sagittal sinus (either encephalitis or meningitis).

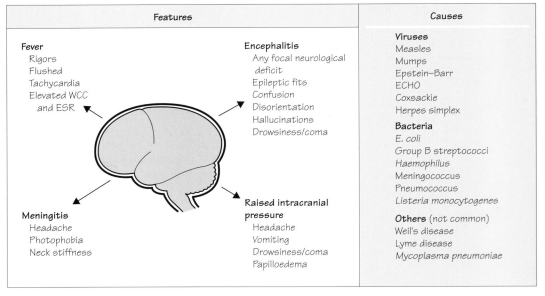

Features

Fever
Rigors
Flushed
Tachycardia
Elevated WCC
and ESR

Encephalitis
Any focal neurological
deficit
Epileptic fits
Confusion
Disorientation
Hallucinations
Drowsiness/coma

Meningitis
Headache
Photophobia
Neck stiffness

Raised intracranial pressure
Headache
Vomiting
Drowsiness/coma
Papilloedema

Causes

Viruses
Measles
Mumps
Epstein–Barr
ECHO
Coxsackie
Herpes simplex

Bacteria
E. coli
Group B streptococci
Haemophilus
Meningococcus
Pneumococcus
Listeria monocytogenes

Others (not common)
Weil's disease
Lyme disease
Mycoplasma pneumoniae

Fig. 15.2 Common acute generalized CNS infections.

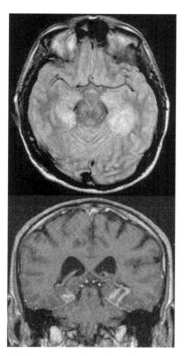

MR brain scan showing changes in both temporal lobes due to oedema and haemorrhage in herpes simplex encephalitis.

Viral infections

In the case of acute viral infections, the clinical picture may be of acute meningitis, acute meningo-encephalitis or acute encephalitis. A mild degree of acute meningo-encephalitis probably occurs in many acute viral infections, certainly in the common exanthematous infections of childhood, especially mumps. In adults with the clinical picture of acute viral meningo-encephalitis, the particular virus may not be identified, though ECHO and coxsackie viruses are those most frequently responsible. Meningo-encephalitis occurs at the time of seroconversion in HIV infection.

Herpes simplex encephalitis, caused by herpesvirus type 1, is the most potentially lethal acute viral infection of the CNS. It can occur at any age, and produces a largely encephalitic clinical picture with or without features of raised intracranial pressure. Brain swelling, especially in the temporal regions, is common, and reflects a highly damaging and necrotic process occurring in the brain tissue. Death, or survival with a significant neurological deficit (intellectual, physical and/or epileptic), are common sequels to this infection. Fortunately, the outcome is significantly improved if the antiviral agent, aciclovir, is given early in the course of the disease. Identification of herpes simplex antigen in the cerebrospinal fluid using the polymerase chain reaction is helpful in early diagnosis, but there is no certain way of knowing early enough in the course of the illness which cases of acute encephalitis are due to herpes simplex virus and which are due to other viruses. For this reason, any patient with acute encephalitis should receive aciclovir immediately, especially where the infection is fulminant and producing brain swelling on CT scan.

Japanese encephalitis is a similar illness caused by a mosquito-borne flavivirus, endemic in India and Asia. There is no specific treatment but the infection can be prevented by vaccination. A related virus causes West Nile viral encephalitis in North America.

Bacterial infections

Acute bacterial infections of the CNS generally give rise to the clinical picture of acute meningitis (also known as bacterial meningitis, purulent meningitis and septic meningitis). It is helpful to remember, however, that these infections are meningo-encephalitic, since confusion or some alteration of the mental state, epilepsy and drowsiness are common features of bacterial meningitis. Furthermore, it is the brain involvement that is so worrying in fulminating infections, e.g. meningococcal meningitis, which may progress to coma within hours. Persistent purulent meningitis is very likely to give rise to CSF absorption problems, so that the clinical features of raised intracranial pressure appear, along with CT scan confirmation of hydrocephalus.

Bacterial meningitis is pre-eminently a disease of neonates and infants. It is a medical emergency. Delay in diagnosis and treatment increases both morbidity and mortality. In neonates, the common organisms tend to be *Escherichia coli* and Group B streptococci, but thereafter the common bacteria are *Haemophilus influenzae*, meningococcus and pneumococcus. The speed with which meningococcal meningitis can evolve requires stressing. Fulminating septicaemia and meningitis, with fever, shock, petechial or purpuric rash, rapid deterioration in conscious level, neck stiffness and a positive Kernig's sign, may evolve with startling rapidity. Doctors should give penicillin to patients with suspected bacterial meningitis before transferring them to hospital. Once in hospital, intravenous treatment with a broad-spectrum antibiotic such as ceftriaxone should be started immediately, without being delayed for tests such as scans or lumbar puncture, and should be continued until there is good evidence that the causative organism is likely to be sensitive to a more specific antibiotic, or the diagnosis of bacterial meningitis has been refuted or the treatment is complete.

In all case of bacterial meningitis, perhaps more so in adults, and especially in any case of recurrent infection, a reason for the infection must be sought. The predisposition to infection may be:

1. local, for example:
   - head trauma involving the floor of the anterior cranial fossa, possibly with CSF rhinorrhoea,
   - head trauma involving the temporal bone, with access of bacteria to the CSF from the ear,
   - shunt devices *in situ* for relief of hydrocephalus.
2. general, for example:
   - diabetes mellitus,
   - immunodeficiency or immunosuppression.

Other infective agents

Apart from viruses and bacteria, other infective agents causing acute meningo-encephalitis are not common in the UK. Two treponemal infections, leptospirosis and Lyme disease, are occasional causes of meningitis. Meningitis may occur at the height of Weil's disease (infection with *Leptospira icterohaemorrhagica*), and the meningitis of Lyme disease (infection with *Borrelia burgdorferi*) is often associated with facial nerve palsy. An infection with *M. pneumoniae* in the lungs may be complicated by a meningo-encephalitis, which is usually not too severe.

Viruses	AIDS
	Rabies
	Subacute sclerosing panencephalitis
	Progressive rubella panencephalitis
	Progressive multifocal leucoencephalopathy
Bacteria	Tuberculous meningitis
	Tetanus
	Leprosy
Spirochaete	Syphilis
Non-infective	Malignant meningitis

Fig. 15.3 Subacute and chronic generalized CNS infections.

Subacute and chronic generalized CNS infections

None of these infections is common in the UK currently. This is because of comprehensive immunization of the population (tetanus, tuberculosis), widespread frequent use of antibiotics (syphilis), or because the condition, though common elsewhere in the world, has not yet reached the UK in significant numbers (rabies). None of the infections will be described in great detail therefore, though some awareness of each of them is certainly justified (Fig. 15.3).

AIDS

AIDS patients are predisposed to three groups of problems from the neurological point of view, as shown in Fig. 15.4. The direct effects of HIV and the secondary effects of immunosuppression are both considerably reduced by highly active retroviral therapy regimens, where these are available. In the UK therefore they tend to occur mainly in people who do not realize that they are infected with HIV. Such patients typically present with headache, focal deficit and epilepsy, with a low lymphocyte count and muted evidence of an inflammatory response to infection. Because the immune system is suppressed, microbiological diagnosis relies more on detecting antigens and DNA from the offending organisms than on identifying antibody responses from the patient. Initially it is often necessary to treat the infection that is most likely on clinical and radiological grounds, considering alternative diagnoses (such as lymphoma) if the response to treatment is poor.

Opportunist infection (see Fig. 15.5)	Opportunist malignancy	Direct effect of HIV
Viruses	Cerebral lymphoma	Early
Herpes simplex		Meningo-encephalitis
Herpes zoster		
Cytomegalovirus		Intermediate
Papovavirus		Meningitis
		Myelopathy
Bacteria		Radiculopathy
Not common		Peripheral neuropathy
		Dementia
Spirochaete		
Syphilis		
		Late
Fungus		Meningitis
Cryptococcus		Myelopathy
		Dementia
Protozoan		
Toxoplasma		

Fig. 15.4 Neurological problems in AIDS patients.

Progressive multifocal leucoencephalopathy

This is a rare condition, occurring in immunocompromised patients, characterized by the subacute accumulation of neurological deficits due to multiple areas of demyelination in the brain, mainly in the cerebral hemispheres. It is caused by opportunistic activation of a human papovavirus (the JC virus) infecting oligodendrocytes.

> • Subacute accumulation of neurological deficits

Rabies

This viral illness is usually contracted because the patient is bitten by an infected dog, which has the virus in its saliva. After a variable incubation period (usually 2–8 weeks, but sometimes much longer), a progressive encephalomyelitis occurs (hallucinations, apprehension, hydrophobia, flaccid paralysis with sensory and sphincter involvement), leading to bulbar and respiratory paralysis. Treatment is difficult, not very specific, prolonged and often unsuccessful. Post-exposure prophylaxis with immunoglobulin may be helpful.

> • Dog bite abroad
> • Incubation period
> • Progressive encephalomyelitis

Subacute sclerosing panencephalitis and progressive rubella panencephalitis

After a latency of some years following measles in early childhood or congenital rubella, a slowly progressive, fatal syndrome characterized by personality change, dementia, myoclonic seizures, and ataxia occasionally occurs.

Specific anti-measles or anti-rubella antibodies become increasingly evident in the CSF during the illness, indicating the presence of viral antigen within the CNS.

> • Dementia
> • Myoclonus
> • Ataxia

Tuberculous meningitis

Tuberculosis is increasing in incidence and becoming more resistant to treatment. Tuberculous meningitis causes the same symptoms as other forms of meningo-encephalitis (shown in Fig. 15.2) but evolves more slowly, over days or weeks. The meningitis is often concentrated around the base of the brain, causing cranial nerve palsies, and interfering with the circulation of CSF. Elevated intracranial pressure and hydrocephalus are common in tuberculous meningitis. It can also cause inflammation of the blood vessels as they leave the meninges to enter the brain, causing strokes.

> • Subacute meningo-encephalitis
> • Cranial nerve palsies
> • Hydrocephalus
> • Evidence of infection

- Deep dirty wound
- Progressively severe muscle spasms

Tetanus

Tetanus occurs worldwide, almost exclusively in people who have never been immunized or who have not had a booster immunization in the previous decade. *Clostridium tetani* spores enter the body through a dirty wound and replicate in anaerobic conditions. The bacteria produce a range of toxins that circulate and bind to targets in the brain, spinal cord, peripheral motor nerves and sympathetic nerves, interfering with inhibitory neurotransmission. This results in increased muscle tone, spasms and seizures. Spontaneous muscle spasms typically begin in the face, referred to as trismus or lockjaw and risus sardonicus. They spread to the trunk and limb muscles, where spasms termed opisthotonus arch the body backwards and may be strong enough to cause crush fractures of the vertebrae or death from respiratory failure and exhaustion. Involvement of the autonomic nerves may cause hypertension and tachycardia.

Debridement of the necrotic wound, antibiotics, tetanus antitoxin, sedation, neuromuscular blocking agents and ventilation may all feature in the management of patients with tetanus, which still has a mortality of more than 10%. Perhaps surprisingly, survivors still require immunization to prevent recurrence.

Leprosy

- Severe sensory loss
- Painless sores
- Muscle weakness and wasting

Leprosy is caused by *Mycobacterium leprae* infection of skin, nerves and mucous membranes. It affects about 600 000 new patients each year, mainly in the Indian subcontinent and parts of Africa and South America. The incidence is falling in response to an international eradication programme, but there are still between 1 and 2 million people worldwide who are disabled by the chronic sequelae of the disease.

The milder, paucibacillary form causes hypopigmented skin macules. The macules have reduced pain and light touch sensation. The more severe, multibacillary form causes larger symmetrical skin lesions, nodules and plaques. Patients with this form of the disease are more likely to get a slowly progressive multifocal neuropathy (Chapter 9, see p. 146). Individual peripheral nerves become thickened and there is wasting, weakness and anaesthesia in the distribution of these nerves.

Treatment requires combination antibacterial therapy, with rifampicin and dapsone, combined with clofazimine in multibacillary cases.

Syphilis

The CNS is involved in the tertiary phase of infection by the spirochaete, *Treponema pallidum*. Neurosyphilis is mainly encountered in patients with AIDS in the UK nowadays. The manifestations of neurosyphilis are:
- optic atrophy;
- Argyll–Robertson pupils, which are small, unequal, irregular, react to accommodation but do not react to light;
- general paralysis of the insane, in which meningo-encephalitic involvement of the cerebral cortex (especially the frontal lobes, including the motor cortex) occurs. It gives rise to a combination of dementia and upper motor neurone paralysis of the limbs;
- tabes dorsalis, in which the proximal axons of the dorsal root ganglion cells, destined to travel in the posterior columns of the spinal cord, become atrophied. The clinical picture is one of proprioceptive sensory loss, especially in the legs. An unsteady, wide-based, stamping gait, and a tendency to fall in the dark, typify patients with tabes dorsalis;
- meningovascular syphilis is perhaps the most frequent clinical expression of neurosyphilis these days. The small arteries perforating the surface of the brain become inflamed and obliterated in the subacute syphilitic meningitis. Acute hemiplegia and sudden individual cranial nerve palsies are the most common clinical events in this form of the disease.

- Optic disc pallor
- Abnormal pupils
- Cranial nerve palsy
- Dementia
- Upper motor neurone signs
- Posterior column sensory loss
- Abnormal gait
- Stroke

Malignant meningitis

This is a relentlessly progressive meningitis, often with cranial nerve and spinal nerve root lesions, and often associated with headache, pain in the spine or root pain. It is due to infiltration of the meninges by neoplastic cells rather than infection. The neoplastic cells may be leukaemic or lymphomatous, or may be derived from a solid tumour elsewhere. Such patients are often immunosuppressed, so the differentiation of malignant meningitis from an opportunistic infection of the meninges may be difficult. Cytological examination of the CSF may be very helpful, the malignant cells showing themselves in centrifuged CSF samples.

- Remorseless progression
- Painful
- Cranial nerve palsies
- Spinal nerve root lesions

CNS infections in immunocompromised patients

The prolonged survival of patients with impaired immunity is becoming more and more commonplace. The number of patients on cytotoxic drugs and steroids for the treatment of malignant disease, and to suppress immunity in connective tissue disorders and after organ transplantation, is increasing. The incidence and prevalence of AIDS are also increasing.

These immunosuppressed or immunodeficient patients are susceptible to infections (Fig. 15.5):

- by organisms which are capable of causing infection in normal individuals, but which cause abnormally frequent and severe infections in the immunocompromised;
- by organisms which are not pathogenic in normal circumstances, so-called opportunistic infections.

The clinical features of these infections are often ill-defined and not distinct from the patient's underlying disease. The different organisms do not create diagnostic clinical syndromes. Intensive investigation, in close collaboration with the microbiology laboratory, is usually required to establish the diagnosis and the correct treatment.

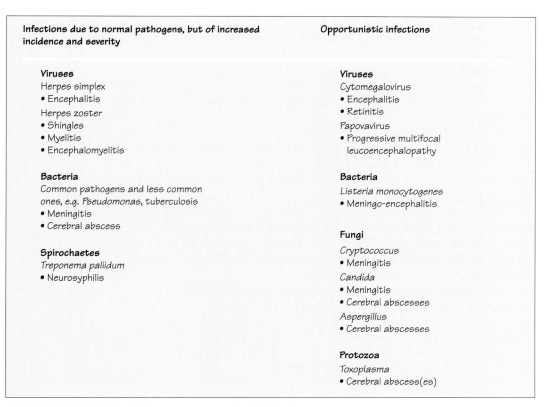

Infections due to normal pathogens, but of increased incidence and severity	Opportunistic infections
Viruses Herpes simplex • Encephalitis Herpes zoster • Shingles • Myelitis • Encephalomyelitis	**Viruses** Cytomegalovirus • Encephalitis • Retinitis Papovavirus • Progressive multifocal leucoencephalopathy
Bacteria Common pathogens and less common ones, e.g. Pseudomonas, tuberculosis • Meningitis • Cerebral abscess	**Bacteria** Listeria monocytogenes • Meningo-encephalitis
Spirochaetes Treponema pallidum • Neurosyphilis	**Fungi** Cryptococcus • Meningitis Candida • Meningitis • Cerebral abscesses Aspergillus • Cerebral abscesses
	Protozoa Toxoplasma • Cerebral abscess(es)

Fig. 15.5 CNS infections in immunocompromised patients.

Management of infections of the nervous system

- Prevent
- Diagnose
- Treat
- Ask why

Prophylaxis

It is not trite to emphasize the importance of the preventive measures which are current in the UK to control CNS infections. We must not become lulled into complacency or lack vigilance over such matters.

- Comprehensive immunization of the population in the case of polio, tetanus and tuberculosis.
- Encouragement of immunization against measles, mumps and rubella.
- Measures to prevent the spread of rabies and AIDS.
- Proper care of patients with compound skull fractures, CSF rhinorrhoea and otorrhoea, otitis media, frontal sinusitis and orbital cellulitis.
- Early active treatment of any infection in diabetic or immunocompromised patients.

Diagnosis

Some infections will be identified from their clinical features alone, e.g. herpes zoster.

In the case of acute meningo-encephalitis, the ideal way to establish the diagnosis is urgent CT scan (to exclude a cerebral abscess mass lesion), followed by immediate lumbar puncture. Blood culture and other investigations are important, but it is the CSF which is usually most helpful in diagnosis, as shown in Fig. 15.6.

In patients with a suspected cerebral abscess, urgent CT brain scan is the investigation of choice, followed by bacteriological diagnosis of pus removed at neurosurgery.

Treatment

Appropriate oral and intravenous antibiotic administration, always in consultation with the microbiology laboratory, constitutes the main line of treatment for pyogenic bacterial, tuberculous, fungal and protozoal infections.

Topical and systemic administration of the antiviral agent aciclovir is used in herpes simplex and zoster infections. Ganciclovir is active against CMV infections. There is now a wide range of drugs active against HIV, and it has been shown that combinations of these drugs are very useful in reducing viral load, maintaining the effectiveness of the immune system and preventing the complications of AIDS. This approach is referred to as HAART (highly active anti-retroviral therapy).

General supportive measures for patients whose conscious

	Polymorph count	Lymphocyte count	Protein conc.	Glucose conc.	Microscopy and culture	Viral antibodies in blood and CSF
Pyogenic bacterial meningitis	↑↑↑	↑	↑	↓	+	—
Viral meningitis or meningo-encephalitis	N or ↑	↑↑	↑	N	—	+
Tuberculous meningitis	N or ↑	↑↑	↑	↓	+	—
Fungal meningitis	N or ↑	↑↑	↑	N or ↓	+	—
Cerebral abscess	Lumbar puncture should not be performed, it is potentially dangerous					

Fig. 15.6 CSF abnormalities in various CNS infections.

level is depressed are often required of medical, nursing and physiotherapy staff (see Fig. 11.7, p. 187).

Reason for the infection

In every patient with a CNS infection, the question must be asked 'Why has this infection occurred in this patient?'. Such a question will detect imperfections of immunization, the presence of diabetes, a state of impaired immunity, a previously undetected site of access or source for infection, a personal contact accounting for the infection, or a visit to a part of the world where the infection is endemic. Such an enquiry is an essential part of the patient's management.

Post-infective neurological syndromes

Figure 15.7 shows this group of rare conditions involving the central or peripheral nervous system soon after an infection; Guillain–Barré syndrome is probably the most common.

Nature of prior infection	Target structure in the nervous system	Syndrome
Many and varied	Myelin around blood vessels in the central nervous system	Acute disseminated encephalomyelitis
Many and varied	Myelin in nerve roots, cranial nerves and peripheral nerves	Guillain–Barré syndrome
Influenza, varicella and other viruses	Mitochondria in brain and liver	Reye's syndrome
Group A streptococci	Basal ganglia	Sydenham's chorea Tourette syndrome Post-encephalitic parkinsonism

Fig. 15.7 Post-infective neurological syndromes.

Acute disseminated encephalomyelitis

Days or weeks after an infection or immunization, a multifocal perivascular allergic reaction in the CNS, associated with perivascular demyelination, may occur.

The clinical expression of such an occurrence varies from mild features of an acute encephalomyelitis, to more major focal or multifocal neurological deficits, to a life-threatening or fatal syndrome with epileptic seizures, major bilateral neurological signs, ataxia, brainstem signs and coma.

Guillain–Barré syndrome

In this condition (fully described in Chapter 10, see p. 163), the post-infectious immunological lesion affects the spinal nerve roots, and the cranial and peripheral nerves. There is damage to the myelin. After a phase of damage, which may show itself by progressive weakness and numbness over 1–4 weeks, the clinical state and pathological process stabilize, with subsequent gradual recovery.

Recovery from Guillain–Barré syndrome is usually complete, whereas persistent deficits are not uncommon after severe acute disseminated encephalomyelitis. Schwann cells can reconstitute peripheral nerve and nerve root myelin with much greater efficiency than oligodendrocytes can repair myelin within the CNS.

Reye's syndrome

In this condition, which occurs in young children, there is damage to the brain and liver in the wake of a viral infection (especially influenza and varicella). Treatment of the child's infection with aspirin seems to increase the chances of developing Reye's syndrome (so avoidance of the use of aspirin in young children has been recommended).

Vomiting is a common early persistent symptom, rapidly progressing to coma, seizures, bilateral neurological signs and evidence of raised intracranial pressure due to cerebral oedema.

The primary insult seems to involve mitochondrial function in both the brain and liver. Abnormal liver function is evident on investigation, with hypoglycaemia, which may clearly aggravate the brain lesion.

Post-streptococcal syndromes

The classic neurological sequel of Group A steptococcal sore throat is subacute chorea, sometimes accompanied by behavioural disturbance, termed Sydenham's chorea or St Vitus' dance. It is usually self-limiting, subsiding after a few weeks. It is now rare in the UK but remains common in some parts of the world such as South Africa (see p. 75).

A different post-streptococcal syndrome is now seen more often in the UK, where the movement disorder is dominated by tics or sometimes parkinsonism, and does not always remit. Such cases can be indistinguishable from Gilles de la Tourette syndrome and post-encephalitic parkinsonism (encephalitis lethargica) respectively, and it is possible that an autoimmune response to streptococcus lies behind these conditions (see p. 76).

In all these conditions, positive streptococcal serology (raised antistreptolysin O or anti-DNAse B titres) points towards the diagnosis.

CASE HISTORIES

Case 1

A 63-year-old warehouse worker with a past history of bronchiectasis is admitted as an emergency after a series of epileptic seizures which begin with jerking of the left leg. He is unrousable but his wife says that over the last 4 days he has complained of severe headache and has become increasingly drowsy and apathetic.

On examination he has a temperature of 37.8°C but no neck stiffness. He does not open his eyes to pain but groans incoherently and attempts to localize the stimulus with his right hand. The left-sided limbs remain motionless and are flaccid and areflexic. His left plantar response is extensor. He does not have papilloedema. General examination is unremarkable apart from crackles in his right lower chest.

a. How would you manage his case?

Case 2

A 18-year-old student spends a month in Thailand on her way back from a gap year in Australia. On returning to the family home she feels lethargic and irritable. She sleeps badly, has no appetite and is losing weight. After 2 weeks she begins to experience continuous dull headaches; she is referred to hospital after a further 2 weeks when she begins to vomit.

She is drowsy but orientated with a normal Glasgow coma score. She looks unwell and has low-grade fever and neck stiffness with no focal neurological deficit. She has a mild neurophilia and a markedly raised CRP. Other routine blood tests, and films looking for malarial parasites, are normal. Her CT brain scan shows no definite abnormality, although there is a suggestion of abnormal enhancement of the meninges around the base of the brain. At lumbar puncture her CSF contains 20 polymorphs and 80 lymphoctytes (normally less than 4), a protein of 1.8 g/dl (normally less than 0.5) and a glucose of 2.2 mmol/l at a time when her blood glucose is 6.6 mmol/l (when normal CSF glucose is at least 50% of the blood level).

a. What is the diagnosis?

(For answers, see pp. 267–8.)

Answers to case histories

Chapter 2

Case 1

a. • CT brain scan, which in this instance showed no definite abnormality, just a suggestion of subarachnoid blood.
   • Lumbar puncture produced unequivocal, uniformly bloodstained CSF.
b. • Neurosurgical referral.
   • Cerebral angiography, which demonstrated a single posterior communicating artery aneurysm on the left.

The patient was started on nimodipine and proceeded to surgery without delay. A clip was placed around the neck of the aneurysm. The post-operative period was complicated by a transient right hemiparesis, which recovered completely after 10 days. The patient's BP settled to 120/80. She has had no further problems.

Case 2

a. Right-sided intracerebral haemorrhage.
b. Right-sided intracerebral haemorrhage.
c. CT brain scan, which shows a large clot of blood centred on the right internal capsule. ECG and chest X-ray both confirm left ventricular hypertrophy.
d. He needs to know that his wife is in a grave situation, with regard to both survival (comatose, obese lady in bed) and useful neurological recovery.

All appropriate care was given to this woman, but she developed a deep vein thrombosis in her left calf on day 2, and died suddenly from a pulmonary embolus on day 4.

Chapter 3

Case 1

a. She has signs of a lesion in the left cerebellopontine angle, with ataxia, loss of the corneal reflex (cranial nerve 5) and deafness (cranial nerve 8). It has come on slowly, starting with deafness, so it is more likely to be an acoustic neuroma than a metastasis from her previous cancer.

An MR scan confirmed this. The neuroma was too large to treat with radiotherapy but was successfully removed, giving her a transient left facial weakness (cranial nerve 7) and permanent complete left deafness.

Case 2

a. It is hard to localize his symptoms to a single part of the brain. There are problems with memory (temporal lobes), behaviour and expressive language (frontal lobes) and spatial ability (parietal lobes). This could indicate a multi-focal process such as metastases, a widespread diffuse process such as a glioma, or just possibly a focal tumour with hydrocephalus.

The drowsiness and papilloedema indicate raised intra-cranial pressure, making a degenerative disease or meta-bolic encephalopathy unlikely. There are pointers towards an underlying systemic disease in the weight loss and lym-phadenopathy.

His CT brain scan showed widespread multifocal areas of high-density tissue in the white matter around the lateral ventricles. The appearances were typical of a primary CNS lymphoma. His HIV test was positive and his CD4 lympho-cyte count was very low, indicating that the underlying disorder was AIDS. He continued to deteriorate despite steroids and highly active anti-retroviral therapy, and died 4 weeks later. The diagnosis of lymphoma was confirmed by autopsy.

Areas with a very high HIV prevalence, such as sub-Saharan Africa, are seeing a huge and increasing burden of neurological disease due to AIDS.

Chapter 4

Case 1

a. Your initial management plan would comprise:
   • admission to hospital;
   • half-hourly neurological observations recorded on a

Glasgow Coma Scale chart by competent staff, regardless of the boy's location, e.g. A & E, ward, CT scanner etc.;
- urgent CT brain scan.

b. When he starts to deteriorate, you should obtain immediate neurosurgical advice and follow it.

The clinical situation strongly suggested a left-sided extradural haematoma which was confirmed by the CT scan and immediately drained in an emergency operation. Thankfully the boy made a full recovery from a potentially life-threatening situation.

Case 2

a. The point here is that you cannot simply assume that his coma is due to alcohol intoxication. People who abuse alcohol are very prone to *head injury* either through accidents or assaults. If they have a long-standing problem their clotting may be defective because of liver disease, increasing the risk of subdural, extradural and intracranial haemorrhage. They have an increased risk of epileptic seizures when intoxicated, when withdrawing from alcohol and as a consequence of previous head injuries, and he could be in a *post-epileptic coma*. A seizure can cause a head injury. Alcohol abuse increases blood pressure and the risk of *stroke*. People with alcohol problems often neglect their health: he could be in a *diabetic coma*. He may be depressed and have taken an *overdose*. He might even have contracted *meningitis* in the back bar. Do not jump to conclusions when assessing an intoxicated patient.

Chapter 5

Case 1

a. She has clearly got parkinsonism, with gait disturbance, bradykinesia and rigidity. Parkinson's disease is quite common at this age, but is not usually symmetrical like this. There are no additional neurological features to suggest a more complex neurodegenerative disease.

The vital part of the history is to establish what pills she is taking. The treatment for her gastro-oesophageal reflux turned out to be the dopamine antagonist metoclopramide. This was stopped and her drug-induced parkinsonism slowly resolved, although it was a year before she felt back to normal.

Case 2

a. This is a very difficult case. The main problem is cerebellar ataxia, with ataxia of gait accompanied by milder limb ataxia and cerebellar dysarthria. But the disease process is affecting several other systems: his optic nerves, causing optic atrophy; his spinal cord, giving extensor plantars; and his peripheral nerves, causing areflexia and impaired distal vibration sense.

b. This is a condition called Friedreich's ataxia. It is a recessively inherited, early-onset form of multisystem degeneration that is classified under the term 'spinocerebellar ataxia'. It is due to a trinucleotide expansion in the frataxin gene, which is believed to have a role in the function of mitochondria. It goes on to affect other systems of the body, causing cardiomyopathy or diabetes mellitus. It is very rare, except in clinical exams.

    You may have considered the possibility of multiple sclerosis, which is a much commoner cause of cerebellar ataxia, optic atrophy and extensor plantars, but rare at this age, not usually gradually progressive and not affecting the peripheral nerves like this. If he was much older you would consider alcohol toxicity. This is a common cause of ataxia and peripheral neuropathy, but would not readily explain the optic atrophy or extensor plantars.

c. Clearly there are going to be a great many difficult matters to discuss with the patient and his family as they face the prospect of a progressive, disabling degenerative disease in early adult life. But there may be particular issues for the parents in relation to the genetics. Firstly, they may feel irrationally guilty that they have unknowingly each carried a genetic mutation that has contributed to their son's illness. Secondly, they will have worries about his younger siblings, who each have a 25% risk of inheriting the illness too. The help of specialists in medical genetics is likely to be invaluable in helping them to approach these issues.

Chapter 6

Case 1

a. You should probably start by examining the patient yourself, but it is perfectly legitimate to say that if you are in doubt you should get advice from a more experienced colleague too.

    The patient has a pattern of weakness that is typical of upper motor neurone weakness in the lower limbs, where the extensor muscles remain relatively strong and the hip flexors, knee flexors and ankle dorsiflexors become weak. The extensor plantar responses also indicate an upper motor neurone problem. It often takes a few days before the reflexes become brisk when upper motor neurone weakness comes on acutely, so you should not worry that the reflexes are still normal here.

In other words, the problem is somewhere in the spinal cord. It is unlikely to be in the neck because the arms are not affected. You need an MR of the thoracic region, not the lumbosacral region, because the cord ends adjacent to the L1 vertebral body (Fig. 6.1).

The sensory signs may be very helpful in this situation. The patient felt pin-prick as blunt in his lower abdomen below his umbilicus and throughout both lower limbs. This is a T9 sensory level, indicating that the cord problem is at or above this dermatome. You call the radiologist back and ask for the appropriate scan. This shows a metastasis compressing the cord in the mid-thoracic region. His pain and neurological deficit improve with high-dose steroids and radiotherapy. Further investigation reveals several other bone metastases from prostate cancer. This is treated medically, with a useful period of palliation.

Case 2

a. The sensory symptoms on neck flexion (so-called L'Hermitte's symptom) help to localize the problem to the neck. Urgency of micturition is also a helpful indicator of a problem in the spinal cord.

   The signs are more specific, indicating pathology at the level of the 5th and 6th cervical vertebrae. He has the segmental sign of absent C5–6 biceps and supinator jerks, and tract signs below this level: brisk C7–8 triceps jerks and upper motor neurone signs in the lower limbs.

b. The most common pathology at this location in someone of this age is cervical spondylosis, with a C5–6 disc bulge and osteophyte formation compressing the cord. This turned out to be the cause here. There are several other rarer possibilities, including a neurofibroma. Because of his delicate manual occupation, he was keen to have decompressive surgery. This stopped his electric shocks and improved the sensation in his hands. The signs in his legs remained unchanged. His bladder symptoms persisted but responded to anticholinergic drugs.

Chapter 7

Case 1

a. This is *not* typical of multiple sclerosis. There is dissemination in time (two separate episodes 4 years apart) but not in place (both episodes seem to arise from the right pons). You need to exclude a structural cause for this.

His MR brain scan showed a vascular anomaly called a cavernoma centred on the right side of his pons, surrounded by concentric rings of altered blood products, suggesting that it had bled repeatedly over the years. There were several other cavernomas elsewhere in the brain. His sister's doctors were, with his permission, told of this unusual, dominantly inherited diagnosis and, after further imaging, her diagnosis was revised to multiple cavernomas too.

b. Both patients were managed conservatively.

MS is common, but you should always consider the possibility of an alternative diagnosis if all the symptoms can be attributed to a lesion in a single place.

Case 2

a. The weakness selectively affects the intrinsic hand muscles supplied by the ulnar nerves. Wasting is an LMN sign not typical of MS, which is a disease of the central nervous system. The likely cause is compression of the ulnar nerves at the elbow by the arm-rests of her wheelchair.

b. Her wheelchair was modified and she was advised to try to avoid resting her elbows on firm surfaces. She declined ulnar nerve transposition.

Chapter 8

a. The problem is in the left optic nerve. The most likely cause is optic neuritis, which comes on rapidly and often causes pain on eye movement. It usually resolves spontaneously but improves rapidly with high-dose steroids.

b. This is most likely to be a right 6th nerve palsy, although a left 3rd nerve palsy or left internuclear opthalmoplegia can all cause the same symptom (see pp. 117–19). Less commonly this symptom reflects weakness of the right lateral rectus or left medial rectus muscles (for example due to myasthenia or thyroid eye disease), and very rarely it is due to a mass in one orbit, displacing the eye. Examination will clarify matters. You can suppress the diplopia with an eye patch and then need to establish the underlying cause.

c. This history of sudden jolts of pain, triggered by touch, in an area supplied by one of the branches of the trigeminal nerve, is typical of trigeminal neuralgia (see pp. 122 and 219). The patient is often unable to wash his face or brush his teeth for fear of triggering the pain. Carbamazepine is usually a very effective treatment.

d. If you were taking this history face-to-face then the left facial weakness would be obvious. The likely cause is a Bell's palsy (see p. 124). This affects the lower motor neurones of the facial nerve, so the whole of the face is affected, including the forehead (unlike upper motor neurone facial weakness, say from a stroke, where the forehead is spared). A short course of oral steroids will improve the chances of a good recovery.

e. This is likely to be a left homonymous hemianopia (see p. 114). Patients are often unaware of the visual field loss so long as the central field is intact. The most likely cause would be a stroke or tumour in the right occipital lobe. He needs to stop driving while you organize a brain scan.

f. The patient is describing positional vertigo and the loss of confidence that accompanies all vestibular disorders. The most likely cause of recurrent brief bouts of positional vertigo is benign paroxysmal positional vertigo (BPPV) (see p. 128) due to particles of debris in one of the semicircular canals of one ear. Ménière's disease causes more prolonged periods of vertigo which are not necessarily provoked by changes in the position of the head and which are accompanied by muffled hearing and tinnitus. Acute vestibular failure or labyrinthitis again causes persistent vertigo, usually with ataxia and vomiting. BPPV can sometimes be cured with a manoeuvre to clear the particles, or the symptoms can be suppressed with vestibular sedative drugs.

Chapter 9

a. Common peroneal nerve palsy or an L5 nerve root lesion.
b. Radial nerve palsy.
c. Carpal tunnel syndrome, i.e. bilateral median nerves.
d. An ulnar nerve lesion at the elbow.

Chapter 10

Case 1

a. He has symptoms and signs of a peripheral neuropathy which is selectively affecting the sensory nerves. The two common causes are excessive alcohol and diabetes mellitus. He is not taking neurotoxic drugs, the length of the history would be against an underlying malignancy, and the lack of motor involvement or family history is against a hereditary neuropathy.

b. The macrocytosis may have made you think of vitamin B_{12} deficiency. This can certainly give rise to neurological problems without causing anaemia, but it typically causes spinal cord pathology in addition to peripheral nerve damage (subacute combined degeneration of the spinal cord, Chapter 6), with extensor plantar responses and a positive Romberg test.

Diabetes mellitus is an important possibility. Even mild diabetes can cause a sensory neuropathy, without the classical symptoms of weight change, polyuria and polydipsia. To exclude diabetes you need a fasting sample, or better still a glucose tolerance test.

But the diagnostic test here was a polite but persistent enquiry into the patient's alcohol history. He had been drinking at least a bottle of wine each day for many years. Alcohol is a common cause of macrocytosis. His liver function tests were also abnormal. Nerve conduction studies were not performed (but might have shown damage to the axons in the form of reduced sensory action potentials).

He was advised to stop drinking, to take vitamin B_1 supplements, and to take care of his numb feet. He eventually managed to do this with considerable psychological help and after 6 months his symptoms of neuropathy started to subside.

Case 2

a. She has the symptoms and signs of a bulbar palsy (see pp. 131 and 156). Her breathlessness could be due to anxiety but could indicate worrying respiratory muscle weakness. You need to clarify this by checking her vital capacity (not her peak expiratory flow rate, which is a test for asthma) as part of your examination.

The most likely cause of this clinical picture in a young woman would be myasthenia gravis. The observation that her speech worsens ('fatigues') as she talks is characteristic of myasthenia. You should not be put off by the absence of myasthenia in her eyes or limbs.

Motor neurone disease is only rarely familial, and in her case the lack of tongue wasting and fasciculation is very reassuring.

b. You should arrange urgent hospital admission to make sure that she does not develop life-threatening bulbar or respiratory weakness. If you are not a neurologist, you should telephone one for advice. If her vital capacity is reduced you should also consider talking to your friendly ITU consultant.

Intravenous edrophonium (Tensilon) gave her a normal voice for a few minutes. She was started on prednisolone and pyridostigmine but continued to deteriorate until she underwent plasma exchange, which helped a great deal. Her acetylcholine receptor antibodies came back 2 weeks later and were strongly positive. CT scans of her thorax revealed a thymus mass which, when resected, turned out to be due to benign hyperplasia. Twelve months later her myasthenia is in remission and she is off all medication.

Chapter 11

Case 1

a. It is always much harder to diagnose blackouts without a witness account, and you would want to make sure that, for example, no fellow dog walker saw the blackout in the park. A description of a minute or two of random limb jerks, cyanosis and noisy breathing would point you towards epilepsy; slumping pale and motionless for several seconds would steer you towards cardiovascular syncope.

b. Without this vital information, we need more information about the parts of the blackouts he can recall. What does he mean by dizziness? Is he describing the lightheadedness of an imminent faint, the déjà vu of a temporal lobe aura, or the ataxia of a vertebro-basilar TIA? We also need to clarify his state after the attacks: did he have any confusion, headache or limb pains to suggest a tonic–clonic epileptic seizure?

c. In this case, and in the absence of any other clues, his rapid recovery from the attacks was suggestive of a cardiovascular cause. His vascular risk factors (smoking and hypertension) provide weak support for this. His ECG showed first-degree heart block (not present in the emergency tracing) and a 24-hour ECG showed evidence of sick sinus syndrome with several prolonged ventricular pauses. A cardiologist confirmed the diagnosis of Stokes–Adams attacks, which she cured with a permanent pacemaker.

Case 2

a. This man is unconscious with a moderately reduced Glasgow coma score of 9 (E2 V2 M5). There no signs of meningitis (fever, neck stiffness) and no focal signs to suggest a localized problem within the brain (encephalitis, abscess, tumour, haemorrhage). The roving horizontal eye movements are helpful, demonstrating that the parts of his brainstem responsible for generating such movements (Fig 8.6, p. 117) are intact. Taken together, these are hopeful signs, suggesting that he has a potentially reversible diffuse problem with his cerebrum, rather than focal disease in his cortex or brainstem.

The only clue to the cause of his coma is the prescription for valproate. He could be in a post-ictal coma after a tonic–clonic seizure or he could have taken an overdose of valproate. Ongoing epileptic states without visible convulsions are very rare. Valproate can cause liver dysfunction but this is accompanied by jaundice.

b. In terms of management, you have already made sure that his airway, breathing and circulation are satisfactory. You check his full blood count, electrolytes, liver function tests and glucose (normal), and start regular observations, monitoring his Glasgow Coma Scale. You are looking for a gradual improvement to confirm your suspicion of a transient post-ictal state but his score actually drops to 7 over the next hour. You are in the process of arranging an EEG, CT brain scan and possible lumbar puncture when his parents arrive and tell you that he has become increasingly depressed since his recent diagnosis of epilepsy, with the loss of his driving licence and his lucrative job as a scaffolder. The diagnosis is a valproate overdose. He recovers with supportive management but needs continuing psychiatric help.

Chapter 12

Case 1

a. She is having brief, stereotyped, repetitive and unprovoked episodes, which should make you think of epilepsy even when the content of the episodes is bizarre. The common manifestations of temporal lobe seizures are a warm, queasy feeling rising from the stomach to the head and disturbances of memory, like déjà vu. Less commonly patients experience olfactory hallucinations, with a brief experience of a strong, unpleasant but indefinable smell. Emotional changes are also less common, and typically take the form of a feeling of impending doom rather than the pleasant calm and omniscience of this case.

b. Her MR brain scan showed a small vascular anomaly called a cavernoma in the right temporal lobe. Neurosurgical advice was that the risk of harming her by removing the cavernoma would be greater than the risk of stroke due to bleeding from it. After learning about the driving regulations, she opted for anticonvulsant therapy. She had completed her family and was not concerned about teratogenic issues. She started treatment with carbamazepine which abolished the attacks.

Case 2

a. The emergency management of status epilepticus starts with the establishment of an airway but it is generally impossible to secure this until you have controlled the seizures. You need to obtain intravenous access and administer intravenous lorazepam (or diazepam) followed by intravenous phenytoin. As the seizures subside you can insert an oral airway.

b. The second phase in the management of status epilepticus is to find out the cause. The commonest is lack of concordance with medication in patients who are known to have epilepsy. When the first manifestation of epilepsy is status epilepticus, the underlying cause is often serious (tumour, stroke, etc.).

The worry here is the persistent fever. It is common to have a fever during status epilepticus because of the heat generated by muscle activity. The white cell count also usually rises. But you would expect the temperature to fall subsequently, rather than to rise. He could have aspirated while fitting and have pneumonia. Ecstasy toxicity can also present in this way. But the priority is to exclude intracranial infection.

His CT brain scan showed no abnormality. At lumbar puncture his CSF pressure was mildly elevated at 26 cm. The CSF contained 110 lymphocytes (normal less than 4), no polymorphs and no organisms on Gram staining. The CSF protein was mildly elevated at 0.6 g/dl and the CSF glucose level was a normal proportion of his blood glucose.

As you will discover in Chapter 15, this CSF picture suggests intracranial infection, most likely viral encephalitis. He was treated with intravenous aciclovir. He subsequently had an MR brain scan which showed signal changes consistent with swelling and haemorrhage in both temporal and frontal lobes, typical of herpes simplex encephalitis. HSV was detected in his CSF using PCR. He rapidly improved but was left with persistent forgetfulness and occasional focal seizures.

Chapter 13

a. This is the typical sudden, severe history that should make you think of subarachnoid haemorrhage.

b. Tension headache gives a constant feeling of pressure in the head, often described in powerful language and accompanied by an overt or unspoken fear of an underlying brain tumour.

c. The predictable diurnal timing and intense orbital pain are typical of cluster headache.

d. This is a textbook, so here is the textbook description of the headache of raised intracranial pressure. Bear in mind that morning headaches are more often due to migraine, hangovers, anxiety about the day ahead or obstructive sleep apnoea, while headaches on stooping are very common in sinusitis, but look hard for signs of raised intracranial pressure when you hear this story.

e. In an elderly patient, a new headache with scalp tenderness and malaise means giant cell arteritis until proved otherwise: ESR and steroids in the meantime.

f. Occasional, intermittent headaches are usually due to migraine.

g. Brief, lancinating pains triggered by stimulation of the face or mouth suggest trigeminal neuralgia.

h. Low-pressure headache is postural and relieved by lying flat.

i. This chronic, unremitting maxillary ache and the accompanying misery in a young or middle-aged woman are typical of the paradoxically named atypical facial pain.

j. Repeated sudden headaches at the moment of orgasms are due to benign sex headache.

Chapter 14

Case 1

a. Possible raised intracranial pressure, due to a mass lesion affecting intellectual function, but not producing any other focal neurological deficit.

b. Urgent neurological assessment and brain scan.

The patient was seen 2 days later by the local urgent neurological service. No new signs had appeared. The urgent CT brain scan revealed a large subdural haematoma on the left. This was evacuated through burrholes by the neurosurgeons (after correcting the prolonged prothrombin time induced by warfarin), and the patient underwent a slow, but entirely satisfactory, recovery.

Case 2

a. The key question is whether this is an acute confusional state or a dementia. In acute confusional states (for example due to infection) the patient is usually drowsy and not fully in touch with their surroundings. In this case the patient is alert; moreover there is a history suggestive of a more gradual dementing process, with poor memory and some visuospatial impairment. This, together with the previous episode of 'confusion', raises the possibility of dementia with Lewy bodies.

You should do your best to settle her by talking to her calmly, reminding her repeatedly that she is in safe hands, and providing a quiet, well-lit environment. If she remains dangerously agitated then you may have to sedate her carefully, for example with a small amount of intravenous lorazepam. You should avoid using conventional neuroleptics because they can cause catastrophic parkinsonism in dementia with Lewy bodies.

Once she is settled, you can rule out causes of acute confusion (full blood count, ESR, electrolytes, urine dipstick, chest X-ray) and can perform a more detailed neurological examination, firstly to make sure that she does not have a focal deficit that would require further investigation and secondly to establish if there is evidence of a dementing process.

In this case the routine tests were all normal. The following day she was found to have problems with memory, language and especially visuospatial function (she could not draw a clock face). She was found to have a stooped, shuffling gait and mild rigidity in the upper limbs. The diagnosis of dementia with Lewy bodies was confirmed and both her hallucinations and her memory problems improved markedly on treatment with rivastigmine, a cholinesterase inhibitor. She went home with support from the community old age psychiatry nurse.

Chapter 15

Case 1

a. The focal onset to the seizures suggests a problem in the right frontal lobe. This is confirmed by finding a left hemiparesis. Remember that it takes several days for the classic upper motor neurone signs of spasticity and hyper-reflexia to develop.

The crucial investigation is therefore an urgent CT brain scan. This showed a ragged ring of enhancing tissue with a low-density centre, surrounded by considerable oedema: a cerebral abscess. There was no evidence of a source of infection in the paranasal sinuses.

Fever is not always a feature of cerebral abscess, especially if there is no active infection elsewhere in the body. Many patients have a low-grade fever after prolonged seizures, and in this case you might also have wondered if the fever was arising from a chest infection. But in a patient with neurological symptoms or signs, a fever should always make you think about infection within the nervous system, and in the presence of focal deficit you should think specifically about cerebral abscess and encephalitis.

He was treated with broad-spectrum intravenous antibiotics, intravenous phenytoin and neurosurgical drainage of the abscess. The organism was not cultured from his blood or the abscess itself, but was assumed to have originated in his chest; chronic suppurative lung disease and congenital heart disease both predispose to cerebral abscess although direct spread from infections in the mastoid or paranasal sinuses is more common.

After a stormy time in the intensive care unit, the patient made a gradual recovery but required long-term carbamazepine therapy for continuing epileptic seizures.

Case 2

a. She has a subacute meningitis, with a predominantly lymphocytic CSF pleocytosis and a low CSF glucose. The most likely cause is tuberculosis, acquired on her travels. Fungal meningitis can cause a similar illness, but is very rare in immunocompetent young people. Malignant meningitis is also rare in young people. The low CSF glucose excludes viral meningitis.

She had not been immunized with BCG. Her Mantoux test was strongly positive and DNA from *Mycobacterium tuberculosis* was detected in her CSF by a PCR technique. She was started on three anti-TB drugs and slowly recovered. CSF culture eventually confirmed the diagnosis 6 weeks later.

Index